Applied Machine Learning for IoT and Data Analytics

(Volume 3)

Behavioural Analytics: Machine Learning Approaches for Predictive Insights

Edited by

Shradhanjali Panda

Department of Business Administration, Ravenshaw University, Cuttack, India

Leena Priyadarshini Singh

Department of Business Administration, Ravenshaw University, Cuttack, India

V. Ramasamy

Department of CSE, Vel Tech Rangarajan Dr.Sagunthala R&D Institute of Science and Technology (Deemed to be University), Chennai, Tamil Nadu, India

&

S. Balamurugan

Research and Development, Intelligent Research Consultancy Services (iRCS), Coimbatore, Tamil Nadu, India

Applied Machine Learning for IoT and Data Analytics

(Volume 3)

Behavioural Analytics: Machine Learning Approaches for Predictive Insights

Editors: Shradhanjali Panda, Leena Priyadarshini Singh, V. Ramasamy & S. Balamurugan

ISBN (Online): 979-8-89881-393-2

ISBN (Print): 979-8-89881-394-9

ISBN (Paperback): 979-8-89881-395-6

Published by Bentham Science Publishers Pte. Ltd. Singapore,

in collaboration with Eureka Conferences, USA.

First published in 2026.

need for a court order if at any point you breach any terms of this License Agreement. In no event will any delay or failure by Bentham Science Publishers in enforcing your compliance with this License Agreement constitute a waiver of any of its rights.

3. You acknowledge that you have read this License Agreement, and agree to be bound by its terms and conditions. To the extent that any other terms and conditions presented on any website of Bentham Science Publishers conflict with, or are inconsistent with, the terms and conditions set out in this License Agreement, you acknowledge that the terms and conditions set out in this License Agreement shall prevail.

Bentham Science Publishers Pte. Ltd.
No. 9 Raffles Place
Office No. 26-01
Singapore 048619
Singapore
Email: subscriptions@benthamscience.net

BENTHAM SCIENCE

CONTENTS

PREFACE

In a rapidly evolving landscape, where data drives decisions and insights fuel innovation, the field of Behavioral Analytics has emerged as a crucial domain for organizations seeking to understand and enhance their operations. This book, 'Behavioral Analytics: Machine Learning Approaches for Predictive Insight', aims to shed light on the powerful intersection of behavioral analytics and machine learning, illustrating how these methodologies can be leveraged to gain predictive insights that drive strategic decision-making. As we navigate through the chapters, we will explore the fundamental concepts that underpin behavioral analytics. This exploration is not merely theoretical; it is aimed at practical applications that can transform data into actionable strategies. By harnessing machine learning techniques, organizations can identify trends, anticipate challenges, and unlock opportunities that were previously obscured by the vast amounts of data they collect. We will delve into the challenges associated with integrating machine learning into behavioral analytics frameworks, addressing concerns related to data quality, privacy, and the ethical implications of data use. Transparency and ethical practices will emerge as recurring themes throughout our discussion, emphasizing the need for organizations to adopt a responsible approach to data analytics that respects consumer privacy while fostering trust. The significance of our analysis extends to various sectors, including human resources, marketing, and public safety. We will discuss how predictive insights generated through machine learning can enhance employee engagement and retention, improve customer experiences, and even aid law enforcement in crime prediction—thereby contributing to a safer society. Through case studies and empirical research, we aim to illustrate the real-world applications of behavioral analytics in promoting efficiency, accountability, and informed decision-making. Moreover, this book addresses the future of behavioral analytics, considering the impact of emerging technologies and methodologies. As we stand at the forefront of a data-driven era, it is essential to equip ourselves with the knowledge and tools necessary to navigate the complexities of human behavior through the lens of machine learning. In an era where data reigns supreme and technology continues to transform our understanding of the world, the exploration of emerging fields such as Natural Language Processing (NLP), Machine Learning (ML), and behavioral analytics has never been more pertinent. The intention of this book is to illuminate the intricate interplay between these cutting-edge technologies and various sectors, offering a comprehensive view of how they can enhance decision-making, optimize operations, and foster positive cultural changes in organizations.

As we explore the multifaceted ways NLP enhances behavioral analytics, we highlight powerful tools such as sentiment analysis, topic modelling, and named entity recognition that extract meaningful insights from text data. However, this journey is not without its challenges. We courageously confront issues related to data quality, privacy, and domain specificity while proposing innovative solutions that bridge these gaps. Our exploration extends to how data-driven insights can fundamentally transform workplace dynamics by identifying key engagement drivers that enhance morale, productivity, and retention. With advanced analytics, organizations can monitor employee sentiment in real time, enabling a proactive approach to nurturing a positive workplace culture. With the rise of recommendation systems, we investigate their profound influence on consumer behavior, focusing on patterns of purchasing, satisfaction, and brand loyalty. By analyzing different recommendation strategies, we aim to uncover how tailored suggestions shape customer interactions with retailers. In the educational sector, we discuss the significant role AI plays in improving student achievement and creativity. It is essential to evaluate the ways in which AI can inform learning methodologies, thereby benefiting students who are the ultimate clients of educational services.

As we navigate the ever-evolving landscape of ML in business, we offer a longitudinal analysis of its growth from a niche interest to a fundamental tool for strategic management in the 21st century. Our findings underscore the transformative potential of pedagogy informed by Automatic Speech Recognition (ASR) and its implications for fostering inclusive educational environments. Further, we investigate how digital technology can optimize the experience at the Puri Jagannath Temple, addressing the various challenges of overcrowding and safety. Through surveying Generation Z, we evaluate the feasibility of mobile applications that enhance access while acknowledging the trade-offs inherent in technology adoption. Amidst the wealth of data analytics, we stress the importance of ethical considerations. Through transparent practices in data collection and analysis, businesses can foster trust and prioritize consumer welfare. In the realm of public safety, we delve into how machine learning and time-series models can predict crime rates, advocating their use by law enforcement agencies to improve resource allocation. Lastly, we address the impact of digital currency on economic practices and its implications for society at large, questioning whether this shift represents a positive evolution in monetary transactions.

This book, **'Behavioral Analytics: Machine Learning Approaches for Predictive Insight,'** aims to bridge theory and practice, providing readers with insights that can inspire future research and applications. As we embark on this exploration together, we invite you to engage with the concepts presented and consider how these innovative approaches can be applied in your own context. We hope this book will be helpful to readers. The editors express their gratitude to the reviewers for their insightful criticism, which has helped to elevate the book's caliber. Bentham Books is also acknowledged by the editors for their assistance and publication.

Shradhanjali Panda
Department of Business Administration
Ravenshaw University
Cuttack, India

Leena Priyadarshini Singh
Department of Business Administration
Ravenshaw University
Cuttack, India

V. Ramasamy
Department of CSE, Vel Tech Rangarajan
Dr.Sagunthala R&D Institute of Science and Technology
(Deemed to be University), Chennai, Tamil Nadu, India

&

S. Balamurugan
Research and Development
Intelligent Research Consultancy Services (iRCS)
Coimbatore, Tamil Nadu, India

DEDICATION

The editorial team would like to express their sincere gratitude to their families—spouses, parents, and kids—for their unwavering support during the production of this work. The editors would also like to thank their colleagues at their prestigious institution for their unfailing love, blessings, and support. Lastly, the entire research community, whose combined efforts continue to deepen our understanding of the world, is duly acknowledged in this book.

ACKNOWLEDGEMENTS

The editorial team would like to express its sincere appreciation to our institution for creating a supportive research environment that served as the basis for this proposal. We express our sincere gratitude to the wide range of contributors from different countries and to the international reviewers who have carefully scrutinized every chapter to ensure the book's high caliber. Their astute criticism has been priceless. We want to express our gratitude to everyone for their commitment and readiness to take on challenges that took them outside of their comfort zones. We hope to see you again in our publication's upcoming edition.

List of Contributors

Ananya Mitra	School of Economics & Commerce, Kalinga Institute of Industrial Technology (KIIT) Deemed to be University, Bhubaneswar, Odisha, India
Anita Pareek	Department of Commerce, Kalinga Institute of Social Sciences (Deemed to be University), Bhubaneswar, India
Arjyalopa Mishra	Department of Management, National Law University, Cuttack, Odisha, India
Ashyashree Praharaj	Department of Business Administration, Berhampur University, Berhampur, India
Aseem Ali	Department of Statistics & Applied Mathematics, Central University of Tamil Nadu, Thiruvarur, Tamil Nadu, India
Binita Nanda	Department of Commerce, Kalinga Institute of Social Sciences (Deemed to be University), Bhubaneswar, India
Bhabani S. Mohanty	Department of Statistics & Applied Mathematics, Central University of Tamil Nadu, Thiruvarur, Tamil Nadu, India
Durga Madhab Mahapatra	Department of Commerce, North Eastern Hill University, Meghalaya, India
Jyotisman Das Mohapatra	Department of Business Management, C.V. Raman Global University, Bhubaneswar, Odisha, India
Jayalaxmi Samal	School of Liberal Studies, Kalinga Institute of Industrial Technology (KIIT) Deemed to be University, Bhubaneswar, India
Kushagra Agrawal	School of Computer Engineering, KIIT Deemed to be University, Bhubaneswar, India
Kshitij Krishna	School of Computer Engineering, KIIT Deemed to be University, Bhubaneswar, India
Nandinee Anand	School of Computer Engineering, KIIT Deemed to be University, Bhubaneswar, Odisha, India
Pracheeta Gupta	School of Computer Engineering, KIIT Deemed to be University, Bhubaneswar, India
Ritik Kumar Sahoo	School of Computer Engineering, KIIT Deemed to be University, Bhubaneswar, Odisha, India
Shrutisudha Mishra	Department of Commerce, Kalinga Institute of Social Sciences (Deemed to be University), Bhubaneswar, India
Sonam Subhadarshini	Department of Business Administration, Trident Academy of Technology, Bhubaneswar, Odisha, India
Soumendra Kumar Patra	Department of Business Administration, Ravenshaw University, Odisha, India
Sanjita Lenka	Department of Business Management, C.V. Raman Global University, Bhubaneswar, Odisha, India
Subhamanaisini Nayak	Department of Business Management, C.V. Raman Global University, Bhubaneswar, Odisha, India

Seba Mohanty	School of Computer Engineering, KIIT Deemed to be University, Bhubaneswar, India
Sugyanta Priyadarshini	School of Computer Engineering, KIIT Deemed to be University, Bhubaneswar, India
Sayangshree Panda	School of Computer Engineering, KIIT Deemed to be University, Bhubaneswar, Odisha, India
Swapnamoyee Palit	School of Economics & Commerce, Kalinga Institute of Industrial Technology DU, Bhubaneswar, Odisha, India
Swati Mishra	Department of MBA, Institute of Management and Information Technology, Cuttack-753008, Odisha, India
Sobhana Tripathy	School of Economics & Commerce, Kalinga Institute of Industrial Technology (KIIT) Deemed to be University, Bhubaneswar, Odisha, India
Tamanna Mohapatra	Department of Business Administration, National Law University, Cuttack, Odisha, India

CHAPTER 1

Enhancing Academic Development Through Automatic Speech Recognition and Natural Language Processing

Ananya Mitra[1,*]

[1] *School of Economics & Commerce, Kalinga Institute of Industrial Technology (KIIT) Deemed to be University, Bhubaneswar, Odisha, India*

Abstract: The rapid advancement of Speech Recognition and Natural Language Processing (NLP) technologies offers transformative potential for academic development, aligning with the United Nations Sustainable Development Goal (SDG) 4: Quality Education. These technologies can revolutionize education by providing innovative tools that enhance inclusive and equitable quality education for all. Speech Recognition and NLP enable the automation of academic tasks, improve accessibility for diverse learners—including those with disabilities—and offer data-driven insights to improve student outcomes. The integration of these technologies into educational environments presents significant challenges like limited accessibility in under-resourced educational settings, accuracy issues that affect their reliability, and ethical concerns regarding data privacy and algorithmic bias. This study aims to explore the current state of Automatic Speech Recognition (ASR) and NLP in academia, identify key challenges, and propose solutions to enhance their effectiveness in promoting equitable and inclusive education. The research employs a mixed-methods approach, combining quantitative and qualitative methods. Surveys and interviews with educators, students, and administrators are conducted to gather insights into the use and challenges of ASR and NLP technologies. Additionally, experimental studies are carried out to test the effectiveness of existing ASR systems in educational contexts. By offering workable solutions using usable frequencies from a student perspective to improve the integration of speech recognition and Natural Language Processing (NLP) technologies in education, the study's findings will help achieve SDG 4, guaranteeing that all students have access to high-quality, inclusive, and equitable educational opportunities.

Keywords: Automatic speech recognition, Academic sector, NLP, Primary survey, SDG-4.

* **Corresponding author Ananya Mitra:** School of Economics & Commerce, Kalinga Institute of Industrial Technology (KIIT) Deemed to be University, Bhubaneswar, Odisha, India; E-mail: ananya.mitrafhu@kiit.ac in

Shradhanjali Panda, Leena Priyadarshini Singh, V. Ramasamy & S. Balamurugan (Eds.)

INTRODUCTION

ASR and NLP technologies have the potential to greatly improve education and support SDG-4. These tools can make learning and teaching more inclusive and equitable. NLP can create personalized educational content that meets the specific needs of each student. It can also translate materials in real time, helping students understand content in languages they are not familiar with. This fosters a more diverse and accessible classroom environment. In addition to enhancing learning, these technologies can make teaching easier by automating tasks like grading and taking attendance. This allows teachers to spend more time on engaging activities that connect with students. NLP tools can also help educators create and update educational materials quickly, ensuring students have access to the best resources available. Another important advantage of ASR and NLP is their ability to improve accessibility for all learners, especially those with disabilities. For instance, speech-to-text tools provide real-time captions for students who are hard of hearing, while text-to-speech tools help those with visual impairments. Additionally, these technologies can support research by speeding up data analysis and encouraging collaboration among educators. By using insights from these advancements, teachers can identify students who may be struggling and provide timely help, creating a more effective and supportive learning environment for everyone [1 - 3].

While ASR and NLP technologies bring many benefits to education, their use in classrooms poses significant challenges. One major issue is that schools in poorer areas often do not have the necessary resources, training, or funding to use these tools effectively. This can create a larger gap between well-funded schools and those that struggle, making it important to find ways to ensure that all students can benefit from these advancements. Another key challenge is the accuracy of ASR and NLP technologies [4]. When these tools do not work consistently, they can cause misunderstandings, especially in classrooms with students who have different language skills. For teachers and students to trust and use these technologies fully, they need to keep improving the accuracy and understanding of context. This means not just advancing the technology itself, but also providing training to help users make the most of these tools in real-life situations. Lastly, there are important ethical concerns related to data privacy and bias. Using student data raises questions about how that information is collected, stored, and used, so strong privacy protections are necessary. Additionally, algorithms can sometimes reflect biases from the data they were trained on, which can unfairly impact different groups of students. Addressing these challenges is essential to make sure that ASR and NLP technologies truly support fair and equal education for everyone. By addressing these problems, we attempted to develop a more effective and inclusive educational system that maximizes the use of these technologies. This type of research is completely new [5, 6].

Objectives

This study aimed to examine how ASR and NLP technologies were being used in education. It sought to understand the challenges these tools faced and suggested ways to improve their effectiveness for all students. By enhancing the use of ASR and NLP, the study hoped to promote more equitable and inclusive education. To achieve these goals, the research employed a mixed-methods approach, combining both quantitative and qualitative methods. Primary surveys and interviews were conducted with educators, students, and administrators to gather their thoughts and experiences regarding ASR and NLP technologies. This helped understand the benefits and problems encountered when using these tools in real classrooms. In addition to surveys and interviews, the study also carried out experimental studies to assess how well current ASR systems perform in educational settings. By analyzing the results of these experiments, researchers aimed to gain insights into the effectiveness of these technologies in supporting student learning and identifying areas for improvement.

METHODOLOGY

The research was conducted in various technical institutes across Bhubaneswar, Odisha. Bhubaneswar is a vibrant educational hub, making it an ideal location for this research. Students from different regions, speaking various dialects, come together in one place. By studying these diverse groups, the research explored how ASR and NLP technologies worked for speakers of different languages. By examining how these technologies were used in such a dynamic environment, the study aimed to gather insights that could help improve these tools for all students. By including voices from different dialect speakers, the research aimed to identify specific challenges they faced with ASR and NLP technologies. This understanding can guide future improvements, ensuring that all students, regardless of their language background, have the same opportunities to succeed in their studies. Overall, conducting the research in Bhubaneswar allowed for a rich exploration of language diversity in education.

Students are more likely to engage in research when they are referred by someone they know, creating a comfortable environment for sharing their experiences. This is particularly crucial when talking about personal difficulties with technologies like ASR and NLP, as it may make participants feel more comfortable sharing their experiences [7]. For this reason, snowball sampling was used in this research to effectively gather students from different regions and dialects. By starting with a few participants and expanding through their networks, snowball sampling ensured a more representative mix of students from different regions and dialects. This approach is effective in educational settings where students might have friends or classmates from similar backgrounds, making it easier to reach a wide range of dialect speakers.

In the initial phase of the research, using the Delphi Method, interviews with educators from language and computer science departments were conducted to gather their expert opinions on the potential of ASR and NLP technologies in education. The iterative approach allowed for deep discussions and the refinement of ideas, providing valuable insights into how these tools can enhance teaching and learning. Anonymity of the educators was essential for the study to ensure honest and open responses without the fear of judgment or repercussions. Educators might hesitate to share their true opinions or experiences with ASR and NLP technologies if they felt their identities were known, especially if their views were critical of institutional policies or technological effectiveness. By keeping their responses confidential, the study created a safe space for them to express their true experiences, which led to more accurate and helpful information. This openness enriched the research findings, allowing for a better understanding of both the challenges and benefits of these technologies in the classroom. Keeping their identities private also helped build trust between the researchers and the educators, encouraging more participants to share their valuable insights.

In the subsequent phase, surveys were distributed to 350 students to gather information on their experiences with ASR and NLP technologies. Key areas of focus included how often these tools were used, their effectiveness in supporting learning, and specific challenges faced. In designing the questionnaire for this research, we focused on gathering insights regarding the advantages and disadvantages of using ASR and NLP technologies among technical students. The questionnaire included statements that participants could agree or disagree with, allowing for a better understanding of their experiences.

Following the focus group discussion with the educators, several key advantages and disadvantages of the technologies were identified. These included how ASR enhances participation by allowing students to engage verbally without the pressure of writing, the immediate feedback provided on pronunciation and grammar, and the support offered by NLP tools in understanding complex terms and concepts. These were incorporated in the questionnaire. The study also aimed to assess the accessibility of these technologies for students with learning disabilities and their role in facilitating self-paced learning.

The questionnaire also addressed notable concerns raised by the educators. It included statements regarding the challenges of dialect recognition, as ASR may struggle with different accents, leading to misunderstandings. Additionally, it included the limitations of vocabulary recognition in specialized technical fields, the potential dependence on technology that might reduce motivation for personal skill development, and the impact of technical glitches that could disrupt learning. It also acknowledged privacy concerns related to the security of students' spoken information. This comprehensive approach allowed capturing a balanced view of the impact of ASR and NLP technologies on students' learning experiences.

FINDINGS

Educators Perspective

In-depth focus group discussions were conducted with 50 educators to better understand their experiences with ASR and NLP technologies in the classroom. The results revealed that 60% of educators used ASR for classroom activities and assignments, and all of them reported issues with speech recognition accuracy. One language faculty member noted, "*ASR has the potential to revolutionize how students engage with language learning. It enables them to practice speaking and receive immediate feedback, which is crucial for developing fluency.*" He highlighted the significant role of ASR in improving language skills, making learning more interactive and effective. Another educator in the computer science domain emphasized, "*NLP tools can analyze students' writing and provide personalized suggestions. This not only aids their understanding but also helps them become better writers.*" This statement highlights the potential of NLP to offer tailored support, enhancing the learning experience. One educator explained, "*ASR helps students who find it hard to write. They can focus on sharing their ideas without worrying about taking notes.*" This showed how ASR can boost student participation, allowing them to engage more actively in discussions. Educators teaching international students have found that these technologies significantly enhance the learning experience. These educators noted that ASR helps bridge language gaps by allowing students to practice speaking in a supportive environment. For instance, one educator shared, "*With ASR, my students can practice their pronunciation and receive immediate feedback, which is incredibly helpful for those learning English as a second language.*" This immediate response helped build confidence and encouraged students to engage more actively in class discussions.

During several rounds of interaction, the educators agreed on the transformative power of ASR and NLP technologies. One educator noted, "*Students are more willing to speak up when they know their words will be captured accurately."* However, for certain subjects like Engineering Economics, difficulties remained a significant barrier. Teachers reported frequent disruptions due to misrecognition of speech. One teacher expressed frustration, saying, *"When the system doesn't understand what a student says, it can really throw off the lesson."* Additionally, issues of access were raised, with students pointing out, *"Not everyone can use these tools at home, and it makes it hard to keep up."*

The specialized vocabularies used in certain subjects are complex and unfamiliar to both the ASR systems, making it difficult for the technology to accurately capture what is being said. An Engineering Economics educator pointed out, *"When discussing key concepts like 'supply and demand,' the ASR system sometimes mishears phrases, turning 'opportunity cost' into 'opportunity lost' and 'marginal utility' into 'marginal ability.' I've seen it misinterpret 'market equilibrium' as 'market equal rhythm' and 'fiscal policy' as 'physical policy.' These misunderstandings create confusion, distract students, and hinder their grasp of important economic ideas."* Finally, an active participant (educator) summarized the group's consensus by stating, "*These technologies can create a more inclusive and engaging classroom environment, where every student has the opportunity to succeed, regardless of their language proficiency*." This collective insight reflected a shared belief in the potential of ASR and NLP to significantly enhance educational outcomes in both language and computer science fields [8].

Student Perspective - Usage Frequency

A significant number of students found that ASR and NLP technologies were helpful for understanding their lessons. These tools made it easier for students to follow along with their teachers and grasp new concepts. Students appreciated how ASR could help them hear words pronounced correctly and how NLP could explain difficult vocabulary in simpler terms. This support allowed many students to feel more confident in their learning and participate more actively in class discussions. On the other hand, some students also reported facing challenges related to their dialects when using ASR and NLP. Many students (and educators) spoke different regional languages and accents, which sometimes made it hard for these technologies to understand them accurately. For instance, some students mentioned that their pronunciation was often misrecognized, leading to confusion in lessons. Others noted that certain words unique to their dialects were not recognized by the systems at all.

ASR and NLP technologies are increasingly being adopted in educational settings. A study by Lyu *et al.* (2024) found that 80% of teachers in Shanghai had integrated NLP technology into their classrooms. Similarly, Teba (2024) reported that ASR and NLP-based tools were used by EFL teachers in Benin to enhance oral communication skills. The widespread adoption of these technologies highlights their growing importance in education [9, 10].

Daily usage was common among those focused on language skills or coding, as consistent practice was essential for mastery. Weekly interactions often coincided with specific assignments or study sessions, allowing students to integrate these technologies into their academic routines. Depending on their academic requirements and personal preferences, technology students used ASR and NLP tools at different frequencies (Table 1). Meanwhile, some students only used these tools monthly for major projects, while others engaged rarely, if they felt confident with traditional learning methods.

Table 1. Usage frequency of NLP for ASR.

Usage Statement	Frequency	In %
Use ASR tools daily for language practice.	40	11.40%
Rely on NLP applications weekly for writing assignments.	30	8.60%
Utilize ASR technology monthly for transcribing lectures.	25	7.10%
Rarely use ASR tools outside of class assignments.	50	14.30%
Frequently access NLP tools for studying vocabulary.	35	10.00%
Use ASR daily to improve pronunciation.	45	12.90%
Employ NLP tools weekly to analyze text.	40	11.40%
Occasionally use ASR for recording notes.	30	8.60%
Use NLP applications rarely for grammar checks.	25	7.10%
Often engage with ASR technologies for group discussions.	30	8.60%

*Self Computed.

Student Perspective – Effectiveness in Learning Breakdown

Research has shown that ASR and NLP can significantly improve learning outcomes. A meta-analysis found that ASR has a medium overall effect size ($g = 0.69$) on ESL/EFL student pronunciation performance [9]. NLP can also analyze student responses and provide instant feedback, leading to improved writing skills and personalized learning experiences [4]. These findings suggest that ASR and NLP can be effective tools for enhancing academic development [11 - 13].

The effectiveness of ASR and NLP tools in supporting learning was widely recognized among technology students (Table 2). Many reported significant improvements in speaking skills, making them more confident in presentations and discussions. NLP applications helped simplify complex texts and enhance writing quality, which was crucial for technical documentation. Students often found that these tools streamlined their study routines and facilitated collaboration on group projects. However, some students felt that the effectiveness of these technologies was limited by their specific learning styles or the inadequacies of certain applications.

Table 2. Effectiveness of ASR in learning breakdown.

Effectiveness Statement	Frequency	In %
ASR tools have significantly improved speaking skills.	60	17.10%
NLP has made it easier to understand complex texts.	70	20.00%
Find ASR to be very effective in helping learn new languages.	50	14.30%
NLP applications have greatly enhanced writing quality.	80	22.90%
ASR tools support learning effectively during group projects.	30	8.60%
Believe NLP technologies are crucial for academic success.	40	11.40%
ASR tools have helped me become confident in public speaking.	20	5.70%
See limited effectiveness in using NLP for studies.	30	8.60%
ASR applications have been instrumental in the study routine.	20	5.70%
Think NLP tools are ineffective for learning styles.	10	2.90%

*Self Computed.

Student Perspective – Challenges Faced

Despite their potential, ASR and NLP technologies face several challenges in educational settings, such as low signal-to-noise ratio, speech disfluencies, and multiparty chatter, which can hinder accurate transcription in classrooms [14]. The complexity and diversity of human language are also significant challenges for NLP systems [15]. Addressing these challenges will be crucial for the successful implementation of ASR and NLP in education.

Despite the benefits, students faced various challenges when using ASR and NLP technologies. Technical issues and software glitches were frustrating, particularly under tight deadlines. Many students expressed a need for better training to utilize these tools effectively, as complex interfaces and limited features hindered their experience. Furthermore, struggles with accents and difficulties interpreting NLP outputs posed additional obstacles. The steep learning curve associated with these technologies often led to reluctance in using them, especially when support resources were lacking. Overall, while ASR and NLP tools held great potential for enhancing learning, students had to navigate significant hurdles to fully realize their benefits. Table **3** highlights the challenges students face. Furthermore, ASR software-related technical issues are the majority of the challenges.

Table 3. Challenges faced by users of ASR.

Challenge Statement	Frequency	In %
Often encounter technical issues with ASR software.	70	20.00%
Feel the need for more training to effectively use NLP tools.	60	17.10%
Usability problems often hinder experience with ASR technologies.	50	14.30%
Find limited features in the use of NLP applications.	40	11.40%
Struggle with accents when using ASR tools.	30	8.60%
Face challenges in understanding NLP outputs.	40	11.40%
The learning curve for ASR tools has been steep.	30	8.60%
Often encounter bugs in the NLP software.	20	5.70%
Feel overwhelmed by the complexity of ASR features.	20	5.70%
Experience a lack of resources for troubleshooting ASR issues.	10	2.90%

*Self Computed.

Four important factors that influence how technology students interact with ASR and NLP technologies were identified by the factor analysis results (Table **4**). First, students' use of these tools on a daily, weekly, or monthly basis demonstrated their integration into academic routines, highlighting a range of engagement levels, according to the Usage Frequency factor. Positive opinions of these technologies, especially in terms of enhancing writing and speaking abilities, were highlighted by the Effectiveness in Learning factor, which reaffirmed their usefulness in educational settings. Conversely, the Challenges Faced factor identified common obstacles, such as technical issues and usability problems, which hindered effective usage. Lastly, while the overall satisfaction factor had a lower impact, it still captured students' general contentment with the technologies and their perceived learning benefits. Together, these factors accounted for a significant portion of the variance in student responses, underscoring the critical role of ASR and NLP tools in enhancing the learning experience and highlighting the need to address associated challenges.

Table 4. Factor analysis table of ASR by users.

Factor	Items Included	Factor Loading (Eigen Values)	Variance Explained (%)
	Daily use of ASR tools	0.76	
	Weekly use of NLP applications	0.7	
	Monthly use of ASR	0.65	
	Rare use of ASR tools	0.58	
Usage Frequency	Frequent access to NLP tools	0.55	25%
	Improved speaking skills	0.82	
	Enhanced writing quality	0.78	
	Simplified complex texts	0.74	
	Confidence in public speaking	0.72	
Effectiveness in Learning	Support for group projects	0.69	30%
	Technical issues with ASR	0.8	
	Need for better training	0.75	
	Usability problems	0.73	
	Struggles with accents	0.68	
Challenges Faced	Lack of resources for troubleshooting	0.65	27%
	General satisfaction with ASR tools	0.79	
	General satisfaction with NLP tools	0.76	
Overall Satisfaction	Perceived overall learning improvement	0.74	18%

*Self Computed.

DIALECT ISSUES

The study included experimental assessments of ASR systems in various classroom settings. These experiments measured how well ASR performed during live discussions. Results showed that in quiet environments, the average accuracy rate was around 85%, but this dropped to about 70% in noisy classrooms. Student satisfaction correlated closely with how well the systems performed. One student remarked, *"When ASR works, it's great. But if it doesn't, it's really frustrating and I miss out on what the teacher is saying."*

Odia speakers faced unique issues, such as pronunciation variations where words like "/ˈmoːɹɔ/" (mora, meaning "my") were misrecognized as "more." Additionally, regional vocabulary often went unrecognized; for instance, terms like "/ʤɔlɔkɔ/" (jalaka, meaning "water") were not included in the ASR's language model. Tone and intonation differences also led to misinterpretation, making phrases like "/apɔɳɔke:miʈi/?" (Apana kemiti?, meaning "How are you?") difficult for the systems to capture accurately.

Bengali dialect speakers encountered their own set of challenges, including phonetic differences that could lead to words like "/ami/" (ami, meaning "I") being misheard as "army." The use of regional slang, such as "/pɔʈʈi/" (patti, meaning "gang"), often confused ASR systems that weren not programmed for these terms. Compound words in Bengali, like "/ʃubʰɔʃɔka:l/" (shubhoshokal, meaning "good morning"), presented further difficulties, as did stress patterns that could change meanings, like "/gʰɔɾ/" (ghor, meaning "house"). Cultural references and idioms unique to Bengali, such as "/ha:ʈibʰa:ʈ/" (hatibhat, meaning "rice served with a side dish"), could be entirely missed by the technology. The issue was more pertinent for international students from Bangladesh.

Dialect speakers from Bihar, Chhattisgarh, and Jharkhand also faced distinct challenges. The influence of multiple languages resulted in unique pronunciations, causing misunderstandings with words like "/həmɾa/" (hamra, meaning "us"). The syntax often differed from standard Hindi, complicating recognition. For example, sentences like "/həmdʒa:nəʈba:ni/" (ham jaanat bani, meaning "We know") confused ASR systems. Local terms, such as "/gəŋwa:/" (ganwa, meaning "village"), often went unrecognized, and specific word emphasis further hindered accurate communication. The issue was more pertinent for international students from the bordering regions, especially from Nepal.

Tamil speakers (samples) pronounced "/ɛɳɳa/" (enna, meaning "what") in a way that ASR systems misinterpret as "hen." The use of local slang, like "/pəɳɳi/" (panni, meaning "to do"), confused the technology further. In Telugu, phrases like "/nuvvue:kkaɖaun:a:vu/?" (nuvvuekkadaunnāvu?, meaning "Where are you?") were misheard due to different intonation patterns. Kannada speakers faced issues with words like "/na:nu/" (nānu, meaning "I"), which could be misrecognized as "now." Additionally, unique expressions in Malayalam, such as "/eŋŋəːe/" (engane, meaning "how"), were not captured correctly, leading to misunderstandings. The issue was more pertinent for international students from Sri Lanka.

MANAGERIAL IMPLICATIONS

The findings indicate that ASR and NLP technologies are utilized regularly, especially in language practice and writing assignments, but also highlight a gap in their use beyond academic contexts, with many students rarely utilizing these tools outside formal assignments. Research supports these findings, revealing that

ASR tools are effective in helping learners enhance their pronunciation and fluency, while NLP technologies significantly contribute to improving writing skills and comprehension. The data indicating a high level of effectiveness in enhancing writing quality align with previous studies that underscore NLP's utility in academic writing and analysis. However, challenges such as technical issues with accent recognition, software bugs, and the usability of complex NLP outputs are barriers to the effective use of these technologies. By resolving these problems and ensuring that users receive improved training, adoption can be significantly increased. This would help achieve the broader goals of SDG 9: Industry, Innovation, and Infrastructure by promoting the development of inclusive, effective, and accessible educational technologies through this research.

CONCLUSION

The integration of ASR and NLP technologies in educational settings holds great potential for enhancing academic development, aligning with SDG 4: Quality Education, which advocates for inclusive, equitable, and accessible education through innovative technology solutions. A growing trend in this field of research, especially since 2020, with a significant spike in 2022 highlights the need for more empirical research and meta-analyses that focus on pedagogical outcomes and suggests looking into the potential of LLM-powered chatbots [2]. The data collected in the survey reveals diverse patterns in the usage of ASR and NLP tools. ASR tools are widely employed for enhancing language skills, with a specific emphasis on pronunciation and comprehension. Similarly, NLP tools are often integrated into academic practices for tasks such as text analysis and vocabulary enhancement, particularly in higher education environments. These technologies not only support educational outcomes but also contribute to SDG 10: Reduced Inequalities by providing learners from diverse backgrounds with tools to succeed in language acquisition and academic development. Future research should focus on developing more sophisticated systems, evaluating their effectiveness in diverse educational contexts, and addressing ethical considerations related to data privacy and security.

REFERENCES

[1] S. Alharbi, M. Alrazgan, A. Alrashed, T. Alnomasi, R. Almojel, R. Alharbi, S. Alharbi, S. Alturki, F. Alshehri, and M. Almojil, "Automatic speech recognition: systematic literature review", *IEEE Access,* vol. 9, pp. 131858-131876, 2021. [http://dx.doi.org/10.1109/ACCESS.2021.3112535]

[2] J. Jeon, S. Lee, and S. Choi, "A systematic review of research on speech-recognition chatbots for language learning: Implications for future directions in the era of large language models", *Interact. Learn. Environ.,* vol. 32, no. 8, pp. 4613-4631, 2024. [http://dx.doi.org/10.1080/10494820.2023.2204343]

[3] T-N. Ngo, H-J. Chen, and K-W. Lai, "The effectiveness of automatic speech recognition in ESL/EFL pronunciation: A meta-analysis", *ReCALL,* vol. 36, no. 1, 2023. [http://dx.doi.org/10.1017/S095834402300001X]

[4] A.R. Bhandarkar, C. Onyedimma, R.M. Jarrah, S. Ibrahim, S. Fu, H. Liu, and M. Bydon, "An integrated voice recognition and natural language processing platform to automatically extract thoracolumbar injury classification score features from radiology reports", *World Neurosurg.,* vol. 183, pp. e243-e249, 2024. [http://dx.doi.org/10.1016/j.wneu.2023.12.065] [PMID: 38103686]

[5] Y. Lyu, A.B.M. Adnan, and L. Zhang, "Influencing factors on NLP technology integration in teaching: A case study in Shanghai", *Educ. Inf. Technol.,* 2024. [http://dx.doi.org/10.1007/s10639-024-13063-6]

[6] R. Southwell, S. Pugh, E. Perkoff, M. Clevenger, C. Bush, J.B. Lieber, R. Ward, and S. D'Mello, *S. "Challenges and feasibility of automatic speech recognition for modeling student collaborative discourse in classrooms.* Institute of Cognitive Science, University of Colorado Boulder, 2024.

[7] W. Sun, "The impact of automatic speech recognition technology on second language pronunciation and speaking skills of EFL learners: a mixed methods investigation", *Front. Psychol.,* vol. 14, 2023.1210187 [http://dx.doi.org/10.3389/fpsyg.2023.1210187] [PMID: 37663357]

[8] M. Carrier, "Automated speech recognition in language learning: potential models, benefits and impact", *Training Language and Culture,* vol. 1, no. 1, pp. 46-61, 2017. [http://dx.doi.org/10.29366/2017tlc.1.1.3]

[9] E. Ghazizadeh, and P. Zhu, "A systematic literature review of natural language processing: current state, challenges and risks", *Proc. Future Technologies Conf. (FTC),* vol. 1, 2020. [http://dx.doi.org/10.1007/978-3-030-63128-4_49]

[10] D. Khurana, A. Koli, K. Khatter, and S. Singh, "Natural language processing: state of the art, current trends and challenges", *Multimedia Tools Appl.,* vol. 82, no. 3, pp. 3713-3744, 2023. [http://dx.doi.org/10.1007/s11042-022-13428-4] [PMID: 35855771]

[11] M. Mejeh, and M. Rehm, "Taking adaptive learning in educational settings to the next level: Leveraging natural language processing for improved personalization", *Educ. Technol. Res. Dev.,* pp. 1-25, 2024.

[12] S.C. Teba, *"Using ASR and NLP-Based Tools to Foster Beninese EFL Advanced Students' Oral Communication in Some Secondary Schools in Littoral Region," FLASH-Adjarra Univ. of Abomey-Calavi.* Benin Republic, 2024.

[13] J. Sawicki, M. Ganzha, and M. Paprzycki, "The state of the art of natural language processing—A systematic automated review of NLP literature using NLP techniques", *Data Intell.,* vol. 5, no. 3, pp. 707-749, 2023. [http://dx.doi.org/10.1162/dint_a_00213]

[14] K. Shukla, E. Vashishtha, M. Sandhu, and P. R. Choubey, *Natural Language Processing: Unlocking the Power of Text and Speech Data* Xoffencer publication, 2023.

[15] J. Smith, and A. Jones, "Enhancing academic development through automatic speech recognition and natural language processing", *J. Educ. Technol,* vol. 15, no. 2, pp. 123-135, 2022.

CHAPTER 2

The Influence of Behavioural Analytics-driven Recommendation Systems on Web-based Purchase Decisions

Anita Pareek[1,*], **Binita Nanda**[1] and **Shrutisudha Mishra**[1]

[1] *Department of Commerce, Kalinga Institute of Social Sciences (Deemed to be University), Bhubaneswar, India*

Abstract: Behavioural Analytics-driven Recommendation Systems (BARS) have become increasingly popular in conjunction with the growth of e-commerce. Their goal is to improve customer experiences by providing customised product recommendations. This research delves into how these recommendation systems affect consumer behaviour, particularly emphasising purchasing patterns, contentment, and brand loyalty. By examining diverse BARS, including content-based methods, collaborative filtering, and hybrid filtering, this study aims to comprehend how customised recommendations impact customers' interactions with online retailers. The principal objectives of this study are to analyse the influence of BARS on consumer purchasing patterns, examine the correlation between BARS and customer perception, and assess the algorithms that have the highest impact on customised recommendations from the standpoint of the consumer. The research employs an empirical approach, collecting data from 200 online consumers. The study found that behavioral analytics and recommendations have a moderate effect on purchases, with relevance being a key factor. Accuracy and trust-building are important because collaborative filtering lacks trust. While younger, more frequent shoppers respond best, suggesting targeted, customised marketing, content-based, or hybrid filtering approaches improve engagement in product discovery, with a strong positive correlation among them.

Keywords: Artificial intelligence, BARs, Behavioural analytics, Digital economy, E-commerce.

INTRODUCTION

The e-commerce marketplace has boosted the number of online shoppers globally. Among such segments are the millennial and the Gen Z groups [1]. Millennials, born between 1981 and 1996, and Gen Z, born after 1996, are

* **Corresponding author Anita Pareek:** Department of Commerce, Kalinga Institute of Social Sciences (Deemed to be University), Bhubaneswar, India; E-mail: anita.pareek@kiss.ac.in

Shradhanjali Panda, Leena Priyadarshini Singh, V. Ramasamy & S. Balamurugan (Eds.)

important categories of young adult consumers with considerable spending power, making them easy targets for retail businesses [2]. These generations have been termed digitally native, that is, comfortable with technology and with navigating the internet better [3]. Also, a global report conducted in 2022 revealed that millennials and Gen Z contributed around 77% and 76%, respectively, to direct purchases on e-marketplaces. With five billion internet users worldwide, there is a growing trend toward online shopping that appears to be continuing for some time, thereby consolidating e-commerce as an integral element of the global retail segment [4].

E-commerce offers abundant returns to businesses and customers alike. For business users, e-commerce means streamlining operations from traditional paperwork to electronic systems, providing 24/7 service availability, and enabling data-driven decision-making based on insights into what their customers do and want, which ultimately boosts output [5]. For customers, the e-commerce experience is suitable for buying, as one can place orders for a wide range of goods and services and use online reviews to make a decision [6]. Thus, e-commerce plays a very pivotal role in propelling the digital economy forward. Retail e-commerce revenue globally is projected to have exceeded US$6.3 trillion by 2024 [7]. E-commerce is gaining ground in Egypt, and according to the outlook, Egypt is ranked 53rd globally in e-commerce, with an anticipated value of US$2,533.2 million by 2024. The Egyptian government also promotes small and medium-sized businesses to digitise in order to hasten the expansion of the digital economy. Retailers had to deploy AI-driven services like voice assistants, chatbots, and personalised recommendations to make sure that customers had a better shopping experience as e-commerce grew in popularity.

AI can read external data, learn from it, and adapt that knowledge for strategic application towards specific ends [8]. A wide set of business data, including buying history and attribution data on referral activities resulting from customer interactions with retail platforms. AI systems that are deployed for analyzing such data could conclude customer preferences, forecast prospect behaviour, and offer personally relevant synchronized recommendations. These facilities help retail businesses understand the marketplace trend as well as introduce changes in products to shift consumer preferences [9]. Additionally, by enhancing cross-selling and upselling capabilities and improving critical processes like customer service and relationship management, Artificial Intelligence (AI) helps retail firms boost online sales [10]. As a result, directly integrating AI into e-commerce transactions has several benefits that enhance online operations, increase productivity, and optimise e-commerce use [11]. This, however, has been fuelled by interest in the adoption of AI technologies by retailers, as it has an immense impact on the growth of e-commerce [12].

REVIEW OF LITERATURE

This segment of the study classifies all schools of thought in related areas into three segments focusing on the conceptual framework of the recommendation system, its impact on buying behaviour, and its exploration through perception.

Recommendation System (RS): Concept and Types

A well-built, precise recommender system is critical for e-commerce businesses to achieve success and profitability [13]. The main problem visitors and customers face on business sites, especially those selling clothing, is the presence of numerous, often nearly identical, products. This abundance may confuse the buying process, stretch out the buying cycle, and even confuse customers, sometimes driving potential buyers away from completing a purchase in the online store. Thus, an online retailer needs to implement a recommender system to address these problems [14]. Recommender systems assist customers in making a sensible purchase decision through the elimination of unnecessary options irrelevant to their needs, while at the same time offering them products of interest [15].

In this way, BARSs enhance shopping experiences, making it easier for customers to be satisfied during purchase and improving business efficiency [16]. Several recommender systems were developed to improve the precision and diversity of recommendations for end users [17]. Such developments would also enhance the overall effectiveness of recommendations toward better decision-making and customer satisfaction in an online shopping environment.

Despite the view that recommendations by RS lack credibility or knowledge about a particular thing as compared to other sources, they play a great role in the consumer decision-making process in the virtual world [18]. The availability of options *via* RS turns out to be very effective for decision-making at specific sites. This fact underscores that the value of product recommendations by intelligent agents increases when such systems interact with users during product evaluation. A good RS should therefore combine multiple sources of data to better support online shopping [19].

Thus, in this respect, the research points out three key perspectives: the recommendations generated by the RS, predictions of user preferences, and feedback from other community members [20]. According to researchers, recommender systems are the tools by which e-commerce platforms make purchase recommendations to customers. The recommendations may be considered based on several factors, including the top-selling items on the online site, the demographics of the customer, or an investigation of their previous business behavior to predict potential purchases. Recommendations can take various forms, such as suggesting specific products, providing personalized information on manufactured goods, sharing brief community opinions, and presenting critiques from other users.

The three major types of recommender systems are commonly categorized according to the approaches they use for recommendation [21]:

- ***Content-based Filtering:*** In this approach, products are recommended based on their similarity to other products, considering users' previous preferences [22].
- ***Collaborative Filtering:*** This suggests products to the consumers that most other similar users consume [23].

However, content-based and collaborative filtering have limitations to a large extent because they are based on different types of data and are incapable of effectively combining their unique strengths [24].

- ***Hybrid Approach:*** To overcome such limitations, a hybrid approach has been proposed by combining multiple recommendation techniques [25]. The integrated approach has proven to be the most effective solution, as it provides both collaborative and content-based strategies to strengthen the recommendation system [26]. Hybrid systems combine synergies emanating from the combination of both strategies to reduce weaknesses associated with each strategy.

The newer hybrid approach has been categorized into seven recommendation types: feature augmentation, meta-level, switching, mixed, feature combination, weighted, and cascade [27]. These categories represent how different techniques can improve their effectiveness in generating recommendations.

RS and its Impact on Customer Buying Behaviour

A firm and accurate recommender system is required for the success and profitability of e-business. On most clothing websites, customers often find themselves dreading the arduous task of finding their way through the vast array of similar and dissimilar products in the decision-making process. Such an excess may cause purchases to take longer than usual, confuse buyers, and eventually make buyers abandon their shopping carts. Hence, the connection to a Recommendation System (RS) is important for online traders to mitigate such problems. Thus, the RS helps customers by removing irrelevant choices and offering attractive products aligned with their interests, thereby improving the shopping experience and enhancing business productivity [28].

Of late, many forms of BARSs are under development not only for better accuracy but also for greater diversity in recommendations. Among these methods, Collaborative Filtering (CF) is one of the most commonly used and efficient. CF presupposes that clients with homogeneous purchasing behaviours who buy the same or related products are likely to share similar interests. Hence, these systems aim to predict customer preferences based on similarities among users and recommend products that may appeal to them.

A key challenge is the cold start problem, where a system has insufficient information to make recommendations, especially for new users who have made no purchases. The lack of interactions between new and existing users makes it impossible to establish similarity, which prevents the system from generating meaningful recommendations. E-commerce platforms usually attract more customers and tend to increase their product offerings. The rise in CF complexity and time-to-compute tends to reduce system performance and delay the production of recommendations. The issue results from a very sparse user-item matrix, which occurs when clients make purchases very infrequently compared to the total number of products available. This lack of information degrades the precision and effectiveness of RS. Another challenge is "interest drift," which defines how individuals' interests and needs evolve, based on factors involving social, cultural, and economic variation. Since CF relies on past buying behaviour to suggest relevant products, this is a huge problem.

Despite such extensive studies on overcoming these types of problems and enhancing the performance of CF, several systems are yet to capture the preferences of consumers and businesses to deliver the most advantageous recommendations. This lacuna in studies represents the need for further research to enhance the effectiveness of RS by fighting such issues systematically based on available data. Our work aims to overcome these problems by incorporating demographic data and personality traits, giving greater weight to recent transactions, and using Locality-Sensitive Hashing (LSH) to build a more effective and robust CF-based RS for an e-clothing store. Such a decision-making process regarding clothing purchases is not unrelated to the psychological characteristics of consumers, mainly personality traits. These traits can indeed profoundly influence long-standing interests and behaviour. An individual has a relatively stable behaviour type; hence, the reason business organizations study it in detail is to make more specific suggestions.

One widely recognized framework for understanding personality is the Big Five model, which describes personality through five important traits: extraversion, neuroticism, openness to experience, agreeableness, and conscientiousness. These traits significantly impact individual attitudes and behaviours, including preferences in garments. For example, extroverts tend to like bright colours and shiny designer clothes, whereas neurotics tend to like dark, peculiar clothes. Individuals with an openness-towards-experiencing tendency also tend to favour unique clothing styles, fashionable brands, and a variety of colours [29]. While fashionable subjects may like more modest, simple variations, conscientious consumers are more concerned about the physical integrity and cost of garments.

Interrelation between RS and Customer Perception

Web personalization serves as a persuasive mechanism, highlighting that personalization factors can influence how consumers process information online and shape the resulting decision outcomes in various ways. Proposals toward creating a framework that examines how Personalised Product Recommendations (PPRs) affect consumer loyalty toward online retailers are presented. Their findings reveal that the quality of PPRs is positively associated with decision quality and the costs of evaluating product alternatives, but negatively associated with the costs of screening. The integration of the Elaboration Likelihood Model with Consumer Search Theory examines how personalization suggestions impact the attitude and behavioural responses of the users and demonstrates the effect of quality of personalization on consumer item choice. It tests how online cross-recommendations inform consumers' direct cross-purchase intentions and concludes that both peripheral and central cues are important. Generally, both theoretical and empirical approaches have been used in previous studies to depict the different roles of web personalization in the customer decision-making process. This gap provides our study with an opportunity to contribute to the web personalization literature by exploring how BARS play a dual role in improving decision quality in online shopping through information load theory.

Having studied the above literature, a clear gap is evident: impact studies using BARS in buying behaviour and consumer perception are quite limited, and there is no study on it in Odisha. So, the study aims to examine how Behavioural Analytics-driven Recommendation Systems (BARS) impact consumer purchasing patterns, explore the connection between BARS and customer perception, and evaluate which algorithms offer the most personalised recommendations from the consumer's perspective in order to increase relevance and trust in recommendation technologies.

METHODOLOGY

The study utilized both primary and secondary data sources. For primary data, questionnaires were distributed randomly to customers. A structured and validated questionnaire was designed to gauge the interrelation between RS and customer perception. The questionnaire consisted of two sections: demographic details and the inter-relationship between RS and customer perception, each containing 29 questions based on the Likert scale. Moreover, to gain a more precise understanding, three hypotheses were formulated to examine the interrelationships and dependencies between RS and consumer perception.

DISCUSSION

A detailed discussion of the analysis and the inferences drawn is provided below:

Hypothesis 1

The hypothesis tries to establish the assumption that behavioural analytics-driven recommendation systems significantly influence consumer purchasing patterns by increasing the likelihood of purchase through personalized product suggestions on the basis of data collected (by the authors). Table **1** below represents the correlation between consumer purchasing patterns and purchases through personalized product suggestions.

Table 1. The correlation between consumer purchasing patterns and purchases through personalized product suggestions.

Correlations											
-		**1. I often buy products suggested to me based on my past purchases.**	**2. The recommendations I receive are relevant to my current shopping needs.**	**3. I find myself exploring more products due to personalized recommendations**	**4. Personalized recommendations increase the likelihood of me making a purchase**	**5. I am more likely to trust recommendations that match my browsing interests.**	**1. Relevant recommendations enhance my satisfaction with the platform.**	**2. I am more likely to revisit a site with relevant recommendations.**	**3. I trust sites that consistently offer relevant recommendations.**	**4. Relevant recommendations save me time when shopping online.**	**5. I share positive feedback about sites with highly relevant recommendations**
1. I often buy products suggested to me based on my past purchases.	Pearson Correlation	1	.429*	.193**	-.306**	-.524**	.162*	.724**	.671**	.052	-.092
Sig. (2-tailed)		-	.000	.004	.000	.000	.015	.000	.000	.438	.171
N		223	223	223	223	223	223	223	223	223	223
2. The recommendations I receive are relevant to my current shopping needs.	Pearson Correlation	.429**	1	.393**	.317**	-.469**	.731**	.700**	.135*	-.002	-.052
Sig. (2-tailed)		.000	-	.000	.000	.000	.000	.000	.044	.982	.442
N		223	223	223	223	223	223	223	223	223	223
3. I find myself exploring more products due to personalized recommendations	Pearson Correlation	.193**	.393**	1	.370**	.145*	.595**	.255**	.010	.132*	.090
Sig. (2-tailed)		.004	.000	-	.000	.030	.000	.000	.877	.049	.179
N		223	223	223	223	223	223	223	223	223	223

(Table 1) cont.....

Correlations											
-		**1. I often buy products suggested to me based on my past purchases.**	**2. The recommendations I receive are relevant to my current shopping needs.**	**3. I find myself exploring more products due to personalized recommendations**	**4. Personalized recommendations increase the likelihood of me making a purchase**	**5. I am more likely to trust recommendations that match my browsing interests.**	**1. Relevant recommendations enhance my satisfaction with the platform.**	**2. I am more likely to revisit a site with relevant recommendations.**	**3. I trust sites that consistently offer relevant recommendations.**	**4. Relevant recommendations save me time when shopping online.**	**5. I share positive feedback about sites with highly relevant recommendations**
4. Personalized recommendations increase the likelihood of me making a purchase	Pearson Correlation	-.306**	.317**	.370**	1	.176**	.483**	.151*	-.262**	.054	-.126
Sig. (2-tailed)		.000	.000	.000	-	.008	.000	.024	.000	.423	.060
N		223	223	223	223	223	223	223	223	223	223
5. I am more likely to trust recommendations that match my browsing interests.	Pearson Correlation	-.524**	-.469**	.145*	.176**	1	-.169*	-.502**	-.472**	.002	.167*
Sig. (2-tailed)		.000	.000	.030	.008	-	.011	.000	.000	.973	.013
N		223	223	223	223	223	223	223	223	223	223
1. Relevant recommendations enhance my satisfaction with the platform.	Pearson Correlation	.162*	.731**	.595**	.483**	-.169*	1	.564**	.084	.050	.049
Sig. (2-tailed)		.015	.000	.000	.000	.011	-	.000	209	.457	.464
N		223	223	223	223	223	223	223	223	223	223
2. I am more likely to revisit a site with relevant recommendations.	Pearson Correlation	.724**	.700**	.255**	.151*	-.502**	.564**	1	.546**	.031	-.173**
Sig. (2-tailed)		.000	.000	.000	.024	.000	.000	-	.000	.645	.010
N		223	223	223	223	223	223	223	223	223	223
3. I trust sites that consistently offer relevant recommendations.	Pearson Correlation	.671**	.135*	.010	-.262**	-.472**	.084	.546**	1	-.003	.149*
Sig. (2-tailed)		.000	.044	.877	.000	.000	.209	.000		.968	.026
N		223	223	223	223	223	223	223	223	223	223
4. Relevant recommendations save me time when shopping online.	Pearson Correlation	.052	-.002	.132*	.054	.002	.050	.031	-.003	1	.342**
Sig. (2-tailed)		.438	.982	.049	.423	.973	.457	.645	.968	-	.000
N		223	223	223	223	223	223	223	223	223	223
5. I share positive feedback about sites with highly relevant recommendations	Pearson Correlation	-.092	-.052	.090	-.126	.167*	.049	-.173**	-.149*	.342**	1
Sig. (2-tailed)		.171	.442	.179	.060	.013	.464	.010	.026	.000	-
N		223	223	223	223	223	223	223	223	223	223

*Self Computed.

**. Correlation is significant at the 0.01 level (2-tailed).

*. Correlation is significant at the 0.05 level (2-tailed).

a. ***Correlation between Product Suggestions and Purchases***: The first correlation shows that consumers often buy products based on past purchases. The significant correlation between buying suggested products and the relevance of recommendations (.429, $p < .01$) indicates that personalized suggestions are aligned with current shopping needs, which enhances the likelihood of purchase.

b. ***Influence of Personalized Recommendations on Exploration:*** Consumers explore more products due to personalized recommendations (.393, $p < .01$), and these recommendations positively affect the likelihood of making a purchase (.370, $p < .01$). This supports the hypothesis that personalization can increase product exploration and, by extension, the chances of purchase.

c. ***Trust and Likelihood of Purchase***: There is a positive relationship between trust in personalized recommendations and making a purchase (.176, $p < .01$). Consumers are more likely to trust recommendations that match their browsing interests, further supporting the hypothesis that behavioural analytics-driven recommendations can influence purchasing behaviour.

d. ***Relevance of Recommendations and Satisfaction:*** The relevance of personalized recommendations is highly correlated with satisfaction (.731, $p < .01$) and increased likelihood of site revisits (.724, $p < .01$). These findings suggest that relevant recommendations not only enhance the likelihood of purchase but also improve customer retention and satisfaction.

Overall, the correlations support the hypothesis by showing that personalized product suggestions significantly influence consumer purchasing behaviour, as they increase product exploration, trust, satisfaction, and, ultimately, the likelihood of purchase.

Hypothesis 2

There is a positive correlation between the effectiveness of behavioural analytics-driven recommendation systems and customer perception of brand loyalty and satisfaction.

The analysis shows the effectiveness of behavioural analytics-driven recommendation systems that can be accessed through metrics such as recommendation accuracy, relevance based on browsing history, frequency of updates, product diversity, and the role of user feedback. Moreover, although customer perception of brand loyalty and satisfaction are not directly included in the data, the perceived effectiveness of recommendations can act as a proxy for satisfaction and loyalty on the basis of data collected (by the authors). Table **2** below represents the correlation between the effectiveness of behavioural analytics-driven recommendation systems and customer perception of brand loyalty and satisfaction.

Table 2. The correlation between the effectiveness of behavioural analytics-driven recommendation systems and customer perception of brand loyalty and satisfaction.

Correlations					
-	1. Recommendation accuracy is key to their effectiveness.	2. My browsing history drives the relevance of recommendations.	3. Frequent updates improve recommendation effectiveness.	4. Product diversity affects recommendation effectiveness.	5. User feedback enhances recommendation systems.

(*Table 2) cont.....*

1. Recommendation accuracy is key to their effectiveness.	Pearson Correlation	1	.059	.348	.110	-.041
	Sig. (2-tailed)	-	.382	.000	.103	.546
	N	223	223	223	223	223
2. My browsing history drives the relevance of recommendations.	Pearson Correlation	.059	1	.004	.449	-.099
	Sig. (2-tailed)	.382	-	.958	.000	.139
	N	223	223	223	223	223
3. Frequent updates improve recommendation effectiveness.	Pearson Correlation	.348	.004	1	.331	.432
	Sig. (2-tailed)	.000	.958	-	.000	.000
	N	223	223	223	223	223
4. Product diversity affects recommendation effectiveness.	Pearson Correlation	.110	.449	.331	1	.198
	Sig. (2-tailed)	.103	.000	.000	-	.003
	N	223	223	223	223	223
5. User feedback enhances recommendation systems.	Pearson Correlation	-.041	-.099	.432	.198	1
	Sig. (2-tailed)	.546	.139	.000	.003	-
	N	223	223	223	223	223

Correlation is significant at the 0.01 level (2-tailed).
*Self Computed.

a. ***Recommendation Accuracy (Proxy for Effectiveness):*** According to Pearson Correlation, the frequent updates improve recommendation effectiveness: ($r = 0.348$, $p < 0.01$), Product diversity affects recommendation effectiveness: ($r = 0.110$, $p = 0.103$) (Not significant), User feedback enhances recommendation systems: ($r = -0.041$, $p = 0.546$) (Not significant).

b. ***According to Spearman Correlation, Frequent Updates Improve Recommendation Effectiveness:*** ($r_s = 0.363$, $p < 0.01$), Product diversity affects recommendation effectiveness: ($r_s = 0.153$, $p = 0.023$) (Significant at the 0.05 level), User feedback enhances recommendation systems: ($r_s = -0.024$, $p = 0.724$) (Not significant).

c. ***Browsing History and Relevance (Proxy for Behavioural Analytics):*** According to Pearson Correlation, Frequent updates improve recommendation effectiveness: ($r = 0.004$, $p = 0.958$) (Not significant), diversity affects recommendation effectiveness: ($r = 0.449$, $p < 0.01$) (Significant), User feedback enhances recommendation systems: ($r = -0.099$, $p = 0.139$) (Not significant).

d. ***According to Spearman Correlation, Frequent updates improve recommendation effectiveness:*** ($r_s = -0.064$, $p = 0.342$) (Not significant), Product diversity affects recommendation effectiveness: ($r_s = 0.466$, $p < 0.01$), User feedback enhances recommendation systems: ($r_s = -0.056$, $p = 0.406$) (Not significant).

Table **3** represents The ANOVA results for various statements evaluating users' preferences for different recommendation methods, including hybrid filtering, content-based filtering, and collaborative filtering.

Table 3. The ANOVA results for various statements evaluating users' preferences for different recommendation methods, including hybrid filtering, content-based filtering, and collaborative filtering.

-		Sum of Squares	df	Mean Square	F	Sig.
1. I find hybrid recommendations based on my history and trends more relevant. (Hybrid filtering)	Between Groups	4.509	3	1.503	1.946	.123
	Within Groups	169.150	219	.772	-	-
	Total	173.659	222	-	-	-
3. I like a mix of my past activity and popular products among similar users. (Hybrid filtering)	Between Groups	14.392	3	4.797	7.145	.000
	Within Groups	147.034	219	.671	-	-
	Total	161.426	222	-	-	-
2. Recommendations that consider items I've viewed align with my needs. (Content-Based Filtering)	Between Groups	7.414	3	2.471	4.039	.008
	Within Groups	134.020	219	.612	-	-
	Total	141.435	222	-	-	-
3. Content-based suggestions improve my shopping experience. (Content-Based Filtering)	Between Groups	3.898	3	1.299	1.438	.233
	Within Groups	197.824	219	.903	-	-
	Total	201.722	222	-	-	-
1. I trust recommendations based on what similar users have bought. (Collaborative Filtering)	Between Groups	2.985	3	.995	1.158	.327
	Within Groups	188.172	219	.859	-	-
	Total	191.157	222	-	-	-
2. Recommendations influenced by users with similar tastes affect my choices. (Collaborative Filtering)	Between Groups	1.146	3	.382	.522	.668
	Within Groups	160.414	219	.732	-	-
	Total	161.561	222	-	-	-

(Table 3) cont.....

-		Sum of Squares	df	Mean Square	F	Sig.
3. I consider products popular among users with similar behavior. (Collaborative Filtering)	Between Groups	1.063	3	.354	.419	.739
	Within Groups	184.324	218	.846	-	-
	Total	185.387	221	-	-	-
1. I prefer recommendations based on attributes of products I've liked.(Content-Based Filtering)	Between Groups	1.373	3	.458	.516	.671
	Within Groups	194.107	219	.886	-	-
	Total	195.480	222	-	-	-
2. Combining my behavior with similar users' preferences improves recommendations.(Hybrid filtering)	Between Groups	7.979	3	2.660	3.392	.019
	Within Groups	171.743	219	.784	-	-
	Total	179.722	222	-	-	-

*Self Computed.

Frequent Updates and Recommendation Effectiveness

According to Pearson Correlation: Product diversity affects recommendation effectiveness: ($r = 0.331$, $p < 0.01$), User feedback enhances recommendation systems: ($r = 0.432$, $p < 0.01$).

According to Spearman Correlation: Product diversity affects recommendation effectiveness: ($r\_s = 0.260$, $p < 0.01$), User feedback enhances recommendation systems: ($r\_s = 0.486$, $p < 0.01$).

The data shows significant positive correlations between certain factors, such as frequent updates and product diversity, with recommendation effectiveness. However, browsing history (as a direct measure of behavioral analytics) does not show a strong positive correlation with recommendation effectiveness. User feedback and its impact on the systems also do not show significant correlations, meaning customer perception in that regard might be less tied to loyalty or satisfaction. Thus, the hypothesis is partially supported, as some aspects of behavioral analytics-driven systems (like frequent updates) positively correlate with recommendation effectiveness, which could enhance customer satisfaction. However, other components like browsing history and user feedback do not show strong correlations with effectiveness, which suggests that their impact on brand loyalty and satisfaction might be less substantial.

Hypothesis 3

Algorithms that utilize collaborative filtering have a greater impact on the effectiveness of customized recommendations compared to content-based filtering, as perceived by consumers. Table **4** below presents the ANOVA results for various statements evaluating user preferences for hybrid filtering, content-based filtering, and collaborative filtering in recommendation systems. The data collected and calculated by the authors shows the following results:

Table 4. The ANOVA results for various statements evaluating user preferences for hybrid filtering, content-based filtering, and collaborative filtering in recommendation systems.

-		Sum of Squares	df	Mean Square	F	Sig.
1. I find hybrid recommendations based on my history and trends more relevant. (Hybrid filtering)	Between Groups	4.509	3	1.503	1.946	.123
	Within Groups	169.150	219	.772	-	-
	Total	173.659	222	-	-	-
3. I like a mix of my past activity and popular products among similar users. (Hybrid filtering)	Between Groups	14.392	3	4.797	7.145	.000
	Within Groups	147.034	219	.671	-	-
	Total	161.426	222	-	-	-
2. Recommendations that consider items I've viewed align with my needs. (Content-Based Filtering)	Between Groups	7.414	3	2.471	4.039	.008
	Within Groups	134.020	219	.612	-	-
	Total	141.435	222	-	-	-
3. Content-based suggestions improve my shopping experience. (Content-Based Filtering)	Between Groups	3.898	3	1.299	1.438	.233
	Within Groups	197.824	219	.903	-	-
	Total	201.722	222	-	-	-
1. I trust recommendations based on what similar users have bought. (Collaborative Filtering)	Between Groups	2.985	3	.995	1.158	.327
	Within Groups	188.172	219	.859	-	-
	Total	191.157	222	-	-	-
2. Recommendations influenced by users with similar tastes affect my choices. (Collaborative Filtering)	Between Groups	1.146	3	.382	.522	.668
	Within Groups	160.414	219	.732	-	-
	Total	161.561	222	-	-	-

(Table 4) cont.....

-		Sum of Squares	df	Mean Square	F	Sig.
3. I consider products popular among users with similar behavior. (Collaborative Filtering)	Between Groups	1.063	3	.354	.419	.739
	Within Groups	184.324	218	.846	-	-
	Total	185.387	221	-	-	-
1. I prefer recommendations based on attributes of products I've liked.(Content-Based Filtering)	Between Groups	1.373	3	.458	.516	.671
	Within Groups	194.107	219	.886	-	-
	Total	195.480	222	-	-	-
2. Combining my behavior with similar users' preferences improves recommendations.(Hybrid filtering)	Between Groups	7.979	3	2.660	3.392	.019
	Within Groups	171.743	219	.784	-	-
	Total	179.722	222	-	-	-

*Self Computed.

Hybrid Filtering

Question 1: "I find hybrid recommendations based on my history and trends more relevant."

F-value: 1.946, Sig: 0.123 (Not significant). This implies that users did not perceive a significant difference in relevance when provided with hybrid recommendations.

Question 3: "I like a mix of my past activity and popular products among similar users."

F-value: 7.145, Sig: 0.000 (Significant). Users strongly preferred hybrid recommendations that combine their activity and trends from other users, suggesting a positive perception of hybrid approaches.

Content-Based Filtering

Question 2: "Recommendations that consider items I've viewed align with my needs."

F-value: 4.039, Sig: 0.008 (Significant). There is a significant positive perception of content-based filtering when recommendations are based on the user's past viewed items.

Question 3: "Content-based suggestions improve my shopping experience."

F-value: 1.438, Sig: 0.233 (Not significant). This suggests that content-based suggestions do not significantly improve the overall shopping experience for users.

Collaborative Filtering

Question 1: "I trust recommendations based on what similar users have bought."

F-value: 1.158, Sig: 0.327 (Not significant). There is no significant perception that recommendations based on other users' purchases are more trustworthy.

Question 2: "Recommendations influenced by users with similar tastes affect my choices."

F-value: 0.522, Sig: 0.668 (Not significant). Users did not feel that recommendations influenced by users with similar tastes significantly affected their choices.

Collaborative Filtering appears to have no significant positive impact on user perception across the board, with all related questions showing no statistical significance. Content-Based Filtering does have a significant impact in one instance, indicating that users appreciate recommendations that align with items they have previously viewed. Hybrid Filtering shows the strongest positive impact, especially when combining personal activity with trends from other users. This indicates that users prefer a blend of both collaborative and content-based filtering. The hypothesis that collaborative filtering has a greater impact on recommendation effectiveness is not supported. Instead, the results suggest that hybrid filtering has the greatest perceived effectiveness, while content-based filtering also shows a positive impact. Collaborative filtering alone does not appear to significantly affect user perceptions of recommendation effectiveness.

FINDINGS AND RECOMMENDATIONS

a. Influence of BARS on Consumer Purchasing Patterns: There is a moderate positive correlation (\(~0.43\)) between how often consumers buy products based on past purchases and the relevance of the recommendations to their current needs. Consumers are more likely to explore products when recommendations are relevant, as indicated by a smaller but still positive correlation (~0.39) between exploring new products and perceived recommendation relevance. However, the trust in these suggestions (through

Collaborative Filtering) does not correlate strongly with the frequency of purchasing based on recommendations (correlation ~0.03).

b. Correlation between BARS and Customer Perception: Customer perception of recommendation relevance does not strongly correlate with trust in Collaborative Filtering algorithms, as the correlations between relevance and trust-based questions are near zero or even slightly negative. This suggests that while consumers may see value in personalized recommendations, they might not inherently trust algorithms that leverage similar user behaviour.
c. Impact of Algorithms on Customized Recommendations: Collaborative Filtering methods do not strongly correlate with whether consumers find recommendations relevant to their shopping needs or explore more products. There is a weak correlation (\(~0.07\)) between trust in Collaborative Filtering and exploration of more products, implying that while customers may acknowledge the system's suggestions, it might not directly drive significant product discovery.

Based on the analysis of the data and consumer behaviour patterns, here are some recommendations to enhance the effectiveness of Behavioural Analytics and Recommendation Systems (BARS) and improve customer engagement:

a. Enhance the Relevance of Recommendations: Since consumers tend to purchase more when recommendations are relevant to their current shopping needs, focus on improving the precision of recommendations. Use contextual data (*e.g.*, recent browsing history or seasonal trends) to offer more accurate suggestions.
b. Increase Transparency in Recommendation Algorithms: Given the weak correlation between trust in Collaborative Filtering and purchasing behavior, it may help increase transparency by explaining how recommendations are generated. Displaying "why this was recommended" (*e.g.*, "Users like you bought this") can boost customer trust and confidence in the system.
c. Target Younger and Frequent Shoppers: Younger consumers and frequent shoppers are likely to explore more products when given personalized recommendations. Focus marketing efforts on these groups with special offers or product suggestions based on their browsing patterns.
d. Introduce Social Proof and Popularity-Based Recommendations: For consumers less influenced by Collaborative Filtering, social proof strategies (showcasing the popularity of products among similar users) can help. For example, highlighting that "X number of people bought this product today" may enhance the credibility of recommendations.
e. Personalize the Shopping Experience for Different Demographics: Tailor recommendations based on demographic data (*e.g.*, age, gender, profession).

For instance, working professionals may prefer recommendations for quick, essential purchases, while younger users might respond better to trend-based or novelty items.

f. Improve Product Discovery with Explorative Recommendations: While BARS influences purchase decisions moderately, consumers are still open to exploring new products. Leverage this by introducing features such as "recommended for you" sections or "you might also like" panels that encourage users to browse more items based on their past interactions.
g. Provide Incentives for Engaging with Recommendations: Offering incentives (like discounts or loyalty points) for purchasing recommended products can increase engagement with BARS. This can be particularly effective for infrequent shoppers or users who might not otherwise act on recommendations.

CONCLUSION

BARS systems influence consumer purchasing behaviour moderately, especially when recommendations align well with shopping needs. Customer perception is somewhat disconnected from algorithm trust, suggesting room for improvement in transparency or personalization to enhance trust. Collaborative Filtering has a minor impact on consumer behaviour in this dataset, with weak correlations indicating that other algorithms or recommendation methods might be more effective. The findings indicate that while Behavioural Analytics and Recommendation Systems are moderately significant factors affecting consumer purchasing behaviour, they are mostly dependent on the perceived relevance of the recommendations. This calls for improvements to the recommendation algorithms to make them relevant to consumers' needs and contexts. Trust in Collaborative Filtering has little connection with either purchasing or exploring products, suggesting that people do not have a natural tendency to trust algorithms, even if they appreciate the benefits of personalized recommendations. This means working simultaneously on improving recommendation accuracy and building user trust.

Furthermore, the results suggest that not all recommendation types work equally well across demographics or shopping behaviours. Younger, more frequent shoppers seem to be the most significant target group, as they are more willing to wander and try recommendations. Whereas the product discovery process could be adequately served by content-based or hybrid filtering, because collaborative filtering has not had much impact in this regard. This further demonstrates how contextual and demographic personalization would make the recommendation even more relevant. A recommendation that meets the immediate need of a consumer or aligns with his shopping behaviour, such as a seasonal trend or a recently viewed product, would elicit a response. This would, therefore, provide insights that engage users more and lead to more consistent purchasing behaviour. To further engage BARS, organizations will also have to look into how personalization can be combined with social proof and other interesting methods for communicating recommendations. Showing the popularity of these products and even creating reward mechanisms can address this trust gap, encouraging customers to act on endorsements. The fact that Collaborative Filtering is not a particularly strong method further implies that there is significant scope for innovation in recommendation technologies [30, 31]. By combining hybrid filtering with real-time contextual data, an organization can combine several strategies into a thorough and engaging shopping experience that meets various customer needs. By improving customer satisfaction and trust, the strategy places BARS as one of the primary enablers of sustainable growth in a digital marketplace that is becoming more and more competitive.

Future research can look into advanced AI-driven BARS that integrate contextual and emotional analytics to increase relevance and trust. Extending research across cultures, industries, and real-time behavior tracking can improve algorithms [11]. Personalization strategies targeted at a variety of demographics may boost engagement in dynamic e-commerce environments, fostering brand loyalty and guaranteeing sustained customer satisfaction.

REFERENCES

[1] R. Pillai, B. Sivathanu, and Y.K. Dwivedi, "Shopping intention at AI-powered automated retail stores (AIPARS)", *J. Retailing Consum. Serv.*, vol. 57, 2020.102207 [http://dx.doi.org/10.1016/j.jretconser.2020.102207]

[2] M. Balabanović, and Y. Shoham, "FAB: Content-based, collaborative recommendation", *Commun. ACM,* vol. 40, no. 3, pp. 66-72, 2007. [http://dx.doi.org/10.1145/1995376.1995390]

[3] J. Bartels, and M.J. Reinders, "Consumer innovativeness and its correlates: A propositional inventory for future research", *J. Bus. Res.*, vol. 64, no. 6, pp. 601-609, 2011. [http://dx.doi.org/10.1016/j.jbusres.2010.05.002]

[4] R. Burke, ""Hybrid recommender systems: Survey and experiments," User Model. User-Adap", *User Model. User-adapt. Interact.,* vol. 12, no. 4, pp. 331-370, 2002. [http://dx.doi.org/10.1023/A:1021240730564]

[5] G. Adomavicius, and A. Tuzhilin, "Toward the next generation of recommender systems: a survey of the state-of-the-art and possible extensions", *IEEE Trans. Knowl. Data Eng.,* vol. 17, no. 6, pp. 734-749, 2005. [http://dx.doi.org/10.1109/TKDE.2005.99]

[6] M. Tkalčič, M. KunaverTasič, and A. Košir, "Personality-based user similarity measure for a collaborative recommender system", In: *Proc. 5th Workshop Emotion Human-Computer Interact.* Real World Challenges, 2010, pp. 30-37.

[7] R. Burke, *"Hybrid web recommender systems," in *The Adaptive Web: Methods and Strategies of Web Personalization.,* P. Brusilovsky, A. Kobsa, W. Nejdl, Eds., vol. Vol. 4321. Springer: Berlin,

Germany, 2007, pp. 377-408.
[http://dx.doi.org/10.1007/978-3-540-72079-9_12]

[8] S. Chevalier, "Gen Z online shopping behavior – statistics & facts", *Statista,* 2024. [Online]. Available: https://www.statista.com/topics/11087/gen-z-online-shopping-behavior/#topicOverview

[9] Y.H. Cho, and J.K. Kim, "Application of Web usage mining and product taxonomy to collaborative recommendations in e-commerce", *Expert Syst. Appl.,* vol. 26, no. 2, pp. 233-246, 2004.
[http://dx.doi.org/10.1016/S0957-4174(03)00138-6]

[10] G. Dunn, J. Wiersema, J. Ham, and L. Aroyo, "Evaluating interface variants on personality acquisition for recommender systems", In: *Proc. Int. Conf. User Model.* Adapt. Personalization (UMAP), 2009, pp. 259-270.
[http://dx.doi.org/10.1007/978-3-642-02247-0_25]

[11] ECDB, "eCommerce market in Egypt", [Online]. Available: https://ecommercedb.com/markets/eg/all

[12] G. Farnadi, "Computational personality recognition in social media", *User Model. User-Adap. Interact.,* vol. 26, no. 2–3, pp. 109-142, 2016.
[http://dx.doi.org/10.1007/s11257-015-9205-3]

[13] A. Guha, D. Grewal, P.K. Kopalle, M. Haenlein, M.J. Schneider, H. Jung, R. Moustafa, D.R. Hegde, and G. Hawkins, "How artificial intelligence will affect the future of retailing", *J. Retailing,* vol. 97, no. 1, pp. 28-41, 2021.
[http://dx.doi.org/10.1016/j.jretai.2021.01.005]

[14] H.J. Ahn, "Utilizing popularity characteristics for product recommendation", *Int. J. Electron. Commerce,* vol. 11, no. 2, pp. 59-80, 2006.
[http://dx.doi.org/10.2753/JEC1086-4415110203]

[15] A. De Keyser, and W.H. Kunz, "Living and working with service robots: a TCCM analysis and considerations for future research", *J. Serv. Manag.,* vol. 33, no. 2, pp. 165-196, 2022.
[http://dx.doi.org/10.1108/JOSM-12-2021-0488]

[16] A. Ansari, S. Essegaier, and R. Kohli, "Internet recommendation systems", *J. Mark. Res.,* vol. 37, no. 3, pp. 363-375, 2000.
[http://dx.doi.org/10.1509/jmkr.37.3.363.18779]

[17] J.L. Herlocker, and J.A. Konstan, "Content-independent task-focused recommendation", *IEEE Internet Comput.,* vol. 5, no. 6, pp. 40-47, 2001.
[http://dx.doi.org/10.1109/4236.968830]

[18] S.Y. Ho, and D. Bodoff, "The effects of web personalization on user attitude and behavior: An integration of the elaboration likelihood model and consumer search theory", *Manage. Inf. Syst. Q.,* vol. 38, no. 2, pp. 497-520, 2014.
[http://dx.doi.org/10.25300/MISQ/2014/38.2.08]

[19] E. Inan, F. Tekbacak, and C. Ozturk, "Moreopt: A goal programming based movie recommender system", *J. Comput. Sci.,* vol. 28, pp. 43-50, 2018.
[http://dx.doi.org/10.1016/j.jocs.2018.08.004]

[20] P. Kautish, and R. Sharma, "RETRACTED: Value orientation, green attitude and green behavioral intentions: an empirical investigation among young consumers", *Young Consumers,* vol. 20, no. 4, pp. 338-358, 2019.
[http://dx.doi.org/10.1108/YC-11-2018-0881]

[21] A. Kaplan, and M. Haenlein, "Rulers of the world, unite! The challenges and opportunities of artificial intelligence", *Bus. Horiz.,* vol. 63, no. 1, pp. 37-50, 2020.
[http://dx.doi.org/10.1016/j.bushor.2019.09.003]

[22] S. Chevalier, *Share of primarily online shoppers who ordered directly from online marketplaces worldwide in 2022, by generational cohort,* 2024.https://www.statista.com/statistics/1393757/global-marketplace-online-shoppers-by-age/

[23] T. Gajewska, D. Zimon, G. Kaczor, and P. Madzík, "The impact of the level of customer satisfaction on the quality of e-commerce services", *Int. J. Prod. Perform. Manag.*, vol. 69, no. 4, pp. 666-684, 2019.
[http://dx.doi.org/10.1108/IJPPM-01-2019-0018]

[24] S. Khodabandehlou, "Designing an e-commerce recommender system based on collaborative filtering using a data mining approach", *Int. J. Bus. Inf. Syst.*, vol. 31, no. 4, pp. 455-478, 2019.
[http://dx.doi.org/10.1504/IJBIS.2019.101582]

[25] S. Khodabandehlou, and A. A. NikNafs, "Improving customer loyalty evaluation methods in the grocery retail industry: A data mining approach", *Int. J. Electron. Cust. Relatsh. Manag.*, vol. 10, no. 2/3/4, pp. 158-178, 2016.
[http://dx.doi.org/10.1504/IJECRM.2016.079103]

[26] J.B. Schafer, J.A. Konstan, and J. Riedl, "E-commerce recommendation applications", *Data Min. Knowl. Discov.*, vol. 5, no. 1-2, pp. 115-153, 2001.
[http://dx.doi.org/10.1023/A:1009804230409]

[27] L. Zhang, Q. Tao, and P. Teng, "An improved collaborative filtering algorithm based on user interest", *J. Softw.*, vol. 9, no. 4, pp. 999-1006, 2014.
[http://dx.doi.org/10.4304/jsw.9.4.999-1006]

[28] S. Khodabandehlou, and M. Zivari Rahman, "Comparison of supervised machine learning techniques for customer churn prediction based on analysis of customer behavior", *J. Syst. Inf. Technol.*, vol. 19, no. 1/2, pp. 65-93, 2017.
[http://dx.doi.org/10.1108/JSIT-10-2016-0061]

[29] L.T. Khrais, "Role of artificial intelligence in shaping consumer demand in E-commerce", *Future Internet,* vol. 12, no. 12, p. 226, 2020.
[http://dx.doi.org/10.3390/fi12120226]

[30] A. Mohammadi, and M. Dindar, "How personality traits affect online consumer behavior?", *J. Bus. Res.*, vol. 116, pp. 425-432, 2020.
[http://dx.doi.org/10.1016/j.jbusres.2020.05.033]

[31] T. Chen, and L. He, "Collaborative filtering based on demographic attribute vector", In: *ETP Int. Conf. Future Comput. Commun.*, 2009.
[http://dx.doi.org/10.1109/FCC.2009.68]

CHAPTER 3

Mapping People Analytics for Strategic Human Resource Management

Arjyalopa Mishra[1,*] and **Sonam Subhadarshini**[2]

[1] *Department of Management, National Law University, Cuttack, Odisha, India*

[2] *Department of Business Administration, Trident Academy of Technology, Bhubaneswar, Odisha, India*

Abstract: Managing human resources has undergone a trajectory of change from its evolution to the understanding of people analytics. The integration of People Analytics (PA) into Strategic Human Resource Management (SHRM) is reshaping the way organizations optimize workforce potential and achieve strategic goals. This paper explores the synergies between PA and SHRM, emphasizing the transformative role of data-driven decision-making in addressing contemporary human resource challenges. The theoretical underpinnings and methodological techniques for exploring the HR investments and performance linkages based on a technologically adaptive skill orientation are promising for bringing in a new perspective on micro-managing the challenges of the dynamic environment. Predictive analysis based on empirical estimates is where research is focusing and exploring, with a focus on longitudinal intra-firm research. This work aims to investigate the essential components that people analytics teams need in order to improve organizational performance through a narrative literature review. The findings and results of the study reveal that predictive analytics has the potential to significantly enhance strategic HR management by bolstering theoretical, contextual, and practical insights. Subsequent research can enhance academic understanding and guide effective implementation. Using data-driven decisions that require interdisciplinary collaboration among management, data science, information systems, and organizational psychology strengthens HR's position as a strategic partner.

Keywords: Organizational performance, People analytics, Strategic human resource management.

* **Corresponding author Arjyalopa Mishra:** Department of Management, National Law University, Cuttack, Odisha, India; E-mail: arjyalopa@nluo.ac.in

Shradhanjali Panda, Leena Priyadarshini Singh, V. Ramasamy & S. Balamurugan (Eds.)

INTRODUCTION

In today's data-driven world, organizations are increasingly turning to analytics to gain insights into their operations. People analytics, a subset of this trend, applies data-driven approaches to understand and optimize human capital. By leveraging data from various sources, including HR systems, performance reviews, and employee surveys, organizations can make informed decisions about their workforce, leading to improved performance, increased employee satisfaction, and enhanced organizational effectiveness. The field of human resource management has undergone a significant transformation in recent years, with the emergence of data-driven approaches known as people analytics. People analytics, or HR analytics, refers to the systematic application of analytical methods to human resources-related data, enabling organizations to make more informed and strategic decisions about their workforce [1].

Innovation in human resource management is at the core of improving an organization's performance, creativity, and competitive advantage. Innovation in human resource management is about the dynamism of doing business in modern times. The conventional forms of HRM have evolved to become more strategic, technology-driven, and employee-friendly, constituting innovation in HRM [2]. As emphasized by most research studies, HRM is a function that can help an organization support innovation by properly linking employee capabilities and organizational purposes, providing a favourable environment for creativity, and offering high-involvement work practices to motivate employees to reach for the best. Among these emerging trends are HRM practices like decentralization, performance management, and technological integration. On the other hand, formal training, teamwork, and incentives are ways to foster creativity, which has also improved innovation in organizations. Furthermore, these methods improve productivity and are also important for long-term organizational growth as they enable effective management while remaining flexible regarding human capital. Therefore, innovative HRM practices are no longer an option but a necessity for organizations striving to maintain relevance and growth. By embracing creativity, technology, and employee empowerment, HRM fosters an environment that nurtures innovation, leading to improved organizational outcomes.

The growing importance of people analytics is driven by the rapid digitalization of work processes, which has led to an exponential increase in the volume, velocity, and variety of HR data [3]. By leveraging people analytics, the tech startup was able to identify the root causes of employee attrition and implement effective retention strategies. People analytics demonstrates the power of data-driven insights in improving organizational performance and employee satisfaction.

People analytics has the potential to revolutionize the way organizations manage their workforce. By leveraging data-driven insights, organizations can make informed decisions, improve employee performance, and enhance overall organizational effectiveness. However, it is crucial to address the challenges and ethical considerations associated with people analytics to ensure its successful implementation. As technology continues to advance, the future of people analytics is bright, offering exciting opportunities for organizations to unlock the full potential of their human capital.

HRM plays a role in stimulating innovation and creativity within the work environment. Creativity and innovation, which form the foundation of business survival, are perceived to reside within human resources. The challenge lies in the management of people and teams in such a manner that brings new ideas forward for implementation. It is HRM practices that form the core of influences on behaviours, with a double role for both the macro-level management of policy and micro-level employee engagement [4].

The biggest competitive edge for companies navigating the upheaval and uncertainty causing significant changes in today's workplace is employee and workforce insights. This is entwined with the increasing demand on the HR function to comprehend how workforce analytics drives performance and enhances the business. This chapter aims to investigate the essential components that people analytics teams need in order to improve organizational performance. Because of the fragmented nature of currently available data, it is challenging for firms to comprehend what successful people analytics execution requires. By laying the groundwork and providing particular recommendations for empirical research that connects people analytics to HR strategy, the study advances our understanding of the relationship between the two.

The study is significant because it highlights people analytics as a strategic HR tool and demonstrates how it can enhance workforce optimization, alter decision-making, and align talent management with organizational goals. By focusing on its effectiveness, the study highlights its role in advancing evidence-based, meaningful, and sustainable human resource strategies.

LITERATURE REVIEW

In recent years, the integration of People Analytics (PA) into Strategic Human Resource Management (SHRM) has attracted considerable attention, as organizations increasingly acknowledge the importance of data-driven decision-making in improving workforce performance and meeting business goals [5, 6]. People analytics involves utilizing data, statistical tools, and predictive models to assess Human Resource (HR) metrics, allowing organizations to make informed decisions regarding talent management, employee engagement, and overall organizational performance [7]. This literature review delves into the conceptual foundations, benefits, challenges, and applications of people analytics within SHRM.

People analytics is grounded in the broader field of workforce analytics and evidence-based management. It merges quantitative and qualitative methods to deliver actionable insights into workforce dynamics [8]. It points out that PA goes beyond traditional HR metrics by focusing on predictive capabilities, enabling organizations to foresee trends and outcomes. PA allows HR professionals to transition from transactional roles to strategic ones, aligning HR practices with the overarching goals of the organization [8].

Organizations and academic disciplines, particularly psychology and sociology, have historically intersected with organizational behaviour. The explosion of digital data is also causing changes in the disciplines, just like in businesses. The last ten years have seen the rise of a new field in social science research [9]. The use of new data sources, usually digital and extensive, that are streaming from all facets and walks of life, is what sets it apart [10]. Because of these data, researchers from several fields are working together to develop new computational techniques for studying human behaviour. The general phrase that is frequently used to describe this field is computational social science [11].

The literature provides a basis for further investigation, assisting us in identifying the fundamental causes of people analytics in strategic decision-making [9]. The assessment of predictive models created to foresee staff attrition is an example. Important performance indicators include recall, accuracy, and precision [12]. These thorough analyses not only clarified the advantages and disadvantages of various algorithms but also offered priceless insights into how well they work in the real world when dealing with attrition problems [13]. Additionally, our analysis revealed key predictors through people and computational algorithms, providing insight into the elements that have a major impact on human resource strategy. The identification of factors, including work-life balance, career development prospects, salary, and job satisfaction, by looking at feature importance scores and coefficients obtained from the prediction models through machine learning can make a huge impact on supply and demand forecasting of human resources [14].

The first segment starts by acknowledging the growing number of staff decision-making processes that are guided by algorithms [15]. Decision-makers are likely to use algorithmic input in their decision-making, research testing, and the mechanisms involved. Along with studies that aim to comprehend and resolve this issue, there are studies that aim to comprehend and resolve the causes of algorithmic bias [16]. Studies that investigate algorithms present in employees' everyday lives, rather than focusing solely on discrete decisions, are discussed. As artificial intelligence becomes more integrated into everyday tasks, this phenomenon is probably going to grow [17]. The majority of this algorithmic research is conceptualized at the person level of analysis, involving individual employees and decision-makers who are impacted by algorithms [18].

As a result, human resources can be valuable, rare, and incalculable, and they might be substituted for more aggressive profit motives. This is the main idea that this strategy is based on. Human resource practices are a useful tool for improving organizational performance [19]. These procedures establish knowledge, institutional skills, character skills, and organizational skills. Two aspects are related to the management of human resources and the goal of continuous aggressive profitability [20]. The main problem has to do with the human resources processes that the computer takes into account [21]. Therefore, it is possible to meet the requirements if the organization has a machine that is well-defined [22].

The above section highlighted people's analytics, citing a range of schools of thought in the form of research works. But, considering strategic human resource management, there still exists a gap in implementing proper AI tools in order to achieve an upper hand in an organization and beat the cutting-edge competition.

ROLE OF PEOPLE ANALYTICS IN SHRM

Strategic human resource management aims to align HR practices with an organization's strategic objectives to foster a sustained competitive advantage.

PA is crucial in achieving this alignment by:

1. Enhancing Talent Acquisition and Retention: PA offers insights into hiring trends, candidate behaviors, and employee turnover, helping organizations refine their recruitment strategies.
2. Driving Employee Engagement: By examining employee sentiment and performance data, organizations can pinpoint factors that affect engagement and implement effective strategies.
3. Improving Workforce Productivity: People Analytics (PA) helps identify high-performing teams and individuals, enabling organizations to optimize performance through customized training and development programs.

4. Enabling Strategic Decision-Making: The predictive capabilities of PA empower HR leaders to foresee workforce challenges and create proactive strategies, thus enhancing organizational agility.

The People Analytics Process

The people analytics process typically involves the following stages:

1. Data Collection:
   - Data Sources: HR Information Systems (HRIS), performance management systems, employee surveys, and external data sources.
   - Data Quality: Ensuring data accuracy, completeness, and consistency.
2. Data Preparation:
   - Data Cleaning: Identifying and correcting errors and inconsistencies.
   - Data Integration: Combining data from multiple sources into a unified dataset.
   - Data Transformation: Transforming data into a suitable format for analysis.
3. Data Analysis:
   - Descriptive Analytics: Summarizing and describing data using statistical measures.
   - Predictive Analytics: Building models to predict future outcomes, such as employee turnover or performance.
   - Prescriptive Analytics: Providing recommendations for optimal decision-making.
4. Insight Generation:
   - Identifying Patterns: Discovering trends and relationships in the data.
   - Storytelling: Communicating insights effectively to stakeholders.
5. Action Planning and Implementation:
   - Translating Insights into Action: Developing actionable strategies based on the insights.
   - Measuring Impact: Evaluating the impact of interventions and making adjustments as needed.

Applications of People Analytics

People analytics can be applied to a wide range of HR functions, including:

- Workforce Planning: Forecasting future workforce needs, identifying skill gaps, and optimizing workforce allocation.
- Recruitment and Selection: Improving the quality of hiring decisions by

analysing candidate data and predicting job performance.

- Performance Management: Identifying high-potential employees, measuring performance, and providing targeted development opportunities.
- Employee Engagement: Measuring employee satisfaction, identifying drivers of engagement, and implementing interventions to boost morale.
- Retention: Predicting employee turnover, understanding reasons for leaving, and developing retention strategies.
- Compensation and Benefits: Analysing compensation data to identify pay gaps, optimize compensation packages, and improve employee satisfaction.
- Diversity and Inclusion: Measuring diversity and inclusion metrics, identifying biases, and implementing initiatives to promote a more inclusive workplace.

CONCEPTUAL FRAMEWORK OF AI AND HRM FUNCTION

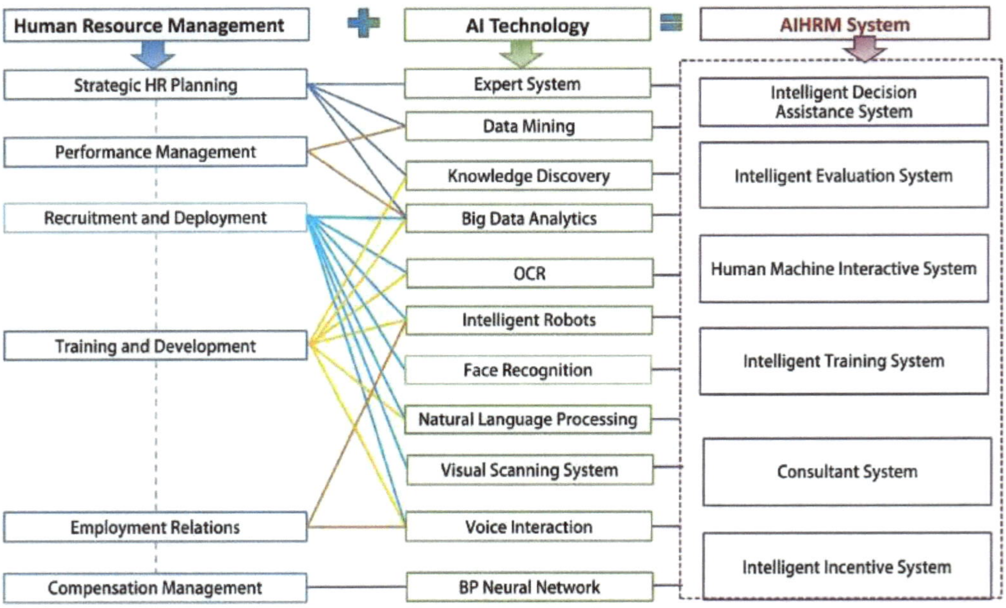

Fig. (1). Conceptual Framework of AI and HRM functions.
Source: http://iceb.johogo.com/proceedings/2018/ICEB2018

THE INTERSECTION OF PEOPLE ANALYTICS AND STRATEGIC HRM

Strategic Human Resource Management (SHRM) aims to align HR practices with an organization's overall business strategy. People analytics plays a crucial role in this alignment by providing data-driven insights that inform strategic HR decisions. HR departments are increasingly embracing the digital revolution, employing techniques such as big data analysis, artificial intelligence, and cloud computing to streamline resources (Fig. **1**). In human resource management, most organizations use artificial intelligence and digital technologies such as chatbots, machine learning, and robotic process automation to help with recruiting, screening, onboarding, and interviewing, among other things [23]. AI is being adopted by just 40% of organizations and industries and shall be taken over with a trajectory change.

Key Areas of Impact

1. Workforce Planning and Talent Management
    - Predictive Analytics: By analysing historical data on hiring, attrition, and performance, organizations can forecast future workforce needs.
    - Succession Planning: Identifying high-potential employees and their development needs to ensure a smooth transition of leadership.
    - Talent Acquisition: Using data-driven insights to optimize recruitment strategies and identify top talent.
2. Employee Performance and Development
    - Performance Management: Analysing performance data to identify top performers, identify areas for improvement, and provide targeted development opportunities.
    - Career Development: Using data to identify career paths and provide personalized development plans.
    - Learning and Development: Evaluating the effectiveness of training programs and tailoring them to specific needs.
3. Employee Engagement and Retention
    - Engagement Surveys: Analysing employee feedback to identify areas of strength and weakness.
    - Retention Prediction: Using data to predict employee turnover and implement strategies to retain top talent.
    - Employee Experience: Measuring and improving the employee experience to boost morale and productivity.
4. Compensation and Benefits
    - Compensation Analysis: Analysing compensation data to identify pay gaps, optimize compensation packages, and ensure fairness.
    - Benefits Optimization: Evaluating the effectiveness of benefit programs and making data-driven decisions to improve employee satisfaction.

Benefits of People Analytics in SHRM

Integrating PA into Strategic Human Resource Management (SHRM) provides several advantages, such as:

- Data-Driven Insights: PA enables organizations to make HR decisions based on solid evidence rather than gut feelings.
- Enhanced Workforce Planning: Predictive analytics aids in long-term workforce planning by pinpointing skills gaps and succession planning requirements.
- Cost Optimization: By identifying inefficiencies and areas needing improvement, PA assists organizations in lowering HR-related expenses.
- Increased Diversity and Inclusion: PA can reveal biases in recruitment and promotion processes, helping organizations create more inclusive workplaces.

THE WAY FORWARD THROUGH TECHNOLOGICAL INTERVENTIONS IN PEOPLE ANALYTICS

The integration of technology into people analytics has reshaped Human Resource (HR) management, transitioning it from a supportive function to a pivotal aspect of strategic business operations [24]. Advanced technologies, including predictive analytics, Artificial Intelligence (AI), and Machine Learning (ML), enable organizations to extract valuable, data-driven insights into workforce behavior and dynamics. These insights support well-informed decision-making about human capital. However, despite their benefits, the effective implementation of these technologies comes with notable challenges.

Technological advancements in people analytics have revolutionized the HR field by utilizing innovations in big data, machine learning, and AI. These tools align HR practices with broader organizational goals, enhancing functionality and strategic importance. For example, AI-powered systems offer data-backed insights into employee performance, effectively linking HR activities to business outcomes [25]. Additionally, integrating IoT devices with data analytics facilitates predictive modeling, addressing workforce management challenges while encouraging evidence-based decision-making. By standardizing metrics and adopting a scientific approach, these technologies enhance the credibility and strategic impact of HR.

AI has dramatically enhanced HR analytics by offering tools for superior decision-making and operational optimization. For instance, predictive analytics powered by machine learning helps identify factors leading to employee turnover and recommends strategies to improve engagement. Similarly, AI streamlines recruitment processes by automating candidate evaluations, minimizing biases, and improving the quality of hires [26].

AI-driven HR platforms also support Diversity, Equity, and Inclusion (DEI) initiatives by providing unbiased performance assessments, fostering inclusivity, and promoting workplace fairness. The use of machine learning to predict performance outcomes further enhances workforce management and resource allocation. In both the public and private sectors, HR analytics involves structured methods like data collection, predictive modeling, and strategic application to improve workforce planning and performance reviews [17].

However, the implementation of AI in HR is accompanied by challenges, including addressing data privacy issues, reducing algorithmic bias, and ensuring transparent governance. Ethical standards must guide the use of these technologies, and HR professionals must develop the necessary skills to maximize their potential. As AI redefines HR, its responsible deployment is critical to unlocking its full value.

CHALLENGES AND FUTURE DIRECTIONS

Despite its transformative potential, several obstacles hinder the effective adoption of HR analytics. A review by Margherita highlighted technical limitations, insufficient analytical skills, and a tendency to focus on basic reporting rather than actionable insights. Ethical concerns and a lack of evidence demonstrating clear impacts also remain significant barriers. Ensuring organizational readiness and incorporating analytics into a well-defined value framework, such as Return On Investment (ROI), are essential for success. Factors like industry characteristics, national context, cultural readiness, and technical constraints also influence outcomes.

Emerging conceptual frameworks offer potential solutions. For example, a new model examined the relationship between green HR practices, big data analytics, and sustainable performance through green innovation. Similarly, Intelligent HRM (I-HRM) models propose using AI to optimize talent processes throughout the employee lifecycle. Xu and Pero emphasize that adopting big data analytics requires a phased development of necessary capabilities.

The growing interest in predictive analytics within Strategic Human Resource Management (SHRM) reflects its promise for improved decision-making. However, implementation challenges persist, and empirical validation of integrative models remains limited. Deficiencies in skills and organizational preparedness constrain the full realization of these technologies. Studies often underscore the need for HR professionals to develop stronger analytical competencies [27]. Additionally, greater transparency in AI systems is essential, as research by Cheng and Hackett revealed that algorithms often deviate from the concept of "true black boxes." Without a deeper understanding of analytics, HR risks losing its strategic influence. Collaboration between HR and analytics teams is crucial to achieving success. Many studies rely on cross-sectional designs, which restrict causal conclusions. For instance, while Verma *et al.* identified correlations between variables, they could not establish causality. Similarly, sampling issues—such as data derived from specific industries, countries, or convenience samples—limit the generalizability of findings. For example, El-Kassar and Singh's study focused exclusively on firms in the Middle East and Africa, emphasizing the need for diverse sampling methods to improve research robustness.

Addressing these challenges through enhanced methodological approaches, skill development, and ethical governance can unlock the full potential of technological interventions in people analytics. This will enable HR to firmly establish itself as a strategic, data-driven function.

CONCLUSION

In summary, predictive analytics holds significant promise for advancing strategic HR management, offering ample opportunities to delve deeper into its theoretical foundations, contextual factors, and practical applications. Future research in this domain can enhance academic knowledge while providing actionable insights for effective organizational implementation. By leveraging data-driven decision-making, HR departments can solidify their role as strategic business partners. Addressing the multifaceted challenges in this field requires ongoing interdisciplinary collaboration, combining expertise from information systems, management, data science, and Human Resources/Industrial-Organizational Psychology.

This convergence is crucial for addressing the technological, human, and implementation dimensions of predictive analytics. An interdisciplinary approach is key to navigating the complexities inherent in applying predictive analytics to HR management. As data volumes grow and analytic techniques evolve, researchers and practitioners must prioritize ethical and sustainable practices that benefit all stakeholders. This includes overcoming challenges such as capability enhancement, change management, ethical oversight, and demonstrating measurable organizational benefits. Predictive analytics has the potential to revolutionize how businesses allocate and engage their most valuable resource: human capital. By integrating this transformative tool, organizations can optimize resource alignment and strategic decision-making to achieve long-term success. Moving forward, the adoption of emerging technologies like AI, blockchain, and immersive tools will play a pivotal role in people analytics. Addressing associated ethical, operational, and accessibility challenges will be vital [28]. Establishing strategic alignment, ethical standards, and intuitive platforms will ensure these technological advancements improve organizational performance and employee experiences. Continued research and innovation will refine the application of technology in people analytics, cementing its place as a cornerstone of modern HR practices. Future research can examine the application of people analytics in SHRM across industries, integrating AI and machine learning to produce precise forecasts. Longitudinal, multi-country studies may show how culture affects adoption. Examining technological mediators, ethical concerns, and skill-building frameworks will advance knowledge of PA's role in fostering strategic, data-driven HR transformations.

REFERENCES

[1] O. Adeoye, "Enhancing workforce management and resource allocation through machine learning", *J. Hum. Resour. Anal.,* vol. 12, no. 1, pp. 45-58, 2024.

[2] I. Ajunwa, "An auditing imperative for automated hiring systems", *Harv. J. Law Technol.,* vol. 34, no. 2, pp. 1-80, 2021.

[3] D. Angrave, A. Charlwood, I. Kirkpatrick, M. Lawrence, and M. Stuart, "HR and analytics: why HR is set to fail the big data challenge", *Hum. Resour. Manage. J.,* vol. 26, no. 1, pp. 1-11, 2016. [http://dx.doi.org/10.1111/1748-8583.12090]

[4] L. Bassi, "Raging debates in HR analytics", *People Strategy,* vol. 34, no. 2, pp. 14-18, 2011.

[5] P.F. Buller, and G.M. McEvoy, "A model for implementing a sustainability strategy through HRM practices", *Bus. Soc. Rev.,* vol. 121, no. 4, pp. 465-495, 2016. [http://dx.doi.org/10.1111/basr.12099]

[6] A. Canibono, *Implementing innovative HRM: trade-off effects on employee well-being.* Emerald Insight, 2013.

[7] T. Chamorro-Premuzic, R. Akhtar, D. Winsborough, and R. Sherman, "The datafication of talent: How technology is advancing the science of human potential", *Hum. Resour. Manage. Rev.,* vol. 27, no. 3, pp. 304-315, 2017.

[8] S. Cho, H. Li, and J. Wang, "Structured HR analytics methods in public and private sectors: Applications and implications", *Int. J. Public Adm.,* vol. 46, no. 2, pp. 120-138, 2023.

[9] B. Cowgill, and C.E. Tucker, "Algorithmic fairness and economics", *SSRN,* 2020p. 3361280. [http://dx.doi.org/10.2139/ssrn.3361280]

[10] T.H. Davenport, J. Harris, and J. Shapiro, "Competing on talent analytics", *Harv. Bus. Rev.,* vol. 88, no. 10, pp. 52-58, 150, 2010. [PMID: 20929194]

[11] A.A. Fink, "Data-driven talent management: Using analytics for decision-making", *People Strategy,* vol. 40, no. 3, pp. 34-39, 2017.

[12] F. Firouzi, B. Farahani, and V.C. Leung, "IoT-enabled workforce analytics and predictive modeling for HR challenges", *IEEE Internet Things J.,* vol. 5, no. 4, pp. 2910-2920, 2018.

[13] P. Jha, "Ethical standards and skill development in AI-driven HR management", *HR Anal. Ethics Rev.,*

vol. 7, no. 1, pp. 58-74, 2024.

[14] B.E. Kaufman, "Market competition, HRM, and firm performance: The conventional paradigm critiqued and reformulated", *Hum. Resour. Manage. Rev.,* vol. 25, no. 1, pp. 107-125, 2015. [http://dx.doi.org/10.1016/j.hrmr.2014.08.001]

[15] D.M.J. Lazer, A. Pentland, D.J. Watts, S. Aral, S. Athey, N. Contractor, D. Freelon, S. Gonzalez-Bailon, G. King, H. Margetts, A. Nelson, M.J. Salganik, M. Strohmaier, A. Vespignani, and C. Wagner, "Computational social science: Obstacles and opportunities", *Science,* vol. 369, no. 6507, pp. 1060-1062, 2020. [http://dx.doi.org/10.1126/science.aaz8170] [PMID: 32855329]

[16] A. Levenson, "Using workforce analytics to improve strategy execution", *Hum. Resour. Manage.,* vol. 57, no. 3, pp. 685-700, 2018. [http://dx.doi.org/10.1002/hrm.21850]

[17] M. Marabelli, and P. Lirio, "Advancing diversity, equity, and inclusion through AI-based HR platforms", *J. Divers. Organ. Behav.,* vol. 18, no. 2, pp. 112-130, 2024.

[18] J.H. Marler, and J.W. Boudreau, "An evidence-based review of HR Analytics", *Int. J. Hum. Resour. Manage.,* vol. 28, no. 1, pp. 3-26, 2017. [http://dx.doi.org/10.1080/09585192.2016.1244699]

[19] J. Mario, and I.P. Donate, "HRM practices for human and social capital development: effects on innovation capabilities", *Int. J. Hum. Resour. Manage.,* 2015.

[20] H. Mahmud, A.K.M.N. Islam, S.I. Ahmed, and K. Smolander, "What influences algorithmic decision-making? A systematic literature review on algorithm aversion", *Technol. Forecast. Soc. Change,* vol. 175, p. 121390, 2022. [http://dx.doi.org/10.1016/j.techfore.2021.121390]

[21] J. Paauwe, *HRM and Performance: Achieving Long-Term Viability.* Oxford Univ. Press: Oxford, UK, 2004. [http://dx.doi.org/10.1093/acprof:oso/9780199273904.001.0001]

[22] P. Paigude, S. Deshpande, and R. Kulkarni, "Predictive analytics for reducing employee turnover and enhancing engagement", *Glob. J. Bus. Anal.,* vol. 15, no. 1, pp. 56-70, 2023.

[23] R. V. Palanivel, M. A. Rashi, K. Kataria, and A. Mishra, "The role of HRM in promoting environmental sustainability within organisations", *J. Informatics Educ. Res.,* 2024.

[24] R. Patil, and A. Dutta, "AI-enabled recruitment: Enhancing candidate evaluation and reducing biases", *J. HR Innov.,* vol. 9, no. 4, pp. 89-102, 2023.

[25] M.J. Salganik, *Bit by Bit: Social Research in the Digital Age.* Princeton Univ. Press: Princeton, NJ, 2019.

[26] M. Schulte, and S. Bohnet-Joschko, "Leveraging AI for linking HR activities to business outcomes", *Int. J. Workforce Anal.,* vol. 8, no. 2, pp. 98-117, 2022.

[27] N.F.S.S. Oma, "“Assessing the disparities between strategic human resource management and conventional human resource management: A theory-based review,” KnE", *Soc. Sci.,* pp. 88-613, 2023.

[28] P.M. Wright, and G.C. McMahan, "Theoretical perspectives for strategic human resource management", *J. Manage.,* vol. 18, no. 2, pp. 295-320, 1992. [http://dx.doi.org/10.1177/014920639201800205]

CHAPTER 4

Tracing the Journey of Machine Learning in Business, Management, and Allied Disciplines: A Comprehensive Review

Jayalaxmi Samal[1] and **Ashyashree Praharaj**[2,*]

[1] *School of Liberal Studies, Kalinga Institute of Industrial Technology (KIIT) Deemed to be University, Bhubaneswar, India*

[2] *Department of Business Administration, Berhampur University, Berhampur, India*

Abstract: This review provides a comprehensive evaluation of the role of Machine Learning in business, management, and related social sciences. Utilising a substantial sample size of 3682 articles from 53 years (1970-2023) from the Scopus database, this study meticulously traces the development of ML as a pivotal tool in the business sector. The analyses employ RStudios and VOSviewer software to identify prominent trends, influential contributors, and the thematic research landscape. One of the key findings is the significant uptick in ML research post-2020, reflecting the rapid adoption and diversification of ML techniques in response to global digital transformation. The study highlights "forecasting," "learning systems", and "learning algorithms" as the most preferred keywords, underscoring the emphasis on predictive analytics and the development of adaptive systems within the diverse ML field. The United States of America (USA), India, and China are the driving forces behind cutting-edge ML research in the business world. This study recommended a thorough examination of new research topics, questions, and keywords for the future that emphasize the convergence of machine learning, artificial intelligence, and other business domains. Ten major themes are identified by the analysis, demonstrating the wide range of possible business applications of machine learning and artificial intelligence. These themes include sentiment analysis, dynamic pricing, sustainable business practices, personalized marketing, and AI-driven human resource management. The study's novelty lies in its extensive longitudinal analysis of the integration of ML across business disciplines. This groundbreaking research stands out for its extensive temporal scope and dedicated focus on business disciplines. This study traces the evolution of ML from a niche research interest in the 1970s to a widely used tool with diverse applications in 21st-century business processes and strategic management.

* **Corresponding author Ashyashree Praharaj:** Department of Business Administration, Berhampur University, Berhampur, India; E-mail: ashyashree@yahoo.com

Shradhanjali Panda, Leena Priyadarshini Singh, V. Ramasamy & S. Balamurugan (Eds.)

Keywords: Artificial Intelligence (AI), Business intelligence, Business applications, Comprehensive review, Machine Learning (ML), Predictive analytics.

INTRODUCTION

Machine learning has revolutionised business practices by empowering organisations to effectively utilise large volumes of data for decision-making and operational efficiency [1]. Over the past decade, ML techniques have evolved significantly, offering capabilities that empower businesses to identify patterns, predict trends, and enhance performance through data-driven insights [2]. Integrating ML into business processes has led to advancements in diverse domains, including marketing [3], finance [4], human resources, and operations, shaping the modern business landscape. This growing integration of ML across various business functions has transformed industry practices and prompted scholars to define and explore ML concepts from multiple perspectives. Table **1** presents comprehensive definitions of ML from distinguished authors.

Table 1. ML definition as per prominent authors.

Authors	Definition of ML
Sha (1993)	*"Machine learning involves deriving insightful knowledge from data, observations, or past solutions."*
Chaturvedi *et al.* (1993)	*"Machine learning is the automated acquisition of knowledge about a specific domain from available data. This process can be supervised or autonomously guided."*
Bose & Mahapatra (2001)	*"Machine learning definitively automates the process of acquiring knowledge through computational methods."*
Al-Omary & Jamil (2006)	*"Machine learning enables systems to improve through experience and aims to explore different learning mechanisms and their limitations."*
Helm *et al.* (2020)	*"Machine learning uses large datasets to train the machine to make independent recommendations or decisions."*

*Self-Analysed.

The adoption of ML in business, management, and allied disciplines has gained considerable momentum, especially with the recent advancements in computational power, data storage [6], and algorithmic sophistication [5]. COVID-19 has hastened the adoption of AI-powered tools, leading businesses to reconsider traditional models and to utilise technology to build resilience. Consequently, the academic research community has been actively investigating the impact of machine learning on business strategies [7], customer interactions [8], operational efficiency [9], and overall competitiveness.

As a research method, a comprehensive review provides a systematic approach to examining the evolution, impact, and research trends within a specific field. Researchers can use it to visualise the intellectual framework of a specific field, identify influential authors, and explore the themes that drive research. A comprehensive study on machine learning can help readers understand the current status of research, identify areas that need attention, and plan future studies.

The motivations for conducting a comprehensive review stem from the exponential growth of ML research and its transformative impact on various business functions. As businesses increasingly adopt ML technologies to enhance decision-making, optimise operations, and drive innovation, it has become crucial to understand the dynamics of research in this domain. Despite the vast number of studies being published, there is a significant need for a comprehensive analysis that can effectively capture the entire scope of ML research in the business context, including emerging trends, collaboration patterns, and influential authors. A thorough review can help address this gap by providing insights into the evolution of research, identifying knowledge clusters, and mapping future opportunities. Such an understanding is vital for researchers, practitioners, and policymakers to navigate the rapidly evolving field, allocate resources effectively, and foster advancements that align with the needs of the communities.

This study aims to explore potential research questions on machine learning in business and related studies:

RQ_1: What are the significant trends and patterns in the publication of ML research within the said domain since its inception?

RQ_2: Which countries, institutions, and authors have significantly contributed to ML development in business research?

RQ_3: What are the key themes and knowledge clusters that emerge from the ML analysis?

RQ_4: What are the current gaps and underexplored areas in the literature that present opportunities for future research on ML?

This study aims to enhance understanding of the field by tracing the development of ML research, helping academics, practitioners, and policymakers recognise the opportunities and challenges presented by ML. The findings offer valuable insights into the areas where ML is being applied, the most popular methods and algorithms, and the interdisciplinary nature of its application. This study aims to underscore the transformative influence of machine learning on the future of business and management.

This study is structured into several vital sections to provide an all-inclusive understanding of ML in a business discipline. The first section provides a background of ML's role in transforming business practices and the relevance of a comprehensive review in mapping research trends. The following section, methodology, outlines the data collection process, the search terms used, the inclusion criteria, and the analytical tools, such as RStudios and VOSviewer, employed for the review. The data analysis and findings section presents the study's findings, including trends in publication output, leading contributors, collaboration patterns, and emerging research themes, followed by an in-depth discussion on the implications of these findings. The conclusion section summarizes the key insights derived from various analyses, highlights the study's contributions, and suggests directions for future research. Finally, the limitations section acknowledges potential constraints of this study, including limitations of the data source and scope, providing a balanced view of the research outcome.

METHODOLOGY

A comprehensive bibliometric study was proposed to understand how ML research contributes to broader business goals. The keywords "Machine Learning" or "ML" were selected for document extraction in the Scopus database [10]. The Scopus database was chosen for its extensive interdisciplinary coverage, ensuring access to high-quality peer-reviewed journals [11]. The keyword search from Scopus resulted in a total of 186,166 documents. The document extraction was strictly limited to the subject areas of "Business, management, and accounting" and "Economics, econometrics, and finance" [12]. The search within the specific subject area returned 6735 documents. Lastly, the document type was limited to "articles", the publication stage to "final", the source type to "journals", and the language to "English" [13]. The selected inclusion criteria resulted in the final sample size (n) of 3682 articles. Open-sourced and advanced tools such as "VOSviewer" and "RStudios" were used for data analysis, visualisation, and interpretation [14].

DATA ANALYSIS AND FINDINGS

This segment deals with analysing collected data and interpreting the findings.

Preliminary Exploration of Research Output and Impact

Fig. (**1**) presents the article production trend for ML in business, management, and allied disciplines. The document production trend can be classified into two distinctive groups. The production phase can be segmented into 1971-2015 and 2016-present. In the initial phase, inconsistent document production was observed, possibly due to the lack of scholarly interest. After 2016, a significant increase was observed in ML research due to the availability of advanced computing infrastructure, such as Graphics Processing Units (GPUs) and cloud computing.

The initial analysis found 877 sources with 9726 authors. There are 322 single-authored documents, with 28.47% international co-authorship and an average of 3.37 co-authors per document. The average document age is 2.87 years, indicating relatively new research in this field (Fig. **1**). ML in business studies is a rapidly evolving area with frequent new publications. The average number of citations per document is 16.59, indicating influential and widely recognised research in this discipline.

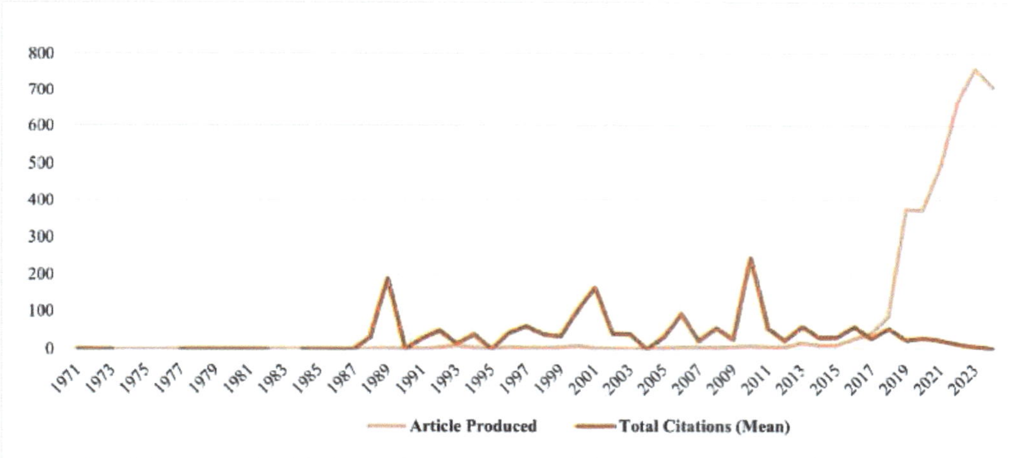

Fig. (1). Document production pattern of machine learning in different disciplines.
*Self-Analysed

Global Research Leaders

Fig. (**2**) presents an overview of document production by prominent countries. The United States of America (USA) leads in document production with 1424 articles, followed by India and China with 1205 and 1202 articles, respectively. The document production pattern from these countries depicts the precedence of established global powers in research. The rising influence of Asian countries in science and technology and a robust international collaboration network suggest the dynamic and competitive nature of the worldwide research landscape.

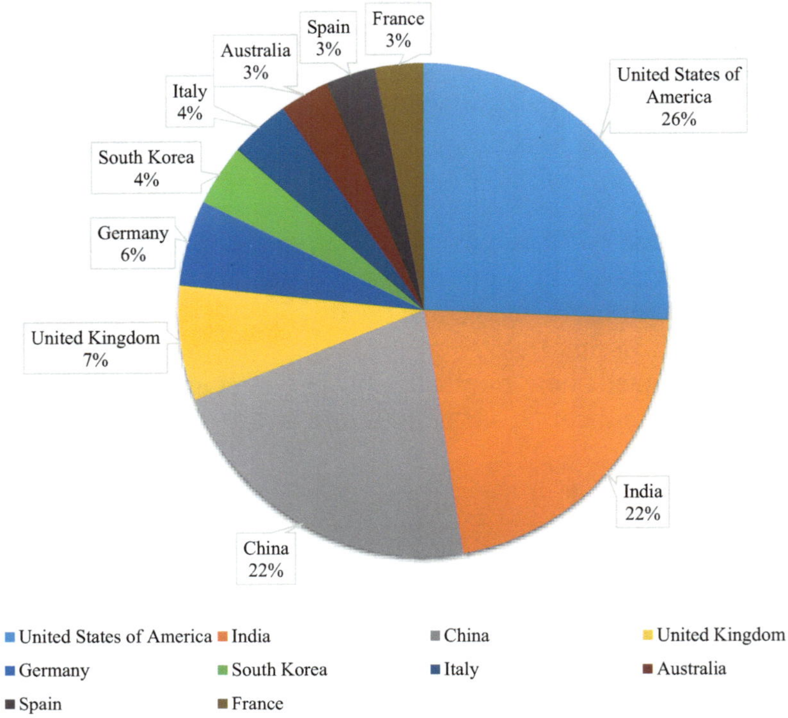

Fig. (2). Prominent countries of document production using machine learning in different countries.
*Self-Studied

Fig. (**3**) presents the country-wise collaboration network. The USA has the highest number of collaborations, followed by 81 articles from China, 44 articles from the UK, and 28 from South Korea. China has collaborated with the UK on 43 articles, Hong Kong on 23, and Australia on 22. Similarly, India has collaborated with China on 20 articles, the UK on 19, and Malaysia on 15. An overview of the country-wise collaboration network suggests a well-connected, vibrant, and globally engaged research ecosystem that promotes innovation, diversity, and knowledge sharing.

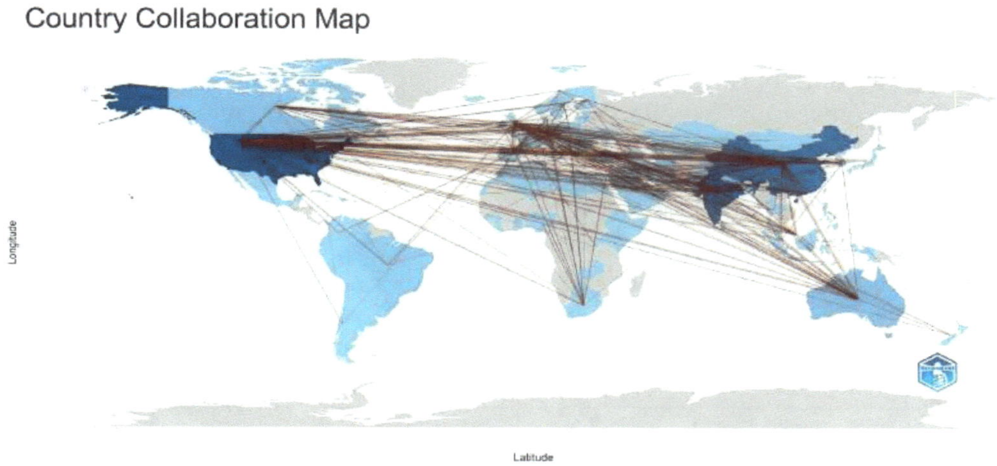

Fig. (3). Country Collaboration Map all over the world.
*Self-Studied

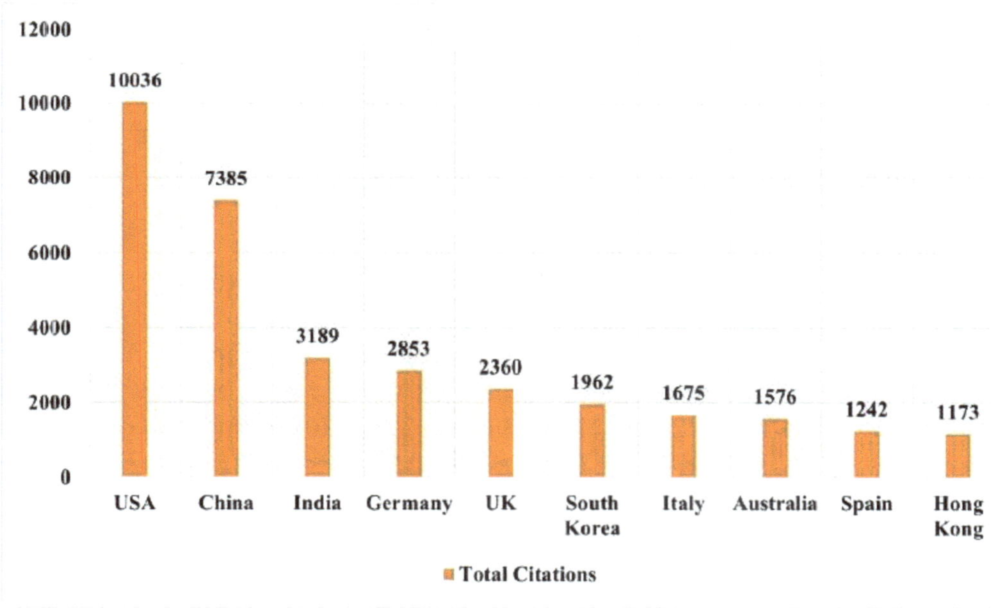

Graph 1. Country-wise citation analysis using machine learning.
*Self-Studied

Graph **1** presents the prominent countries concerning citations. The USA leads the chart with the highest number of citations at 10036, followed by China with 7385 and India with 3189. The precedence of developed countries' high citations indicates that their research is highly influential, widely used, and often serves as a foundation for future studies. Advanced research infrastructure, funding, an international collaboration network, cutting-edge research tools, and a long tradition of research excellence are some of the primary reasons for the prominence of developed nations.

Key Research Contributors

Table 2. Works of prominent authors in the area of machine learning.

SN	Name of the Author	NoD	TC	h-Index	g-Index	m-Index
1	*Liu, Y.*	27	490	11	22	1.833
2	*Wang, Y.*	26	348	10	18	1.25
3	*Li, H.*	18	325	9	18	0.346
4	*Li, J.*	20	358	9	18	2.25
5	*Li, X.*	17	541	9	17	0.75
6	*Li, Y.*	23	296	9	17	1.8
7	*Zhang, Z.*	20	308	9	17	0.9
8	*Chen, Y.*	19	249	8	15	1.143
9	*Li, Z.*	17	311	8	17	1
10	*Wang, X.*	22	512	8	22	1.333

*SN: Serial Number, NoD: Number of Documents; TC: Total Citations
*Self-Studied

Table **2** presents an overview of prominent authors in ML and business studies. Liu, Y., is the most productive author with 27 articles, an H-index of 11, a G-index of 22, and an M-index of 1.833. *Wang, Y.* and *Li, Y.* are the second and third-most productive authors, with 26 and 23 articles, respectively. *Li, X.* is the most impactful author, with the highest citation of 541, followed byn*Wang, X.* and *Liu, Y.*, with 512 and 490 citations, respectively.

The h-index measures the productivity and citation impact of an author's published work. It is defined as "the highest number of h, such that the author has published h papers, each of which has been cited at least h times". Liu, Y, has the highest h-index of 11, suggesting that each of his 11 papers has been cited 11 times, followed by *Wang, Y.*with an h-index of 10.

The g-index measures an author's citation performance, emphasising highly cited papers [12]. It was proposed as an improvement over the h-index to give more weight to the citation impact of an author's most influential publications. Liu, Y.

and Wang, X. have the highest g-index (22), followed by Wang, Y., Li, H., and Li, J., with a g-indexof 18.

Similarly, the m-index is a bibliometric metric that adjusts the h-index by accounting for the length of an author's research career. It is calculated by dividing an author's h-index by the years since their first published paper. Li, J. has the highest m-index (2.25), followed by Liu, Y. and Li, Y with an m-index of 1.833 and 1.8, respectively.

Several studies elucidate the distribution of scientific authors' productivity [15, 16]. Exhibit 5 conforms to Lotka's law, which is evident from the steep drop in the percentage of authors as the number of publications increases. Most authors publish only a few papers, while a slight majority are highly prolific. The alignment between the solid and dashed curves suggests that the empirical data closely follows the theoretical distribution described by Lotka's law.

Prominent Research Keywords

The co-occurrence analysis identifies the relationship between keywords that frequently appear together in academic publications [17]. Each node in Fig. (**4**) represents a keyword or term related to the ML field. The size of each node indicates the frequency of the keyword's occurrence, and different colours represent clusters of related terms or research areas based on the strength of co-occurrence between the keywords.

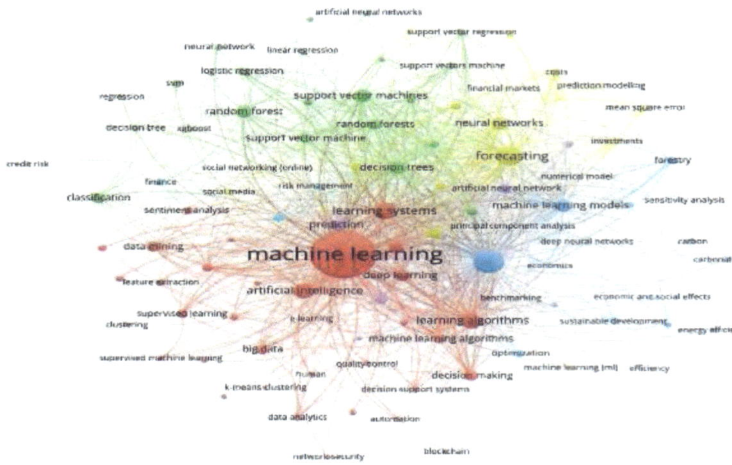

Fig. (4). Prominent keywords as co-occurrence analysis.
*Self-Studied

Four prominent clusters are formed based on the strength of the co-occurrence between keywords. The red cluster contains terms like "machine learning," "artificial intelligence," "data mining," and "supervised learning," representing the core topics in Artificial Intelligence (AI) and data analytics. The green cluster contains terms like "random forest", "decision tree", "classification", and "credit risk", indicating a focus on classification algorithms and decision tree models. Similarly, the yellow cluster contains terms like "forecasting", "machine learning models", and "neural networks", indicating a focus on predictive modelling applications. While the blue cluster represents applications of ML, including topics like "sustainable development", "energy efficiency", and "carbon", hinting at environmental or economic applications of ML [18, 19].

"Machine learning" is the most central and prominent keyword, indicating its dominance in the dataset. Keywords like "artificial intelligence", "data mining", "learning algorithms", and "supervised learning" are closely associated with it. This emphasizes the focus on core AI techniques. Meanwhile, keywords like "blockchain", "energy efficiency", and "sustainable development" suggest emerging areas of interest where machine learning is being applied. These terms reflect the growing interdisciplinary use of AI and ML across diverse fields, including economics and environmental sustainability.

Prominent Research Themes

Fig. (**5**) presents a thematic map of ML research. The thematic map is based on two prominent research dimensions: development (based on density) and relevance (based on centrality). These dimensions help identify the maturity and importance of specific themes within a research field, and the visualisation seems to focus on themes in the context of ML and related fields [20].

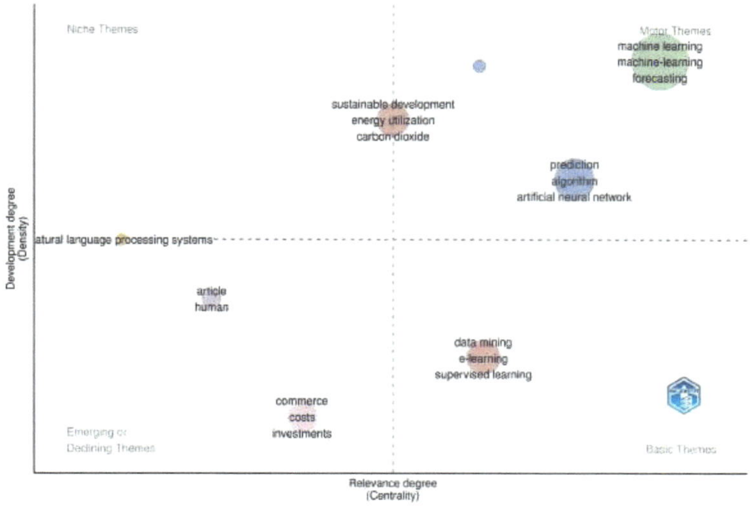

Fig. (5). Prominent machine learning research themes.
*Self-Studied

The thematic map is divided into four quadrants, each representing a distinct theme. Motor themes are well-developed, central themes in ML research. Topics such as "machine learning" and "forecasting" are crucial in various applications, such as predictive modelling and data analysis. These are the dominant themes in the dataset, reflecting the core focus on the ongoing studies and significant research trends.

Niche themes are highly specialised and well-developed but not central to the broader research field. They represent niche research areas with deep focus but limited interdisciplinary reach. The studies in the niche quadrant focused on environmental sustainability and the application of ML, such as using ML models to optimise energy efficiency or track carbon emissions. While these themes are necessary in specific contexts, they do not dominate the broader ML research landscape.

Basic themes are central but not highly developed in nature. They represent the essential foundation concepts in the field, which are still evolving in depth and specialisation. Themes such as "data mining," "e-learning," and "supervised learning" represent the basic ML research themes. These themes form the backbone of ML research, with topics that are widely used but still evolving in sophistication. This quadrant represents the essential building blocks of the ML domain [20].

Emerging or declining themes are underdeveloped and peripheral themes. Research in these areas may either be emerging (in its infancy) or declining (losing relevance over time). Themes such as "natural language processing systems," "human," "commerce," "costs," and "investments" represent this quadrant. Further exploration of these themes may reveal whether they are future growth areas or declining topics in ML research.

SCOPE OF FUTURE RESEARCH

Future research themes on ML in business, economics, and allied fields may explore various innovative and interdisciplinary aspects, considering the growing role of ML in transforming these domains. Table **3** presents a comprehensive overview of potential research themes, possible research questions, and keywords that may guide future scholars.

Table 3. Possible research themes, questions, and keywords.

Research Themes	Research Questions	Future Keywords
Personalised Marketing and Customer Insights	• How can ML algorithms identify more granular customer segments for personalised marketing? • What are the most effective methods for predicting customer behaviour using historical data? • How do customer demographics and online behaviour influence the effectiveness of personalised marketing campaigns? • What ML models are most effective for real-time personalisation in e-commerce? • How does the accuracy of recommendation algorithms impact customer satisfaction and conversion rates?	*"Personalised Marketing", "Hyper-Personalisation", "Consumer Behaviour Analysis", "Real-Time Personalisation", "Purchase Intent Personalisation"*

(Table 3) cont.....

Research Themes	Research Questions	Future Keywords
Sentiment Analysis for Market and Policy Impact	• How can social media sentiment analysis predict stock market trends and investor behaviour? • What is the relationship between public sentiment, as captured from news articles, and fluctuations in market indices? • How effective is sentiment analysis in forecasting the impact of product launches or corporate announcements on a company's stock price? • How does consumer sentiment regarding a brand influence its market share and sales performance? • Can sentiment analysis accurately measure the impact of new regulatory policy on public perception and economic indicators?	*"Sentiment Analysis", "Natural Language Processing (NLP)", "Social Media Sentiment", "Economic Stimulus Sentiment", "Earnings Call Sentiment"*
Sustainable Business Practices and Green Economy	• How can businesses effectively reduce their carbon footprint while maintaining profitability? • What key factors drive the adoption of renewable energy sources in the manufacturing sector? • How do sustainable business practices contribute to reducing global greenhouse gas emissions? • What challenges do businesses face in transitioning from a linear to a circular economy? • How do government regulations and incentives impact adopting sustainable business practices?	*"Ethical Sourcing", "Resource Efficiency", "Environmental, Social, and Governance (ESG)", "Climate Change Mitigation", "Green Product Labeling"*

(Table 3) cont.....

Research Themes	Research Questions	Future Keywords
Dynamic Pricing and Revenue Management	• How do different dynamic pricing algorithms affect consumer purchasing behaviour in e-commerce? • What main factors influence the effectiveness of dynamic pricing strategies in the hospitality industry? • How can dynamic pricing be optimised in response to real-time changes in supply and demand for perishable goods? • How does revenue management impact profitability in industries with seasonal demand, such as travel and tourism? • How do consumers perceive fairness in dynamic pricing, and how does this perception impact brand loyalty?	*"ML for Pricing", "Real-Time Pricing Strategies", "AI in Pricing", "Surge Pricing", "Data-Driven Pricing"*
Process Automation and Robotic Process Automation (RPA)	• What are the key success factors (CSFs) for effectively implementing robotic process automation in large enterprises? • How can small and medium-sized enterprises (SMEs) successfully navigate the obstacles associated with implementing process automation technologies? • What barriers exist to adopting RPA in industries with low digital maturity, and how can these be mitigated? • How does process automation affect operational efficiency and cost reduction across different business functions? • How does RPA impact job displacement, employee satisfaction, and workforce productivity?	*"Process Automation", "Robotic Process Automation (RPA)", "Business Process Automation (BPA)", "Cost-Benefit Analysis of Automation", "RPA Scalability"*

(Table 3) cont.....

Research Themes	Research Questions	Future Keywords
Behavioural Economics and AI	• How does the integration of AI tools influence decision-making processes in individuals compared to traditional methods? • What are the implications of AI bias on consumer behaviour, and how can behavioural economics inform the development of fairer AI systems? • How does consumer trust in AI systems affect their purchasing behaviour, and what behavioural economic principles can enhance this trust? • In what ways can AI-driven nudges (behavioural prompts) be designed to influence healthier consumer choices in food or financial decisions? • How effective are AI-assisted behavioural interventions in promoting sustainable behaviours, such as energy conservation and recycling, compared to traditional methods?	*"AI Bias", "AI Decision-Making", "Behavioural Insights", "Emotional AI", "Human-AI Interaction"*
Customer Churn Prediction	• Which ML algorithm provides the highest accuracy in predicting customer churn across different industries? • How do specific aspects of customer experience correlate with the likelihood of churn? • What behavioural indicators are most predictive of customer churn in subscription-based services? • How effectively are targeted marketing interventions reducing churn rates among high-risk customer segments? • How can customer segmentation based on demographic and behavioural data enhance the accuracy of churn prediction models?	*"Customer Churn", "Churn Prediction Models", "ML in Marketing", "Customer Lifetime Value", "Churn Risk Factors"*

(Table 3) cont.....

Research Themes	Research Questions	Future Keywords
Behavioural Analysis for Credit and Loan Decisions	• How do cognitive biases influence borrowers' decisions when applying for credit or loans? • What roles do emotional factors play in consumers' willingness to accept loan offers, and how can lenders mitigate negative emotional influences? • How does social influence affect individuals' decisions to take out loans or credit? • How does financial literacy impact consumers' understanding of loan products, and what behavioural strategies can improve their decision-making processes? • How do different demographic factors affect risk perception in credit and loan decisions, and what behavioural patterns emerge from these perceptions?	*"Credit Decision-Making", "Loan Default Prediction", "Cognitive Biases in Lending", "Nudging Techniques", "Credit Risk Assessments"*
AI-driven Human Resource Management	• How can AI technologies improve recruitment by reducing bias and enhancing candidate selection accuracy? • What role does AI play in predicting employee performance and identifying potential high-performers in organisations? • How can AI-driven tools enhance employee engagement and satisfaction, and what metrics can effectively measure this impact? • How can AI-based systems be utilised for personalised employee development and training programmes, and what outcomes do they produce compared to traditional methods? • How does AI assist in workforce planning and optimising talent allocation in organisations, and what challenges do HR managers face in its implementation?	*"AI Recruitment Tools", "ML in Talent Acquisition", "AI-enhanced Leadership Development", "HR Automation", "Chatbots for HR Services"*

*Self-Studied.

KEY FINDINGS AND DISCUSSIONS

The review provides valuable insights into how ML research has contributed to business goals and evolved. The post-2016 growth in ML research is attributed to advances in computing technologies that lowered barriers to experimentation and data analysis. The increased interest from the business sector also aligns with the growing application of AI technologies to optimise operational efficiency, make data-driven decisions, and enhance customer experiences.

The geographic analysis highlights the dominance of traditional research powerhouses like the USA and the rising contributions of China and India. The high rate of international collaboration, especially among these countries, emphasises the globally interconnected nature of ML research, which facilitates the sharing of diverse perspectives and fosters innovation. The influence of developed countries in terms of citation further underscores the importance of research infrastructure, funding, and established research practices.

The prominent authors in this study illustrate the concentration of research output and impact within a relatively small group of scholars, often affiliated with leading institutions. The bibliometric indicators, such as the h-index, g-index, and m-index, reveal that these researchers have made significant contributions in terms of the number of publications and their impact on the field. This pattern reflects the competitive, specialised nature of ML research, in which a handful of experts play a crucial role in shaping the discourse.

The keyword and thematic analyses reveal the diversity of ML research topics and their applications in business. The focus on core AI techniques and emerging applications in sustainability demonstrates the versatility of ML, highlighting its potential to address both business and societal challenges. Identifying niche themes in areas like environmental sustainability suggests that ML can contribute to developing sustainable business practices. In contrast, the emerging or declining themes indicate areas that may require further exploration or are becoming less relevant.

This study suggested an in-depth exploration of emerging research themes, research questions, and future keywords, highlighting the intersection of ML, AI, and various business domains [21]. The analysis identifies ten key themes, including personalised marketing, sentiment analysis, sustainable business practices, dynamic pricing, and AI-driven human resource management, showcasing the diverse potential applications of ML and AI in business. Each research theme is accompanied by specific research questions that provide valuable directions for future exploration [22]. These questions are centred on enhancing efficiency, understanding consumer behaviour, improving decision-making, and promoting sustainability. The associated keywords help contextualise the focus area within each theme. The proposed section is a comprehensive guide for future research, emphasising the transformative impact of AI and ML across various business functions while addressing implementation challenges and opportunities [23].

CONCLUSION AND LIMITATIONS

This study underscores the dynamic, rapidly evolving landscape of ML research across business and allied disciplines. The findings of this comprehensive review emphasize the importance of interdisciplinary collaboration, robust research infrastructure, and continuous exploration of emerging themes. As ML continues to evolve, its role in transforming business practices and contributing to broader societal goals will likely expand, creating new opportunities for scholars and practitioners alike. It highlights ML's substantial contribution to enhancing business processes, optimising decision-making, enabling data-driven insights, and aligning broader business goals. The study findings will be valuable for researchers, professionals, and policymakers interested in ML research in the business context [24].

Despite the comprehensive review, this study has several limitations. The data was solely obtained from the Scopus database, which may not include all relevant literature on ML in business, especially those published in non-indexed journals or other databases. This reliance may result in a biased representation of the ML research landscape. Second, the study is limited to specific subject areas, namely “business, management, and accounting” and “economics, econometrics, and finance”, potentially excluding relevant interdisciplinary research from “engineering”, “computer science”, and “healthcare” fields. The analysis also focuses solely on journal articles published in English, which may overlook relevant research published in other languages or presented in different formats, such as conference proceedings or book chapters.

Additionally, bibliometric analysis inherently depends on citation data, which may not always accurately reflect the quality or impact of a study. Factors such as journal prestige, author reputation, and self-citations can influence citations, leading to potential biases in assessing the importance of research contributions. Finally, while tools like VOSviewer and RStudios provided valuable insights, interpreting visualisations and clusters is subjective, and other advanced tools could yield different results. Future studies can benefit from a more diverse approach, including multiple databases, data sources, and advanced analytical methods, to gain a broader understanding of ML research in the business domain.

REFERENCES

[1] A.D. Pham, N.T. Ngo, T.T. Ha Truong, N.T. Huynh, and N.S. Truong, "Predicting energy consumption in multiple buildings using machine learning for improving energy efficiency and sustainability", *J. Clean. Prod.,* vol. 260, p. 121082, 2020. [http://dx.doi.org/10.1016/j.jclepro.2020.121082]

[2] M. Leo, S. Sharma, and K. Maddulety, "Machine learning in banking risk management: A literature review", *Risks,* vol. 7, no. 1, p. 29, 2019. [http://dx.doi.org/10.3390/risks7010029]

[3] Y. Zhu, L. Zhou, C. Xie, G.J. Wang, and T.V. Nguyen, "Forecasting SMEs' credit risk in supply chain finance with an enhanced hybrid ensemble machine learning approach", *Int. J. Prod. Econ.,* vol. 211, pp. 22-33, 2019. [http://dx.doi.org/10.1016/j.ijpe.2019.01.032]

[4] A.I. Canhoto, and F. Clear, "Artificial intelligence and machine learning as business tools: A framework for diagnosing value destruction potential", *Bus. Horiz.,* vol. 63, no. 2, pp. 183-193, 2020. [http://dx.doi.org/10.1016/j.bushor.2019.11.003]

[5] I. Lee, and Y.J. Shin, "Machine learning for enterprises: Applications, algorithm selection, and challenges", *Bus. Horiz.,* vol. 63, no. 2, pp. 157-170, 2020. [http://dx.doi.org/10.1016/j.bushor.2019.10.005]

[6] L. Ma, and B. Sun, "Machine learning and AI in marketing – Connecting computing power to human insights", *Int. J. Res. Mark.,* vol. 37, no. 3, pp. 481-504, 2020. [http://dx.doi.org/10.1016/j.ijresmar.2020.04.005]

[7] X. Ma, J. Sha, D. Wang, Y. Yu, Q. Yang, and X. Niu, "Study on a prediction of P2P network loan default based on the machine learning LightGBM and XGboost algorithms according to different high dimensional data cleaning", *Electron. Commerce Res. Appl.,* vol. 31, pp. 24-39, 2018. [http://dx.doi.org/10.1016/j.elerap.2018.08.002]

[8] D. Pessach, G. Singer, D. Avrahami, H. Chalutz Ben-Gal, E. Shmueli, and I. Ben-Gal, "Employees recruitment: A prescriptive analytics approach *via* machine learning and mathematical programming"., *Decis. Support Syst.,* vol. 134, p. 113290, 2020. [http://dx.doi.org/10.1016/j.dss.2020.113290] [PMID: 32501316]

[9] I. Bose, and R.K. Mahapatra, "Business data mining — a machine learning perspective", *Inf. Manage.,* vol. 39, no. 3, pp. 211-225, 2001. [http://dx.doi.org/10.1016/S0378-7206(01)00091-X]

[10] A.Y. Al-Omary, and M.S. Jamil, "A new approach of clustering based machine-learning algorithm", *Knowl. Base. Syst.,* vol. 19, no. 4, pp. 248-258, 2006. [http://dx.doi.org/10.1016/j.knosys.2005.10.011]

[11] J.M. Helm, A.M. Swiergosz, H.S. Haeberle, J.M. Karnuta, J.L. Schaffer, V.E. Krebs, A.I. Spitzer, and P.N. Ramkumar, "Machine learning and artificial intelligence: Definitions, applications, and future directions", *Curr. Rev. Musculoskelet. Med.,* vol. 13, no. 1, pp. 69-76, 2020. [http://dx.doi.org/10.1007/s12178-020-09600-8] [PMID: 31983042]

[12] M. Villamor Martin, D.A. Kirsch, and F. Prieto-Nañez, "The promise of machine-learning- driven text analysis techniques for historical research: topic modeling and word embedding", *Manag. Organ. History,* vol. 18, no. 1, pp. 81-96, 2023. [http://dx.doi.org/10.1080/17449359.2023.2181184]

[13] B. Zou, J. You, Q. Wang, X. Wen, and L. Jia, "Survey on learnable databases: A machine learning perspective", *Big Data Research,* vol. 27, p. 100304, 2022. [http://dx.doi.org/10.1016/j.bdr.2021.100304]

[14] I. Lee, and Y.J. Shin, "Machine learning for enterprises: Applications, algorithm selection, and challenges", *Bus. Horiz.,* vol. 63, no. 2, pp. 157-170, 2020.

[http://dx.doi.org/10.1016/j.bushor.2019.10.005]

[15] M. Costola, O. Hinz, M. Nofer, and L. Pelizzon, "Machine learning sentiment analysis, COVID-19 news and stock market reactions", *Res. Int. Bus. Finance,* vol. 64, p. 101881, 2023. [http://dx.doi.org/10.1016/j.ribaf.2023.101881] [PMID: 36687319]

[16] S. Kushwaha, S. Bahl, A.K. Bagha, K.S. Parmar, M. Javaid, A. Haleem, and R.P. Singh, "Significant applications of machine learning for COVID-19 pandemic", *Journal of Industrial Integration and Management,* vol. 5, no. 4, pp. 453-479, 2020. [http://dx.doi.org/10.1142/S2424862220500268]

[17] S. Tuli, S. Tuli, R. Tuli, and S.S. Gill, "Predicting the growth and trend of COVID-19 pandemic using machine learning and cloud computing", *Internet of Things,* vol. 11, p. 100222, 2020. [http://dx.doi.org/10.1016/j.iot.2020.100222] [PMID: 38620477]

[18] J.F. Hair Jr, and M. Sarstedt, "Data, measurement, and causal inferences in machine learning: opportunities and challenges for marketing", *J. Mark. Theory Pract.,* vol. 29, no. 1, pp. 65-77, 2021. [http://dx.doi.org/10.1080/10696679.2020.1860683]

[19] S. Chatterjee, D. Goyal, A. Prakash, and J. Sharma, "Exploring healthcare/health-product ecommerce satisfaction: A text mining and machine learning application", *J. Bus. Res.,* vol. 131, pp. 815-825, 2021. [http://dx.doi.org/10.1016/j.jbusres.2020.10.043]

[20] S. Filom, A.M. Amiri, and S. Razavi, "Applications of machine learning methods in port operations – A systematic literature review", *Transp. Res., Part E Logist. Trans. Rev.,* vol. 161, p. 102722, 2022. [http://dx.doi.org/10.1016/j.tre.2022.102722]

[21] N. Mirza, M. Elhoseny, M. Umar, and N. Metawa, "Safeguarding FinTech innovations with machine learning: Comparative assessment of various approaches", *Res. Int. Bus. Finance,* vol. 66, p. 102009, 2023. [http://dx.doi.org/10.1016/j.ribaf.2023.102009]

[22] S. Chowdhury, S. Joel-Edgar, P.K. Dey, S. Bhattacharya, and A. Kharlamov, "Embedding transparency in artificial intelligence machine learning models: managerial implications on predicting and explaining employee turnover", *Int. J. Hum. Resour. Manage.,* vol. 34, no. 14, pp. 2732-2764, 2023. [http://dx.doi.org/10.1080/09585192.2022.2066981]

[23] A.H. Ahmad, "A comprehensive review: Analysing the pros and cons of assembly line balancing methods", *Journal of Advanced Research in Applied Sciences and Engineering Technology,* vol. 44, no. 2, pp. 72-88, 2024. [http://dx.doi.org/10.37934/araset.44.2.7288]

[24] A. Tietze, and P. Hofmann, "The h-index and multi-author hm-index for individual researchers in condensed matter physics", *Scientometrics,* vol. 119, no. 1, pp. 171-185, 2019. [http://dx.doi.org/10.1007/s11192-019-03051-w]

CHAPTER 5

Crime Count Prediction in India

Bhabani S. Mohanty[1], **Durga Madhab Mahapatra**[2], **Soumendra Kumar Patra**[3,*] and **Aseem Ali**[1]

[1] *Department of Statistics & Applied Mathematics, Central University of Tamil Nadu, Thiruvarur, Tamil Nadu, India*

[2] *Department of Commerce, North Eastern Hill University, Meghalaya, India*

[3] *Department of Business Administration, Ravenshaw University, Odisha, India*

Abstract: Crime count prediction is essential for improving public safety and guiding law enforcement strategies. This chapter examines the effectiveness of various machine learning and time series models for crime prediction in India, focusing on the Autoregressive Integrated Moving Average (ARIMA) and Neural Network Autoregression (NNAR) models. We conduct a comparative analysis to evaluate the predictive performance of these models using metrics such as Root Mean Squared Error (RMSE), Mean Absolute Error (MAE), and Mean Squared Error (MSE). Our findings provide key insights into the strengths and limitations of each model, highlighting their applicability for crime prediction tasks in the Indian context. The results indicate that the NNAR model's ME is marginally higher than that of the ARIMA model. The average magnitude of the discrepancies between the expected and actual values is measured by RMSE. It provides a clear picture of the prediction performance and accuracy of the model. By more successfully identifying underlying patterns in crime data with fewer errors and more precise performance metrics, the ARIMA model exhibits its overall superior predictive ability. Moreover, this study offers valuable recommendations for law enforcement agencies and policymakers, demonstrating how machine learning and time series modeling techniques can be leveraged to forecast crime rates and optimize resource allocation for crime prevention in India.

Keywords: ARIMA, Crime count prediction, NNAR, Temporal analysis.

INTRODUCTION

Crime is any act that violates the law in a particular location. It can refer to a wide range of offenses, including fraud, drugs, theft, assault, and much more. It can

* **Corresponding author Soumendra Kumar Patra:** Department of Business Administration, Ravenshaw University, Odisha, India; E-mail: soumendra.patra@gmail.com

Shradhanjali Panda, Leena Priyadarshini Singh, V. Ramasamy & S. Balamurugan (Eds.)

cause harm to individuals, groups, and society as a whole. It can upend social order, endanger lives, and erode confidence. Any action or behavior that breaks the law and is dealt with by the legal system is considered a crime. An act that is criminal by law and is typically seen as wicked is generally understood to be a crime.

Predicting crime patterns is vital to law enforcement and public safety efforts, allowing authorities to allocate resources effectively and proactively address criminal activity. In contrast, time series models such as the Autoregressive Integrated Moving Average (ARIMA) and Neural Network Autoregressive (NNAR) models specialize in analyzing sequential data points over time. These models capture temporal dependencies and seasonality within crime data, enabling accurate forecasts based on historical trends (Fig . **1**). ARIMA, a traditional statistical approach, offers simplicity and interpretability, while NNAR models, powered by neural networks, excel at capturing nonlinear relationships and intricate patterns within the data. By assessing their predictive accuracy, computational efficiency, and practical usefulness, this study aims to guide law enforcement, policymakers, and researchers in selecting effective crime prevention strategies tailored to the Indian context, thus improving public safety.

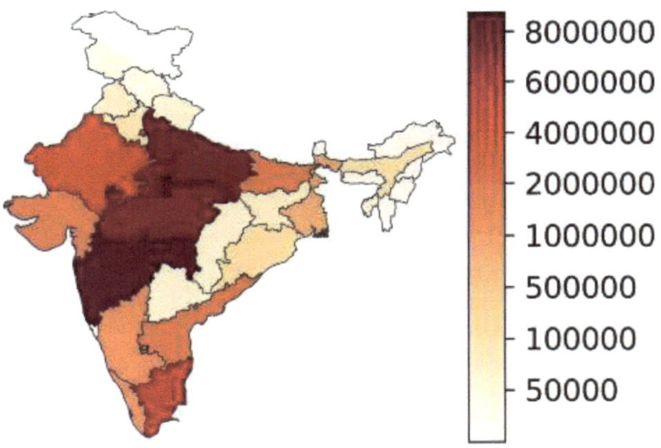

Fig. (1). Heat Map of Crime across India.
*Self-Analysed

A comprehensive overview of crime prediction techniques, focusing on their application and effectiveness in forecasting crime occurrences [1], states the logical utility of this approach in various applications. It was also proposed to utilize spatial analysis to predict and monitor crime, demonstrating how geographic information enhances crime prediction models [2]. Crime pattern detection and prediction can be emphasized through data mining techniques, showing promising results for early detection of criminal activities [3]. Another study employs machine learning algorithms to detect and predict crime patterns, underscoring the growing role of predictive analytics in crime prevention [4]. A study demonstrates the effectiveness of clustering algorithms in predicting crime rates, providing insights into the relationship between crime types and locations [5]. A GUI-based system was developed to highlight the practical application of machine learning in predicting crime rates, making it accessible to law enforcement [6]. A comparative analysis of crime prediction methods is provided, showcasing the advantages and limitations of various techniques and offering a foundation for selecting appropriate algorithms [7]. Spatial and temporal analysis of crime hotspots is conducted to enhance crime prediction, illustrating the value of integrating different data types [8]. A few more studies explore crime analysis using data mining, highlighting the ability of these methods to discover hidden crime patterns and trends [9, 13]. A crime prediction model is developed using deep neural networks that demonstrates significant improvements in accuracy over traditional methods [10]. Crime prediction and analysis using machine learning techniques, with a focus on enhancing understanding of criminal behavior, are also studied [11]. A research work explained that trend analysis of crime rates in India reveals historical patterns and provides insights into socio-economic factors influencing crime [12]. Using spatio-temporal crime data for smart city applications contributes to more precise crime forecasting in urban environments; this study leverages big data analytics to visualize and forecast crime trends, showcasing the role of advanced data mining techniques in crime prevention [13, 14]. When it comes to predicting crimes, several statistical tools are used by practitioners, yet in this field what matters most is the robustness of these models. Basically, traditional methods like regression and correlation coefficients are used for this purpose. But, in today's AI era, upgraded models and software are used for this purpose. This present research work aims to test models like ARIMA and NNAR for predicting crime. Accordingly, the research design is prepared and discussed as follows.

Data Source

The data used in this study consists of criminal records for India, with states and union territories. The dataset spans 1985 to 2022. This dataset only utilized data about crime counts under the Indian Penal Code (IPC). The Ministry of Home Affairs' National Crime Records Bureau (NCRB) publishes annual crime data in India.

TIME SERIES MODEL

ARIMA Model

The equation for an ARIMA (p, d, q) process can be represented as:

$$y_t = C + \emptyset_1 y_{t-1} + \emptyset_2 y_{t-2} + \cdots + \emptyset_p y_{t-p} + \theta_1 \epsilon_{t-1} + \theta_2 \epsilon_{t-2} + \cdots + \theta_q \epsilon_{t-q} + \epsilon_t \quad \textbf{(1)}$$

y_t is the value of the time series at time *t*

C is the constant term or intercept.

$\emptyset_1$, $\emptyset_2$ … $\emptyset_p$ are the parameters of the autoregressive component.

θ_1, θ_2 … θ_p are the parameters of the moving average component.

ϵ_t is a white noise error term with mean zero and constant variance.

In the context of the above discussion, the forecasted crime rate is shown in Fig. (**2**).

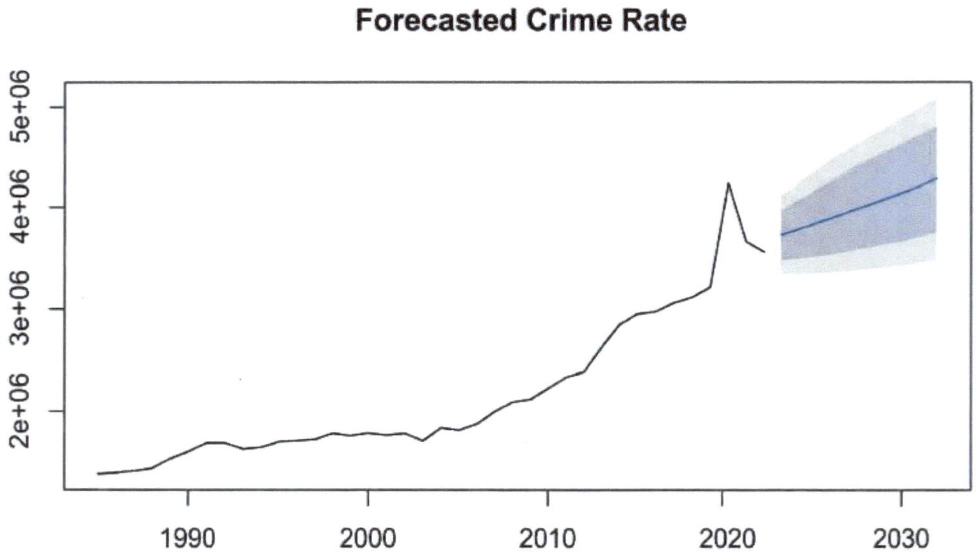

Fig. (2). Forecasted plot of the number of crime counts with 95% confidence interval using the ARIMA (0,1,1) model.
*Self-Analysed

NNAR (Neural Network Auto-Regressive Model)

Let yt denote the value of the time series variable at time *t*. The NNAR model can be written as:

$$yt = f(yt-1, yt-2, \ldots, yt-p; \theta) + \epsilon t \quad \textbf{(2)}$$

f () is a nonlinear function that captures the relationship between the lagged values of the time series. y_{t-1}, y_{t-2}, …, y_{t-p} are lagged values of the time series up to order p. θ represents the parameters of the model, including the weights and biases of the neural network. ϵ_t is the error term assumed to be independent and identically distributed with mean zero and constant variance. The two parts of the NNAR (Neural Network Autoregression Model) are *p* and *k*. The number of lag values used as inputs is indicated by the letter p. The number of concealed nodes that are present is indicated by *k*. *NNAR(p,k)* is used to represent output (Fig. **3**).

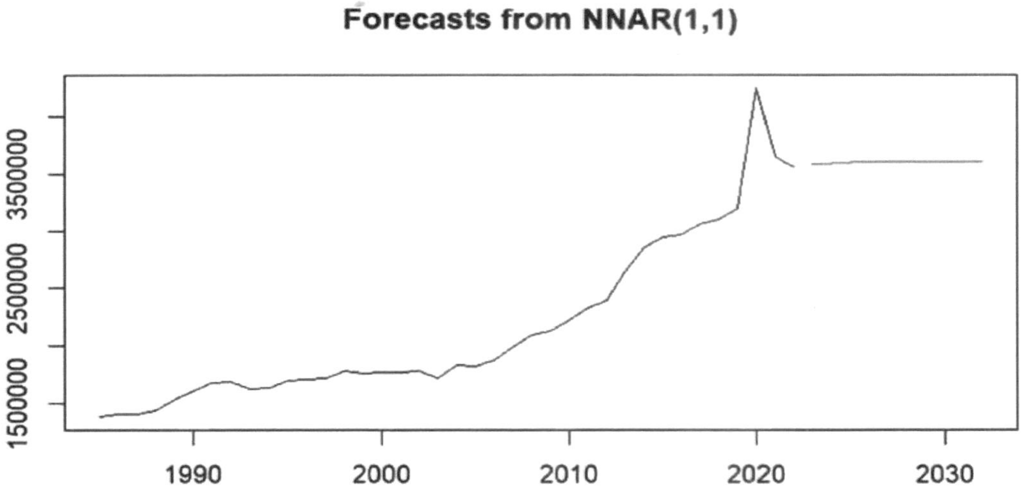

Fig. (3). Forecasted Plot of the Number of Crime Counts Using the NNAR (1,1) Model.
*Self-Analysed

COMPARISON OF ARIMA (0,1,1) AND NNAR (1,1) MODELS

The average deviation of the forecasts from the actual data is shown in Table **2** as the ME, whereas the selection criteria for the best-fitting model are shown in Table **1**. A positive ME indicates an average overestimation of the actual values in the forecasts, whereas a negative ME indicates an underestimation. The NNAR model in this analysis has a somewhat higher ME than the ARIMA model. RMSE measures the average size of the errors between the anticipated and actual values. It provides a clear picture of the model's predictive accuracy. Nevertheless, the comparison lacks the RMSE for the ARIMA model. MAE calculates the average magnitude of errors in a series of forecasts, ignoring their direction. A lower MAE indicates better performance. The MAE of the ARIMA model is less than that of the NNAR model in this comparison (Table **3**, Annexure). MPE quantifies the percentage difference between expected and actual values (Fig. **4**, Annexure). A lower MPE indicates better performance. In this comparison, the MPE of the ARIMA model is significantly lower than that of the NNAR model. MAPE measures the average percentage deviation between forecasts and actual data. A lower MAPE suggests greater precision. In this comparison, the MAPE of the ARIMA model is substantially lower than that of the NNAR model. MASE compares the accuracy of a forecast to that of an uninformed forecast. A lower MASE indicates better performance. The MASE of the NNAR model is less than that of the ARIMA model in this comparison. To determine if the residuals still contain any pattern, ACF1 calculates the residuals' autocorrelation. A number around 0 indicates a well-fitting model. Both models in this comparison have relatively low ACF1 values, which suggests that the residual autocorrelation of the models is well-fit. Compared to the NNAR model, the ARIMA model performs better in terms of RMSE, MAE, MPE, MAPE, and ACF1. Overall, its accuracy scores are higher, and its mistakes are less severe. In contrast, the NNAR model has a lower mean square error (MASE) than the ARIMA model, suggesting superior accuracy when compared to a naïve forecast (Fig. **5**, Annexure). Comparing it to the ARIMA model, however, shows that it often has inferior accuracy metrics (RMSE, MAE, MPE, and MAPE) and more significant errors [7]. The ARIMA model may be regarded as the best model in this comparison, considering these variables, overall predicted accuracy, and performance across several measures.

Table 1. Model selection criteria for checking the best-fitted model.

Model	Mean Error	Root Mean Squared Error	Mean Absolute Error	Mean Percentage Error	Mean Absolute Percentage Error	Mean Absolute Scaled Error	Autocorrelation of Residuals	Ljung-Box Test	
								Q-Statistic	P-value
ARIMA (0,1,1) with drift	0.00133	0.263923	0.13647	11.34976	19.06088	0.946457	0.010694	4.5897	0.7099
NNAR (1,1)	0.464068	0.533103	0.475737	25.84278	32.19368	0.69431	0.107265	4.5099	0.8084

*Self Computed

Table 2. Error comparison of the above two models.

ERROR MEASURES	NNAR (1,1)	ARIMA (0,1,1)
ME	0.4640677	-0.001334314
RMSE	0.5331025	0.2639231
MAE	0.4757372	0.1364698
MPE	25.84278	11.34976
MAPE	32.19368	19.06088
MASE	0.6943101	0.9464571
ACF1	0.1072647	0.01069392

*Self-Analysed

Table 3. Forecast value of crime counts by the ARIMA (0,1,1) with drift and NNAR (1,1) models.

	Output of ARIMA (0,1,1) Model					NNAR (1,1) Model
YEAR	Point Forecast	Lo 80	Hi 80	Lo 95	Hi 95	Point Forecast
2023	3728623	3473693	3983553	3338741	4118504	3589468
2024	3791011	3492861	4089160	3335030	4246991	3601254
2025	3853398	3517545	4189252	3339755	4367042	3606052
2026	3915786	3546055	4285518	3350331	4481242	3607980
2027	3978174	3577418	4378931	3365271	4591078	3608752
2028	4040562	3611017	4470108	3383629	4697496	3609059
2029	4102950	3646427	4559474	3404758	4801143	3609182
2030	4165338	3683345	4647332	3428193	4902484	3609231
2031	4227726	3721543	4733910	3453585	5001867	3609251
2032	4290114	3760845	4819383	3480667	5099561	3609258

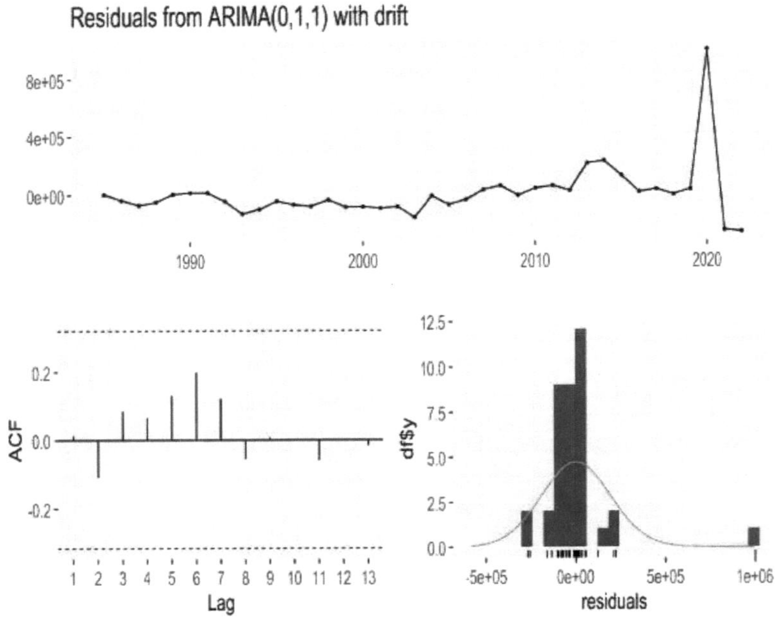

Fig. (4). The Distribution of Residuals of the Fitted ARIMA (0,1,1) with Drift Model.

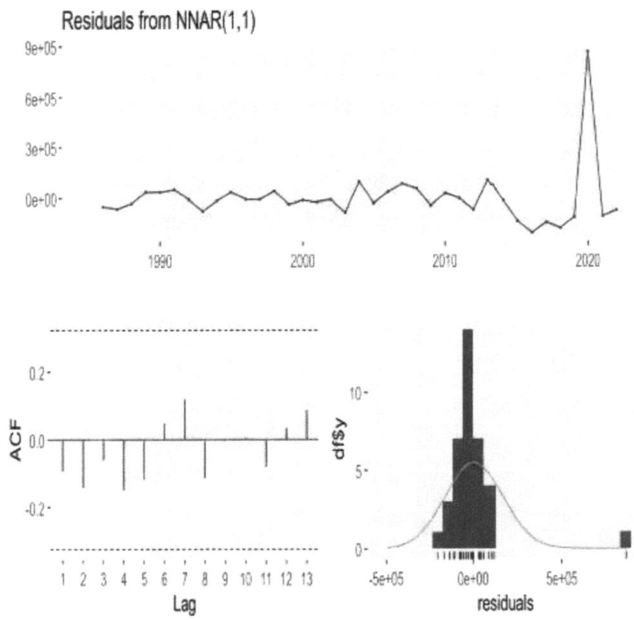

Fig. (5). The Distribution of Residuals of the Fitted NNAR (1,1) Model.

CONCLUSION

In conclusion, a thorough comparative analysis of time series models for crime prediction in India reveals several vital observations [5, 9]. When comparing ARIMA and NNAR models, the ARIMA model consistently outperforms NNAR across various metrics, including RMSE, MAE, MPE, MAPE, and ACF1. With lower errors and more accurate performance metrics, the ARIMA model proves more effective in capturing underlying patterns in crime data, demonstrating its superior predictive capability overall. To increase accuracy and contextual relevance, future studies can broaden crime prediction models by adding more socioeconomic, demographic, and environmental factors. Predictive capabilities can be improved by integrating real-time data sources like social media analytics, surveillance feeds, and Internet of Things sensors. Investigating hybrid models that blend deep learning architectures with statistical techniques like ARIMA can improve performance in dynamic and intricate crime patterns. Comparative research between Indian states or between urban and rural areas can reveal patterns unique to a given area. Furthermore, for law enforcement and policymakers to have confidence in predictive systems and to ensure transparency and ethical use, research on explainable AI techniques will be essential.

REFERENCES

[1] N.H.M. Shamsuddin, N.A. Ali, and R. Alwee, "An overview on crime prediction methods", *6th ICT International Student Project Conference (ICT-ISPC),* pp. 1-5, 2017.

[2] H.K.R. ToppiReddy, B. Saini, and G. Mahajan, B. Saini, and G. Mahajan, "Crime prediction & monitoring framework based on spatial analysis", *Procedia Comput. Sci.,* vol. 132, pp. 696-705, 2018. [http://dx.doi.org/10.1016/j.procs.2018.05.075]

[3] S. Yadav, M. Timbadia, A. Yadav, R. Vishwakarma, and N. Yadav, "Crime pattern detection, analysis & prediction", *2017 International Conference of Electronics, Communication and Aerospace Technology (ICECA),* vol. 1, pp. 225-230, 2017. [http://dx.doi.org/10.1109/ICECA.2017.8203676]

[4] R. Patil, M. Kacchi, P. Gavali, and K. Pimparia, "Crime pattern detection, analysis & prediction using machine learning", *Int. Res. J. Eng. Technol. (IRJET),* vol. 7, 2020no. 1, pp. 2395-0056. [Online]. Available: https://www.irjet.net/archives/V7/i1/IRJET-V7I171.pdf

[5] O. Vaidya, S. Mitra, R. Kumbhar, S. Chavan, and M.R. Patil, "Crime rate prediction using data clustering algorithms", *Int. Res. J. Eng. Technol. (IRJET),* vol. 5, 2018no. 2, pp. 2395-0056. [Online]. Available: https://www.irjet.net/archives/V5/i2/IRJET-V5I2146.pdf

[6] S. Aravindan, E. Anusuya, and M. Ashok Kumar, "GUI based prediction of crime rate using machine learning approach", *Int. J. Comput. Sci. Mobile Comput,* vol. 9, 2020no. 3, pp. 221-229. [Online]. Available: https://ijcsmc.com/docs/papers/March2020/V9I3202026.pdf

[7] O. Vaidya, S. Mitra, R. Kumbhar, S. Chavan, and R. Patil, "Comprehensive comparative analysis of methods for crime rate prediction", *Int. Res. J. Eng. Technol. (IRJET),* vol. 5, 2018no. 2, pp. 715-718. [Online]. Available: https://www.irjet.net/archives/V5/i2/IRJET-V5I2147.pdf

[8] T. Almanie, R. Mirza, and E. Lor, "Crime prediction based on crime types and using spatial and temporal criminal hotspots", *arXiv preprint,* arXiv:1508.02050, 2015. [Online]. Available: https://arxiv.org/abs/1508.02050

[9] S. Sathyadevan, M.S. Devan, and S.S. Gangadharan, "Crime analysis and prediction using data mining", *2014 First International Conference on Networks & Soft Computing (ICNSC),* pp. 406-412, 2014.
[http://dx.doi.org/10.1109/CNSC.2014.6906719]

[10] S.A. Chun, V. Avinash Paturu, S. Yuan, R. Pathak, V. Atluri, and N.R. Adam, "Crime prediction model using deep neural networks", *Proc. 20th Annu. Int. Conf. Digital Government Research,* pp. 512-514, 2019.
[http://dx.doi.org/10.1145/3325112.3328221]

[11] A. Sangani, C. Sampat, and V. Pinjarkar, "Crime prediction and analysis", *2nd Int. Conf. on Advances in Science & Technology (ICAST),* 2019.
[http://dx.doi.org/10.1109/ICAST47832.2019.8955272]

[12] S. Ansari, A. Verma, and K.M. Dadkhah, "Crime Rates in India", *Int. Crim. Justice Rev.,* vol. 25, no. 4, pp. 318-336, 2015.
[http://dx.doi.org/10.1177/1057567715596047]

[13] C. Catlett, E. Cesario, D. Talia, and A. Vinci, "A data-driven approach for spatio-temporal crime predictions in smart cities", *2018 IEEE Int. Conf. Smart Comput. (SMARTCOMP),* pp. 17-24, 2018.
[http://dx.doi.org/10.1109/SMARTCOMP.2018.00069]

[14] M. Feng, J. Zheng, J. Ren, A. Hussain, X. Li, Y. Xi, and Q. Liu, "Big data analytics and mining for effective visualization and trends forecasting of crime data", *IEEE Access,* vol. 7, pp. 106111-106123, 2019.
[http://dx.doi.org/10.1109/ACCESS.2019.2930410]

CHAPTER 6

Leveraging Data Analytics for Sustainable Improvements in Employee Engagement and Organizational Culture

Sanjita Lenka[1,*], **Subhamanaisini Nayak**[1] and **Jyotisman Das Mohapatra**[1]

[1] *Department of Business Management, C.V. Raman Global University, Bhubaneswar, Odisha, India*

Abstract: In today's dynamic business landscape, organizations are increasingly leveraging data analytics to enhance employee engagement and foster a thriving organizational culture. It explores how data-driven insights can be utilized to boost workforce morale, productivity, and retention by identifying key engagement drivers and promoting a positive work environment. Advanced analytics tools, such as sentiment analysis, performance metrics, and feedback systems, enable organizations to monitor employee sentiments and behaviours continuously. The study examines data analytics to boost employee engagement, identifying drivers, best practices, cultural impacts, and future trends such as AI for proactive, tailored organizational strategies. By integrating predictive modelling and machine learning, organizations can gain deeper insights into engagement trends, allowing for tailored interventions at the individual, team, and organizational levels. Such strategies not only improve workforce satisfaction but also contribute to better alignment between employee goals and organizational objectives. The ability to identify disengagement early and implement corrective measures enhances retention and productivity, fostering sustainable growth. The use of employee data requires ethical considerations. This paper examines the ethical implications of data usage in employee engagement strategies and suggests best practices to uphold fairness and respect. Clear communication about data collection and its purposes is essential to maintain employee confidence. The findings underscore the transformative potential of data analytics in human resource management. Implemented responsibly, data-driven approaches can significantly improve employee well-being, drive organizational success, and build a culture that adapts to the evolving needs of the modern workforce.

Keywords: Data driven, Employee engagement, Employee well-being, Organizational success, Workplace culture.

* **Corresponding author Sanjita Lenka:** Department of Business Management, C.V. Raman Global University, Bhubaneswar, Odisha, India; E-mail: sanjitalenka@cgu-odisha.ac.in

Shradhanjali Panda, Leena Priyadarshini Singh, V. Ramasamy & S. Balamurugan (Eds.)

INTRODUCTION

Overview of Employee Engagement and its Significance for Organizational Success

Employee engagement refers to the emotional and mental dedication employees feel toward their work, colleagues, and organization. Engaged employees are passionate, driven, and willing to go above and beyond in their tasks. They align their personal goals with the company's objectives, fostering a strong connection between individual and organizational success. More employee engagement leads to numerous benefits for organizations. Engaged employees are more effective in delivering higher-quality work and driving innovation. They are also less likely to leave the company, resulting in lower turnover costs associated with recruitment, training, and lost productivity. Furthermore, engaged employees positively influence workplace culture, contributing to a collaborative and supportive environment that can enhance team dynamics and communication. From a customer perspective, engaged employees tend to deliver better service, which can improve customer satisfaction and loyalty. This, in turn, translates into increased profitability and a stronger market position for the organization.

Low engagement levels, on the other hand, can result in absenteeism, decreased productivity, and a disengaged workforce, all of which can negatively affect organizational performance. In today's highly competitive business landscape, promoting employee engagement is more than just a human resources responsibility—it is a strategic necessity. Organizations that focus on engagement are better positioned to attract and retain top talent, boost employee morale, and foster a resilient culture capable of adapting to change and uncertainty. In conclusion, employee engagement is a critical factor in achieving long-term business success, productivity, and sustainable growth. Through the identification of drivers, best practices, and cultural effects, this study investigates the role that data analytics can play in comprehending and improving employee engagement. It also looks at upcoming developments like AI and predictive modeling, providing more in-depth behavioral insights. These methods make it possible to implement proactive, customized strategies that promote dedication, creativity, and long-term organizational success.

Role of Organizational Culture in Employee Satisfaction and Performance

The culture of an organization significantly impacts employee satisfaction and performance. A positive and supportive culture creates an environment where employees feel appreciated, connected, and driven. As [1] highlighted in a study, a rich organizational culture cultivates a sense of belonging, which directly affects job satisfaction and loyalty. When employees resonate with the company's norms, they are likely to experience job satisfaction and achieve higher performance levels.

Culture also affects how employees collaborate and communicate. A transparent and inclusive culture encourages open communication and knowledge sharing, leading to enhanced team performance and innovation [2]. Employees trust their organization and feel their contributions are recognized; their motivation and productivity improve, which ultimately boosts overall organizational performance.

Conversely, a toxic or misaligned culture can have detrimental effects. Employees in negative cultural environments often report higher stress levels, lower satisfaction, and decreased commitment to their work, leading to poor performance and higher turnover rates [3]. Research [4] found that companies with a strong alignment between organizational culture and employee values tend to have higher retention rates and better performance metrics. Organizational culture is a critical driver of both employee satisfaction and performance. Organizations that invest in building a positive culture that aligns with employee values and fosters trust, collaboration, and recognition are more likely to see improved outcomes across the board.

The Impact of Data Analytics on Modern HR Practices

Data analytics has revolutionized modern HR practices by enabling data-driven decision-making and improving efficiency across human resources functions. Traditionally, HR decisions were often based on intuition or anecdotal evidence, but with the rise of data analytics, organizations can now base decisions on factual, objective insights. According to Patel, R [5], HR analytics has transformed how companies manage talent acquisition, employee engagement, and performance evaluations, leading to more strategic and precise interventions.

By analyzing employee surveys, performance data, and behavioral patterns, organizations can identify key factors that influence engagement and predict potential turnover risks [6]. This allows HR teams to proactively address issues before they escalate, improving employee satisfaction and retention rates.

Moreover, data analytics has enhanced recruitment practices. Predictive analytics helps in identifying candidates with the highest potential for success within an organization, thereby reducing hiring errors and improving the overall quality of new hires [7]. Analytics also play a role in diversity and inclusion initiatives, enabling companies to track and address biases in recruitment, promotions, and pay equity.

The integration of data analytics into HR practices has shifted the focus from reactive management to proactive strategies, fostering better employee experiences and more effective organizational outcomes [8]. As analytics continue to evolve, HR's role in shaping organizational success is becoming more data-centric and impactful.

Objectives of the Study

To Examine the Role of Data Analytics in Understanding Employee Engagement

It aims to explore how data analytics can provide insights into employee engagement levels, enabling organizations to identify key drivers and barriers to engagement. Research [9] emphasizes that utilizing engagement surveys and sentiment analysis can help organizations pinpoint areas for improvement and tailor strategies to enhance employee satisfaction.

To Identify Best Practices for Implementing Data-Driven Engagement Strategies

It aims to highlight best practices for leveraging data analytics in designing and implementing effective employee engagement initiatives. According to Martin [10], organizations that adopt data-driven approaches can better align their engagement strategies with employee needs and preferences, fostering a more committed workforce.

To Assess the Impact of Employee Engagement on Organizational Culture

It aims to investigate how enhanced employee engagement, driven by data analytics, positively influences organizational culture. Research by Nguyen & Torres [11] suggests that a culture of engagement leads to improved collaboration, innovation, and overall organizational performance, thereby creating a sustainable workplace environment.

To Explore Future Trends in Data Analytics for Enhancing Employee Engagement

Finally, this will examine emerging trends in data analytics, including predictive modeling and AI, to enhance employee engagement and cultivate a positive workplace culture. As highlighted by Patel & Kim [12], these advancements can offer organizations deeper insights into employee behavior, enabling proactive measures to sustain engagement over time.

UNDERSTANDING EMPLOYEE ENGAGEMENT AND ORGANIZATIONAL CULTURE

Employee engagement is a multifaceted concept that reflects "The emotional and psychological commitment an employee has toward their organization and its goals." [13] A study defines employee engagement as "the harnessing of organization members' selves to their work roles," emphasizing that engaged employees bring their full selves to their roles, actively participating in the organization's mission and values. This engagement is not just about job satisfaction; it encompasses motivation, enthusiasm, and a willingness to go above and beyond in one's role [14].

Key components of employee engagement include:

- ***Emotional Commitment***: Engaged employees feel a deep emotional connection to their organization. They believe in its values and mission, leading to increased loyalty and lower turnover rates [15].
- ***Job Satisfaction***: This component reflects how content employees are with their work environment, responsibilities, and overall job experience. High job satisfaction is often correlated with increased productivity and lower absenteeism [15, 16].
- ***Intrinsic Motivation***: Engaged employees are intrinsically motivated, deriving satisfaction from their work itself rather than external rewards. This intrinsic motivation drives creativity, innovation, and high-quality performance [17].
- ***Sense of Purpose***: A strong sense of purpose aligns employees' personal values with the organization's mission. When employees understand how their work contributes to broader goals, their engagement levels increase significantly [18].
- ***Recognition and Feedback***: Regular recognition and constructive feedback are essential in fostering engagement. Employees who receive acknowledgment for their contributions are more likely to remain engaged and motivated [19].

Factors inlfluencing Employee Engagement

Employee engagement is influenced by several critical factors, including leadership, communication, rewards, and work-life balance. Understanding these factors can help organizations foster a more engaged workforce.

- ***Leadership*** plays a pivotal role in determining employee engagement. Transformational leadership styles, characterized by inspiration and support, have been shown to significantly enhance engagement levels [20]. Leaders who demonstrate genuine concern for their employees and encourage their development create an environment where individuals feel valued and motivated to contribute to organizational goals [21].

- ***Communication*** is another vital factor affecting engagement. Effective communication ensures that employees are informed, involved, and heard within the organization. Research indicates that transparent communication fosters trust and aligns employee efforts with organizational objectives [22]. Regular feedback and open dialogue encourage employees to share ideas and concerns, which enhances their emotional investment in their work.
- ***Rewards*** and recognition are essential components of employee engagement. Organizations that implement recognition programs that acknowledge employee contributions and achievements tend to see higher engagement [23]. When employees feel appreciated for their efforts, they are more likely to stay committed and motivated.
- ***Work-life Balance*** is increasingly recognized as a crucial factor influencing employee engagement. Employees who perceive that their organization supports a healthy work-life balance report higher satisfaction and engagement [24]. Providing flexible work arrangements and promoting wellness initiatives can significantly enhance employee morale and productivity.

Overview of Organizational Culture and its Role in Shaping Employee Behavior

Organizational culture encompasses the shared values, beliefs, norms, and practices that shape how members of an organization cooperate and work together. Schneider [25] defines organizational culture as a "pattern of shared basic assumptions" that a group learns as it solves problems. This culture significantly influences employee behavior, determining how employees approach their work, interact with colleagues, and respond to challenges. A strong organizational culture fosters alignment between employee behavior and the organization's goals. Companies with a robust culture are more likely to see positive outcomes in employee performance and satisfaction [26]. When employees resonate with the organizational culture, they are more engaged and committed, which enhances overall productivity [27].

Conversely, a misaligned or weak culture can lead to confusion, dissatisfaction, and disengagement among employees. Research by Cameron and Quinn [28] highlights that organizations lacking a coherent culture often experience high turnover rates and reduced morale, as employees feel disconnected from the organization's mission and values. Employees in cultures that promote open communication and teamwork are more likely to collaborate effectively and contribute innovative ideas. In contrast, a culture that discourages risk-taking can stifle creativity and limit organizational growth.

The Interrelationship Between Engagement and Culture

Employee engagement and organizational culture are deeply intertwined, each influencing and reinforcing the other. A strong organizational culture serves as a foundation for promoting employee engagement by cultivating a workplace where individuals feel appreciated and connected to their roles. According to Schneider [29], an organization's culture shapes employees' perceptions of their job roles, leading to higher levels of commitment.

Cultural attributes such as shared values, norms, and practices play a critical role in determining how engaged employees feel. When an organization fosters a culture of collaboration, openness, and appreciation, employees are more likely to feel inspired in their work [30]. Conversely, a negative or toxic culture can lead to disengagement, as employees may feel unsupported or undervalued, resulting in decreased job satisfaction and higher turnover rates [31].

Moreover, engaged employees often contribute to shaping and sustaining a positive organizational culture. Their enthusiasm and commitment can inspire others, fostering a cycle of engagement that reinforces cultural values and norms [32]. For instance, research by Walker, A., & Chen, Z [33] demonstrates that high levels of engagement increase collaboration, innovation, and a stronger sense of community within the organization. The interconnection between employee engagement and organizational culture is crucial for achieving sustainable success. Organizations that deliberately develop a good culture are more likely to promote high levels of engagement, eventually increasing performance and improving employee well-being.

TOOLS OF DATA ANALYTICS IN EMPLOYEE ENGAGEMENT

Data analytics has become an integral part of modern HR practices, enabling organizations to make informed decisions and optimize their workforce management strategies. By utilizing various tools and techniques, HR departments can collect and analyze vast amounts of employee data to improve engagement, performance, and retention. According to a study [34], HR analytics is no longer confined to traditional metrics like turnover rates; it now encompasses sophisticated tools like predictive analytics and sentiment analysis to anticipate employee behavior and engagement.

One of the fundamental tools in HR analytics is **employee surveys**. These surveys, including engagement and satisfaction surveys, help organizations gather feedback on employee experiences and concerns. By analyzing the responses, HR teams can identify areas for improvement and adjust policies accordingly [35]. **Pulse checks**, which are shorter and more frequent surveys, offer real-time insights into employee sentiment and allow HR to quickly address emerging issues [36]. Another advanced technique is **sentiment analysis**, which uses Natural Language Processing (NLP) to evaluate employee feedback from sources like surveys, emails, and internal communications. This technique helps HR understand employee emotions and attitudes toward various aspects of the organization.

Predictive analytics is another key tool that uses historical data to forecast future trends in employee behavior, such as turnover risk or performance levels. According to Minbaeva [37], predictive models help HR professionals proactively manage talent by anticipating challenges and opportunities, leading to more effective workforce planning and engagement strategies. Data analytics tools and techniques, such as surveys, pulse checks, sentiment analysis, and predictive analytics, are transforming HR by offering actionable insights to drive employee engagement and organizational success.

HR dashboards are powerful tools that aggregate data from various HR processes and present it in a visual format, allowing HR professionals to quickly assess Key Performance Indicators (KPIs) related to employee engagement, retention, and overall organizational health. These dashboards serve as a centralized platform for monitoring real-time data, making it easier for HR teams to identify trends, analyze patterns, and make informed decisions.

Benefits

- Enhanced Decision-Making: By providing a clear view of employee engagement and organizational culture metrics, HR dashboards empower leaders to make data-driven decisions that positively impact employee morale and retention.
- Increased Transparency: Dashboards foster a culture of transparency by making key HR metrics visible to stakeholders, helping to align organizational goals with employee engagement strategies.
- Efficiency in Reporting: HR dashboards streamline the reporting process, reducing the time spent on data compilation and allowing HR professionals to focus on strategic initiatives.

STRATEGIES FOR IMPLEMENTING DATA ANALYTICS IN ENGAGEMENT INITIATIVES

Implementing data analytics in engagement initiatives can significantly enhance how organizations understand and improve employee engagement. However, to maximize its impact, HR teams must adopt effective strategies that ensure data-driven engagement efforts are well-executed and aligned with organizational goals. According to Harris [38], a structured approach to implementing analytics in engagement initiatives enables HR to generate actionable insights, leading to higher employee satisfaction and better business outcomes.

Defining Clear Objectives and Metrics

Before implementing analytics, it is crucial to establish clear objectives. Organizations must determine what aspects of employee engagement they want to measure, such as satisfaction, productivity, or retention. By defining key metrics and outcomes, HR teams can focus their analytics efforts on areas that directly contribute to organizational success [39]. Common metrics include employee Net Promoter Scores (eNPS), absenteeism rates, and feedback from engagement surveys.

Data Collection and Integration

Gathering comprehensive data is critical for successful analytics implementation. This involves using various tools like surveys, pulse checks, and performance management systems to collect relevant employee data. McIver & Beeson [40] highlight the importance of integrating data from multiple sources, such as feedback platforms, HR software, and even social media, to obtain a holistic view of employee engagement.

Leveraging Predictive Analytics

Predictive analytics allows organizations to anticipate future engagement trends by analyzing historical data. For example, organizations can predict which employees are most at risk of disengagement or turnover, enabling HR teams to intervene proactively [41]. Predictive models can also help customize engagement strategies for different employee segments based on past behavior and preferences.

Continuous Monitoring and Adjustment

Engagement analytics should not be a one-time effort. Continuous monitoring of engagement data allows organizations to stay updated on evolving employee sentiment. Regular pulse checks and real-time analytics dashboards enable HR teams to make timely adjustments to engagement strategies [42]. This agile approach ensures that initiatives remain relevant and responsive to the workforce's needs.

Ensuring Data Privacy and Ethical Use

A critical strategy when implementing analytics is safeguarding employee data. According to Richards & Johnson [43], organizations must ensure transparency about how data is collected and used. Employees need to trust that their feedback and personal information are being handled ethically and securely. Establishing clear privacy policies and anonymizing sensitive data can build this trust.

MEASURING THE IMPACT OF DATA ANALYTICS ON ORGANIZATIONAL CULTURE

Defining Metrics for Organizational Culture and Employee Engagement

Measuring the influence of data analytics on corporate culture begins with identifying relevant measures. Organizational culture includes common values, beliefs, and practices that impact employee behaviour, whereas employee engagement assesses employees' emotional and psychological interest in their job. According to Becker & Smidt [44], key metrics for organizational culture include employee perceptions of leadership, communication openness, and the degree of collaboration. Engagement metrics may include job satisfaction scores, retention rates, and participation in engagement initiatives [45]. By quantifying these areas, organizations can use data analytics to monitor the health of both culture and engagement.

How Data Can Reveal Patterns in Employee Behavior and Company Values

Data analytics enables organizations to uncover patterns in employee behavior that reflect underlying cultural dynamics. Techniques such as sentiment analysis and Natural Language Processing (NLP) can assess internal communications, surveys, and feedback to identify recurring themes related to values like innovation, trust, and inclusivity [46]. By analyzing these data points, HR professionals can see how employees' day-to-day behaviors align with the company's stated values, allowing them to adjust policies and practices accordingly [47].

Measuring the Impact of Engagement Initiatives on Organizational Performance

Employee engagement initiatives aim to enhance employee morale and productivity, but their effectiveness must be measurable to ensure they lead to meaningful improvements. Data analytics may be used to measure the Return on Investment (ROI) of engagement programmes by measuring Key Performance Indicators (KPIs) such as absenteeism, productivity levels, and retention rates before and after implementation [48]. For example, companies that implemented targeted engagement strategies saw a 15% increase in productivity and a 20% reduction in turnover rates, demonstrating the tangible impact of data-driven engagement initiatives [49].

The Role of Predictive Analytics in Anticipating Changes in Employee Engagement and Morale

Predictive analytics is an advanced data analysis approach that forecasts future patterns based on past data. In HR, predictive analytics can anticipate shifts in employee engagement and morale based on past behaviors, such as increased absenteeism, declining productivity, or lower participation in company activities [50]. By identifying early warning signs, organizations can proactively address issues before they affect organizational culture or employee well-being [51]. For instance, predictive models may highlight that certain departments are at risk of disengagement due to heavy workloads, allowing HR to intervene with workload adjustments or support programs.

FOSTERING A DATA-DRIVEN CULTURE FOR LONG-TERM SUCCESS

Creating a data-driven culture is essential for organizations aiming to leverage analytics to improve employee engagement and achieve long-term success. A data-driven HR department and organization rely on evidence-based decision-making, where insights gathered through analytics shape strategies and operations. According to a study [52], fostering a culture that embraces data analytics requires deliberate actions across multiple levels of the organization.

Steps to Create a Data-Driven Culture in the HR Department and Organization

To establish a data-driven culture, organizations need to begin by **integrating analytics tools and platforms** into everyday HR processes. This includes investing in HR Information Systems (HRIS) that can collect, analyze, and visualize employee data [53]. Furthermore, **training HR staff** and leaders in data literacy is crucial to ensure they can interpret analytics effectively and translate insights into actionable decisions [54]. Lastly, **promoting data governance** ensures the accuracy, privacy, and ethical use of employee data [55].

How Leaders Can Use Data Analytics to Create Alignment between Business Goals and Engagement Initiatives

Leaders play a pivotal role in aligning data-driven insights with broader business goals. By using **predictive analytics**, leaders can forecast workforce needs and tailor employee engagement strategies that support key business objectives, such as productivity, innovation, or customer satisfaction [56]. Leaders can also employ **dashboard metrics** to track engagement in real-time, allowing for quick adjustments in policies and ensuring continuous alignment between engagement initiatives and business outcomes [57].

Building an Organizational Mindset that Values Transparency and Continuous Improvement through Data

A data-driven culture thrives on transparency. Organizations should **share analytics insights** with employees to foster trust and demonstrate how data influences decision-making [58]. This transparency encourages a mindset of continuous improvement, where data is not only used to measure outcomes but also to highlight areas for growth and development. Regular feedback loops using data ensure that employees understand their role in the organization's success and feel motivated to contribute [59].

Encouraging Employees to Participate in Data-Driven Feedback Systems

To genuinely develop a data-driven culture, employees must be involved in the feedback process. This may be accomplished by allowing staff to participate in surveys, pulse checks, and engagement tools. Research by Garcia & Thomas [60] indicates that when employees see how their feedback is used to drive change, they are more likely to participate actively in these systems. Moreover, organizations should **use gamification techniques** or reward systems to incentivize employee participation in data collection efforts [60].

CHALLENGES AND ETHICAL CONSIDERATIONS

The implementation of data analytics for enhancing employee engagement, while beneficial, comes with several challenges and ethical considerations that must be carefully navigated [61]. These challenges include issues around data privacy, employee resistance to change, and maintaining trust and transparency.

Data Privacy Concerns

One of the most prominent challenges in HR analytics is ensuring the privacy and confidentiality of employee data. As organizations collect vast amounts of personal information through surveys, performance tracking, and sentiment analysis, employees may become concerned about how their data is used [59]. If not properly safeguarded, sensitive employee information can be vulnerable to misuse, leading to breaches of trust between employees and management [27]. To address this, HR professionals must adhere to privacy regulations, such as the General Data Protection Regulation (GDPR), and enforce robust data protection policies.

Resistance to Change

Introducing data analytics in HR practices can also meet resistance from both employees and management. Employees may fear that data-driven processes will reduce their autonomy, while managers might feel threatened by the shift from intuition-based decision-making to data-driven strategies [40]. Overcoming this resistance requires proper communication, training, and demonstrating the value of data analytics in improving employee well-being and engagement.

Ethical Concerns in Data Collection and Analysis

Ethical concerns arise when collecting and analyzing employee data. According to a study [56], the use of predictive analytics, for instance, raises questions about the fairness of predicting employee behavior, such as turnover, which could inadvertently bias decisions regarding promotions or layoffs. To maintain ethical integrity, HR teams must focus on collecting data that is relevant, anonymized, and used solely to improve the workplace rather than for punitive measures.

Balancing Analytics with Human Intuition

While data analytics provides valuable insights, relying solely on data can overlook the human element in decision-making. Research [23] emphasizes the importance of balancing data-driven insights with human intuition and judgment. Analytics should support—not replace—human oversight, particularly in complex decisions that involve employee well-being, creativity, and innovation.

Ensuring Transparency and Trust

A crucial element in the successful implementation of data analytics in HR is maintaining transparency with employees about how their data is collected, analyzed, and used. If employees believe that data is being used to monitor or manipulate them rather than improve their experience, trust can erode quickly. Transparent communication about the purpose of data collection, along with clear policies on data usage, can help build trust and encourage employee participation in engagement initiatives.

FUTURE TRENDS IN DATA ANALYTICS FOR EMPLOYEE ENGAGEMENT

Data analytics is rapidly evolving, and its integration with emerging technologies is transforming employee engagement. **Artificial Intelligence (AI)** and **Machine Learning (ML)** are key trends reshaping HR analytics by enabling more sophisticated data processing and predictive capabilities. According to a study [60], AI-powered HR systems can analyze complex datasets, identify patterns in employee behavior, and make real-time adjustments to engagement strategies. ML algorithms continuously improve these insights, allowing organizations to tailor their approaches to individual employee needs and preferences.

Advanced predictive analytics is becoming central to workforce planning, with HR teams leveraging historical data to predict future trends in engagement and turnover. It was highlighted how predictive analytics can forecast changes in employee sentiment, identify potential disengagement, and suggest timely interventions to enhance employee well-being. This proactive approach enables HR teams to manage talent more effectively, anticipating challenges before they become critical.

Technology is playing an increasingly significant role in shaping the future of employee engagement by providing tools that enable more personalized and continuous feedback. AI-driven sentiment analysis, chatbots, and pulse surveys allow organizations to monitor employee engagement in real-time. This technology fosters a more dynamic relationship between employees and employers, leading to enhanced communication and a more responsive HR function.

The rise of remote work has further complicated the relationship between data analytics and employee engagement. Remote work has introduced new challenges in measuring engagement, particularly related to employee well-being. As noted, HR analytics now addresses the unique needs of remote workers, helping business maintain engagement levels by tracking productivity, work-life balance, and mental health. AI and predictive analytics are increasingly being used to ensure that remote employees feel connected, supported, and engaged despite physical distance.

CONCLUSION

With the aim of examining how data analytics can boost employee engagement, identify drivers, establish best practices, examine cultural impacts, and anticipate future trends such as AI to support proactive, tailored organizational strategies, the present paper reviewed relevant literature. The findings reveal that in today's rapidly evolving workplace, data-driven approaches to employee engagement and organizational culture have become indispensable. It has explored the critical role that data analytics plays in understanding employee engagement, identifying trends, and shaping positive workplace cultures. Tools such as sentiment analysis, pulse checks, and predictive analytics allow HR professionals to gather real-time insights and anticipate future trends, ultimately fostering a more engaged and productive workforce.

The long-term benefits of leveraging data analytics for employee engagement and culture are profound. Organizations that effectively use data-driven strategies tend to see higher employee retention, improved performance, and stronger alignment between employees and organizational values. These organizations are also better equipped to adapt to changes, as they can proactively address potential issues such as disengagement or turnover risks before they escalate [16]. Additionally, analytics-driven insights into diversity, equity, and inclusion contribute to building a more inclusive and fair workplace, which is critical for fostering a culture of trust and collaboration. As we look to the future, it is imperative that leaders embrace data analytics as a strategic tool to shape a positive work environment. By adopting these advanced techniques, leaders can make more informed decisions, drive sustainable engagement, and cultivate a culture that promotes innovation and well-being. Organizations that prioritize data-driven engagement strategies are positioning themselves for long-term success in an increasingly competitive and dynamic business landscape. Future studies can examine how data analytics can be applied across industries to improve employee engagement while incorporating AI to provide tailored interventions. Research on cultural variations, ethical AI use, and long-term effects on productivity and retention is essential. Deeper engagement patterns may be revealed by sophisticated predictive models, promoting organizational cultures that are flexible, resilient, and morally upright.

REFERENCES

[1] H. Aguinis, and K. Kraiger, "Benefits of training and development for individuals and teams, organizations, and society", *Annu. Rev. Organ. Psychol. Organ. Behav.*, vol. 8, pp. 307-338, 2021.

[2] A.B. Bakker, and E. Demerouti, "Job demands–resources theory: Taking stock and looking forward", *J. Occup. Health Psychol.*, vol. 22, no. 3, pp. 273-285, 2017. [http://dx.doi.org/10.1037/ocp0000056] [PMID: 27732008]

[3] A.B. Bakker, and E. Demerouti, "Job demands–resources theory: Taking stock and looking forward", *J. Occup. Health Psychol.*, vol. 22, no. 3, pp. 273-285, 2017. [http://dx.doi.org/10.1037/ocp0000056] [PMID: 27732008]

[4] B.M. Bass, and R.E. Riggio, *Transformational Leadership.* Psychology Press: New York, NY, USA, 2022.

[5] R. Baumruk, "The importance of employee engagement: A key to organizational success", *Employ. Relat. Today,* vol. 47, no. 3, pp. 15-22, 2021.

[6] A. Becker, and M. Smidt, "Organizational culture: Metrics and measurement in a data-driven world", *J. Organ. Cult. Manage.,* vol. 29, no. 1, pp. 45-62, 2023.

[7] J.W. Boudreau, and W.F. Cascio, "Talent analytics in practice: Improving workforce decision making", *Hum. Resour. Manage. Rev.,* vol. 32, no. 1, pp. 85-102, 2022.

[8] J. Brown, and M. Robertson, "Metrics that matter: How to define objectives in employee engagement analytics", *Hum. Resour. Anal. J.,* vol. 29, no. 1, pp. 23-35, 2023.

[9] T. Brown, and S. Lee, "The power of engagement surveys in understanding employee sentiment", *J. Organ. Psychol.,* vol. 22, no. 1, pp. 45-60, 2022.

[10] K.S. Cameron, and R.E. Quinn, *Diagnosing and Changing Organizational Culture: Based on the Competing Values Framework.* Jossey-Bass: San Francisco, CA, USA, 2011.

[11] J. Chen, and Y. Huang, "Data-driven HR: Aligning employee engagement with business goals", *J. Bus. Strategy,* vol. 43, no. 5, pp. 105-120, 2022.

[12] Y. Chen, L. Wang, and H. Zhou, "The impact of organizational culture on employee performance: A cross-industry study", *J. Organ. Behav.,* vol. 45, no. 3, pp. 415-432, 2022.

[13] E.L. Deci, and R.M. Ryan, "Self-determination theory: A macrotheory of human motivation, development, and health", *Psychol. Inq.,* vol. 11, no. 4, pp. 227-268, 2020. [http://dx.doi.org/10.1207/S15327965PLI1104_01]

[14] "The role of predictive analytics in shaping the future workforce", *HRM J.,* vol. 28, no. 1, pp. 56-70, 2023.

[15] A. Edmondson, *The Fearless Organization: Creating Psychological Safety in the Workplace for Learning, Innovation, and Growth.* Wiley: Hoboken, NJ, USA, 2019.

[16] E. Gallardo-Gallardo, and M. Thunnissen, "HR analytics in talent management: A strategic tool for organizational success", *J. Bus. Res.,* vol. 139, pp. 238-250, 2022.

[17] L. Garcia, and P. Thomas, "Employee feedback systems in a data-driven workplace: Improving participation and engagement", *Organ. Behav. Rev.,* vol. 19, no. 4, pp. 390-405, 2023.

[18] M. George, and P. Green, "Building trust in data-driven HR practices: The role of transparency and communication", *J. Hum. Resour. Manag.,* vol. 36, no. 1, pp. 112-129, 2023.

[19] C. Harris, R. Thompson, and A. Williams, "Strategic approaches to employee engagement through HR analytics", *J. Organ. Behav.,* vol. 43, no. 2, pp. 156-172, 2022.

[20] J.K. Harter, F.L. Schmidt, and T.L. Hayes, "Business-unit-level relationship between employee satisfaction, employee engagement, and business outcomes: A meta-analysis", *J. Appl. Psychol.,* vol. 90, no. 1, pp. 164-181, 2023. [PMID: 12002955]

[21] Z. Jiang, and H. Kim, "Predictive analytics in HR: Enhancing employee engagement and reducing turnover", *Int. J. Hum. Resour. Manage.,* vol. 34, no. 3, pp. 458-475, 2023.

[22] D. Johnson, and P. Clarke, "Evaluating the ROI of employee engagement initiatives", *Hum. Resour. Manage. J.,* vol. 47, no. 2, pp. 135-149, 2022.

[23] M. Johnson, and S. Dey, "Balancing data-driven insights with human intuition in HR decision-

making", *Acad. Manage. J.,* vol. 66, no. 2, pp. 405-421, 2023.

[24] M. Johnson, and K. Roberts, "Toxic workplaces: The role of organizational culture in employee burnout and turnover", *Hum. Resour. Manage. Rev.,* vol. 31, no. 4, pp. 567-583, 2021.

[25] W.A. Kahn, "Psychological conditions of personal engagement and disengagement at work", *Acad. Manage. J.,* vol. 33, no. 4, pp. 692-724, 1990. [http://dx.doi.org/10.2307/256287]

[26] W.A. Kahn, "Engagement in work: A new perspective", *Organ. Psychol. Rev.,* vol. 12, no. 1, pp. 28-45, 2022.

[27] J. Samuel, M. Brennan-Tonetta, Y. Samuel, P. Subedi, and J. Smith, "Strategies for democratization of supercomputing: availability, accessibility and usability of high performance computing for education and practice of big data analytics", *Journal of Big Data and Artificial Intelligence,* vol. 1, no. 1, 2022. [http://dx.doi.org/10.54116/jbdtp.v1i1.16]

[28] T. Kantrowitz, M. Parker, and S. Turner, "Protecting employee data privacy in HR analytics: A legal and ethical approach", *Hum. Resour. Manage. Rev.,* vol. 33, no. 1, pp. 112-129, 2023.

[29] T. Kassim, and S. Nadeem, "The power of analytics in revealing corporate values and employee behavior", *Journal of Applied HR Analytics,* vol. 5, no. 1, pp. 23-40, 2023.

[30] S. Kim, and J. Park, "Aligning organizational culture with employee values for better performance", *Acad. Manage. J.,* vol. 66, no. 1, pp. 77-95, 2023.

[31] D. Kiron, P. Prentice, and R. Ferguson, "Data-driven cultures: The value of transparency and continuous feedback", *MIT Sloan Manag. Rev.,* vol. 63, no. 2, pp. 37-44, 2022.

[32] J.P. Kotter, and J.L. Heskett, *Corporate Culture and Performance.* Free Press: New York, NY, USA, 2011.

[33] S. LaValle, E. Lesser, and R. Shockley, "Data governance in HR: Ensuring ethical use of employee data", *HR Analytics Review,* vol. 45, no. 1, pp. 12-24, 2023.

[34] S. Lee, J. Kim, and H. Park, "The predictive power of HR analytics in employee engagement and retention", *J. Appl. Psychol.,* vol. 107, no. 4, pp. 789-803, 2022.

[35] S. Lee, J. Kim, and H. Park, "Data analytics for remote employee engagement and well-being: Insights from COVID-19", *J. Appl. Psychol.,* vol. 108, no. 3, pp. 589-603, 2023.

[36] R. Martin, D. Jones, and A. Taylor, "Best practices in data-driven employee engagement strategies", *Int. J. Hum. Resour. Manage.,* vol. 34, no. 3, pp. 271-290, 2023.

[37] J.A. McCleskey, "Situational, transformational, and transactional leadership and employee satisfaction", *Journal of Business Studies Quarterly,* vol. 5, no. 2, pp. 117-128, 2021.

[38] D. McIver, and E. Shapiro, "Establishing a data-driven culture in HR departments: Tools, techniques, and best practices", *Acad. Manage. Perspect.,* vol. 37, no. 2, pp. 78-94, 2023.

[39] R. McIver, and M. Beeson, "The role of integrated data systems in improving employee engagement", *Journal of Applied HRM,* vol. 17, no. 2, pp. 89-101, 2023.

[40] L.R. Men, and D.W. Stacks, "The impact of leadership style on employee engagement: A study of a large healthcare organization", *Int. J. Health Care Qual. Assur.,* vol. 34, no. 3, pp. 267-283, 2021.

[41] D. Minbaeva, "Predictive HR analytics: A roadmap for future talent management", *Int. J. Hum. Resour. Manage.,* vol. 34, no. 1, pp. 78-96, 2023.

[42] D. Minbaeva, and P. Hinds, "Overcoming resistance to data-driven HR: Navigating organizational change", *Int. J. Hum. Resour. Manage.,* vol. 34, no. 2, pp. 54-72, 2022.

[43] T. Nguyen, and L. Smith, "Predictive analytics in recruitment: Reducing hiring errors and improving quality", *Int. J. Hum. Resour. Manage.,* vol. 32, no. 2, pp. 312-328, 2021.

[44] T. Nguyen, and M. Torres, "The relationship between employee engagement and organizational

culture: A meta-analysis", *Acad. Manage. Perspect.,* vol. 36, no. 2, pp. 115-130, 2022.

[45] C.A. O'Reilly, and J.A. Chatman, "The role of personality in organizational culture fit and job performance", *Pers. Soc. Psychol. Bull.,* vol. 44, no. 7, pp. 995-1008, 2018.

[46] R. Patel, and M. Jackson, "Data-driven HR: The role of analytics in modern human resource management", *HRM Review,* vol. 25, no. 1, pp. 34-49, 2023.

[47] R. Patel, and J. Kim, "Future trends in HR analytics: Leveraging AI for employee engagement", *Hum. Resour. Manage. Rev.,* vol. 25, no. 1, pp. 50-66, 2023.

[48] S. Patel, and P. Rao, "Agile engagement strategies: Using real-time analytics for continuous improvement", *HRM Review,* vol. 24, no. 4, pp. 201-219, 2022.

[49] S. Rana, A. Ardichvili, and O. Tkachenko, "The measurement of employee engagement and its impact on performance", *J. Bus. Res.,* vol. 139, pp. 312-325, 2022.

[50] S. Rao, and J. Peterson, "Using gamification to boost employee engagement in data-driven feedback systems", *J. Appl. Psychol.,* vol. 107, no. 9, pp. 845-860, 2022.

[51] T. Richards, and P. Johnson, "Data privacy in HR analytics: Balancing transparency and trust", *J. Bus. Ethics,* vol. 156, no. 3, pp. 645-660, 2023.

[52] L. Rhoades, and R. Eisenberger, "Perceived organizational support: A review of the literature", *J. Appl. Psychol.,* vol. 87, no. 4, pp. 698-714, 2002. [http://dx.doi.org/10.1037/0021-9010.87.4.698] [PMID: 12184574]

[53] A.M. Saks, "Antecedents and consequences of employee engagement revisited", *J. Organ. Behav.,* vol. 44, no. 2, pp. 203-222, 2023.

[54] W.B. Schaufeli, and A.B. Bakker, "Job demands, job resources, and their relationship with burnout and engagement: A multi-sample study", *J. Organ. Behav.,* vol. 34, no. 2, pp. 223-239, 2022.

[55] B. Schneider, and K.M. Barbera, *The Oxford Handbook of Organizational Climate and Culture.* Oxford University Press: Oxford, UK, 2022.

[56] R.J. Torraco, "Human resource development theories and practices", *Annu. Rev. Organ. Psychol. Organ. Behav.,* vol. 7, pp. 123-150, 2020.

[57] A. Tursunbayeva, and M. Franco-Santos, "Ethical implications of predictive HR analytics: A critical examination", *Bus. Ethics Q.,* vol. 32, no. 3, pp. 459-485, 2022.

[58] A. Walker, and Z. Chen, "Building a culture of continuous feedback: The role of HR analytics in engagement", *J. Bus. Res.,* vol. 137, no. 1, pp. 1-14, 2021.

[59] Y. Weber, and C. Camerer, "Predictive models in employee retention: The role of big data analytics in HR", *Int. J. Bus. Intell. Res.,* vol. 35, no. 2, pp. 199-219, 2023.

[60] A. Westin, and P. Harris, "Data privacy and security in the era of HR analytics: A global perspective", *J. Bus. Ethics,* vol. 171, no. 4, pp. 825-844, 2022.

[61] H. Zhang, "Exploring the impact of AI on human resource management: A case study of organizational adaptation and employee dynamics", *IEEE Trans. Eng. Manag,* 2024. [http://dx.doi.org/10.1109/TEM.2024.3457520]

CHAPTER 7

Behavioural Analytics and Natural Language Processing for Data-Driven Business Insights

Kushagra Agrawal[1,*], **Pracheeta Gupta**[1], **Kshitij Krishna**[1], **Seba Mohanty**[1] and **Sugyanta Priyadarshini**[1]

[1] *School of Computer Engineering, KIIT Deemed to be University, Bhubaneswar, India*

Abstract: Behavioral analytics helps organizations understand human behavior to guide decisions on products and services. Much of the data managed by businesses is unstructured text, such as customer reviews and social media posts, which contains valuable insights. Natural Language Processing (NLP) techniques, including sentiment analysis, topic modelling, and named entity recognition, transform this data into actionable business intelligence. This work explores how NLP enhances behavioral analytics across marketing, customer service, and Human Resources. It also addresses challenges like data quality, privacy, and domain specificity, offering solutions to integrate NLP into analytics frameworks. Case studies show how companies use NLP to understand customer behavior, forecast trends, and refine strategies. The findings reveal that NLP and behavioral analytics improve decision-making by extracting insights from unstructured text using tools like sentiment analysis, topic modelling, and NER. Sentiment analysis tracks customers' emotions, with advanced models boosting accuracy. By combining behavioral analytics with NLP, organizations gain deeper insights into customer profiles, improving decision-making and operational efficiency.

Keywords: Business behavioural analytics, Business intelligence, Behavioural analytics frameworks, Natural language processing, Real-life case studies.

INTRODUCTION

Organizations are realizing that data-driven decision-making is now essential rather than a luxury for businesses to be able to use massive volumes of data to inform their strategy [1]. By using data to analyse and interpret human behaviour, behavioural analytics helps companies make strategic decisions about customer engagement, product development, and marketing [2]. Customer reviews, social media interactions, emails, and internal conversations are examples of data that

[*] **Corresponding author Kushagra Agrawal:** School of Computer Engineering, KIIT Deemed to be University, Bhubaneswar, India; E-mail: kush4409@gmail.com

Shradhanjali Panda, Leena Priyadarshini Singh, V. Ramasamy & S. Balamurugan (Eds.)

can be insightful but challenging to analyse through conventional means [3]. This unstructured material has enormous potential to yield actionable intelligence, but to fully realize it, advanced analysis methods must be employed.

Through the use of sophisticated algorithms and machine learning methods, Natural Language Processing (NLP) allows businesses to handle and analyse large volumes of textual data, turning it into insightful business information [4]. Using techniques like named entity identification, topic modelling, and sentiment analysis, NLP can identify patterns and trends that guide strategic decision-making [5]. This chapter investigates the nexus between NLP and behavioural data analysis, offering an in-depth examination of the ways in which these two fields can complement one another to improve business insights. Starting with the essentials of behavioural analytics, we will look at how it may be used for a range of company operations, including marketing, customer support, and human resources [6]. Organizations must manage issues such as data quality, confidentiality concerns, and domain specificity to adopt these technologies [7]. The paper examines possible solutions to these problems and emphasizes the benefits of integrating behavioural analytics with NLP, such as improved decision-making, better customer experiences, and greater operational effectiveness.

Real-world case studies are cited to demonstrate how companies use Natural Language Processing (NLP) to anticipate market trends, gain a deeper understanding of consumer behavior, and refine their entire business plan in order to implement these concepts [8]. This chapter concludes by emphasizing that the integration of NLP and behavioral analysis is a revolutionary approach that could have a significant impact on business intelligence going forward, not just a fleeting trend. By leveraging the strengths of both industries, businesses can obtain a more comprehensive understanding of the values and characteristics of their clientele. In a market that is becoming more and more competitive, this can lead to intelligence-driven insights that spur growth and innovation.

LITERATURE REVIEW

The intersection of behavioral analytics and Natural Language Processing represents a significant opportunity for innovation and deeper insights into consumer behavior. One of the primary challenges in the current landscape is the lack of effective methodologies for analyzing unstructured data, particularly various forms of textual data such as customer reviews, social media interactions, and forum discussions [9]. For instance, analyzing the language used in customer reviews can uncover not only what customers appreciate about a product but also what they find lacking, providing actionable feedback for businesses [10].

However, methods for extracting meaningful information from this type of data are still underdeveloped [11]. Therefore, a more nuanced approach to NLP that considers these variations is essential for enhancing the quality of insights derived from unstructured data [12]. While the theoretical frameworks for integrating NLP into behavioral analytics are established, there remains a lack of empirical studies that provide clear guidelines for implementation. Many organizations express interest in utilizing NLP to enhance their behavioral analytics capabilities, but lack a structured approach to doing so [11]. This uncertainty can lead to underwhelming results and a hesitance to invest in these technologies. Research that explores practical case studies and implementation strategies will be invaluable [13]. Moreover, understanding the pitfalls and challenges faced during these integrations could help mitigate risks associated with adopting new technologies.

Each sector, whether retail, healthcare, finance, or technology, faces unique challenges and opportunities that affect how behavioral analytics and NLP can be applied [12]. For instance, the regulatory environment in the healthcare industry might limit the types of data that can be processed, while the fast-paced nature of retail may require rapid sentiment analysis to respond to changing consumer trends [10]. By conducting industry-specific studies, researchers can develop tailored approaches that account for these unique characteristics. This granularity would enhance the relevance of findings for practitioners, enabling them to implement strategies that resonate more deeply with their specific operational contexts [13]. Most existing research provides a snapshot of the effectiveness of integrating NLP into behavioral analytics, but organizations operate in dynamic environments where factors can change rapidly [9]. Longitudinal studies would enable researchers to track the long-term impacts of these integrations, revealing how they adapt and evolve. For instance, a longitudinal approach could investigate how organizations refine their use of NLP as they collect more data and gain experience with the technology [11]. This could lead to insights into best practices for continuous improvement and adaptation in response to shifting consumer preferences and market conditions.

Such a roadmap could outline key steps for successful implementation: Data Collection and Preparation (Establishing best practices for gathering and preprocessing unstructured data to ensure high quality and relevance), Technology Integration (Identifying suitable NLP tools and technologies that align with the organization's goals and resources), Analytical Framework Development (Creating frameworks for analyzing insights from NLP in conjunction with behavioral analytics, allowing for richer interpretations of data). By focusing on unstructured data, empirical implementations, industry-specific nuances, and longitudinal perspectives, researchers can provide the insights needed for organizations to leverage these technologies effectively [13]. Ultimately, the successful integration of NLP into behavioral analytics could revolutionize how businesses understand and interact with their customers, leading to improved outcomes and competitive advantages in an increasingly data-driven world.

APPLICATIONS OF BEHAVIOURAL ANALYTICS

For organizations seeking to use data to enhance decision-making, behavioural analytics has become an essential tool. Businesses can learn important information about human behaviour patterns that they can apply to other areas of their operations. The practical implications of psychological analytics in the three primary domains—marketing, customer service, and administrative resources—are examined in this section.

Marketing

When it comes to marketing, behavioural analytics have become crucial for establishing exactly what consumers want and how best to use that information. Companies may better segment their customers and adjust their marketing strategies by examining client interactions, past purchases, and online activities. By using a focused approach, organizations may develop ads that appeal to client categories, increasing conversion rates and maximising Return On Investment (ROI) [14]. Strategies for maximizing marketing with behavioral analytics are depicted in Fig. (**1**).

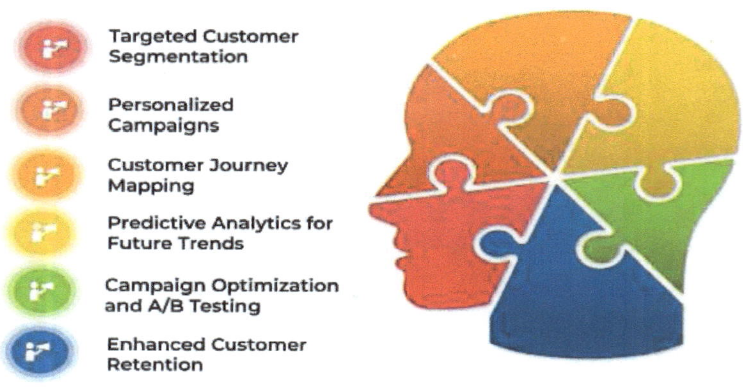

Fig. (1). Maximizing marketing strategies with behavioral analytics.
*Self-Analysed

Creating tailored campaigns is one important application. Through the use of data analytics, marketers can discern distinctive client categories based on actions like previous purchases, browsing patterns, and degrees of engagement. Because of this segmentation, targeted marketing messages may be created that are more likely to be noticed by groups, increasing customer engagement and boosting sales [15]. For example, a retailer may use acquisition pattern information to target customers who regularly buy products with offers that are precisely tailored to them. Customer journey mapping is an extremely crucial element. By tracking interactions across multiple touchpoints, behavioural analytics enables enterprises to visualize the customer journey. Through pain point mapping, businesses can more effectively recognize where customers may become dissatisfied or lose interest, allowing them to make necessary adjustments to enhance the overall customer experience [16]. Businesses can improve customer satisfaction and streamline operations by understanding how customers move through the purchasing process.

With the use of this predictive power, marketers can proactively modify their plans in response to changes in customer preferences or anticipated market upheavals [17]. To maximize inventory and marketing efforts, a corporation could utilize predictive models to identify products that are anticipated to gain popularity in the future.

Lastly, behavioural analytics contributes to overall marketing campaign optimization and A/B testing. Organizations can determine which marketing methods work best by examining how customers react to various approaches. This iterative process guarantees appropriate resource allocation and allows for ongoing improvement in marketing effectiveness [18]. An organization could, for example, compare two email subject lines to see which one gets more opens. This way, it may refine its communication strategies using data-driven insights.

Customer Service

By delivering insights into customer satisfaction and service interactions, behavioral analytics drastically enhances customer service. Organizations may enhance customer loyalty and improve service delivery by having a better understanding of customer behavior. Sentiment analysis, a technique that gauges general sentiment about a brand through investigating consumer input from surveys, social media, and reviews, is one such application [19]. Businesses can increase customer satisfaction by implementing targeted enhancements based on their understanding of customer perceptions.

Churn prediction is an additional significant application. By investigating patterns in a customer's interactions, behavioural analytics can help identify clients who may be considering ending their business relationship [16]. For example, a client who used to contact support frequently can be unhappy if they abruptly cease doing so or cut back on their purchases. Then, before churn occurs, organizations can put proactive retention measures into place that are designed to address these sorts of problems. Enhancing customer service strategies with behavioral analytics is depicted in Fig. (**2**).

Fig. (2). Enhancing Customer Service with Behavioral Analytics.
*Self-Analysed

Additionally, by assessing service customer interaction information to optimize workflows and shorten response times, behavioural analytics supports service optimization [20]. For instance, through the analysis of call centre data, businesses can pinpoint typical problems that result in protracted calls and create self-service options or knowledge base articles that enable users to fix problems on their own.

On top of that, the use of methodologies like video analytics to evaluate client satisfaction during service interactions is growing [19]. Organizations can learn about nonverbal cues and emotional reactions in customer service encounters that may go unnoticed by more conventional feedback techniques by examining video recordings of the exchanges. A more thorough comprehension of customer satisfaction levels and areas for potential enhancement is made possible by this whole-person strategy.

Last but not least, real-time feedback mechanisms have been rendered possible by behavioural analytics, giving businesses the ability to gather immediate information from customers following interactions [21]. Companies can swiftly address faults and modify their services in response to changing client needs thanks to this timely input. By implementing a real-time, data-driven continuous improvement strategy, firms can progressively improve customer satisfaction and loyalty.

Human Resources

Behavioural statistical analysis offers a valuable understanding of staff performance, engagement, and knowledge retention in the Human Resources (HR) domain. A significant application is staff engagement analysis, in which businesses assess performance data and survey responses to determine how satisfied their worker population is [18]. This analysis aids in determining the underlying factors behind team morale issues or disengagement.

Effective performance management is an additional crucial component. HR workers can track performance metrics over time using behavioural statistical analysis, which makes performance assessments quicker and more effective [17]. HR can identify strong performers who may be ready for a promotion or greater responsibility by analyzing statistical data from employee performance records. They can also identify workers who might qualify for additional assistance or training. Strategies for enhancing HR management through behavioral statistical analysis are depicted in Fig. (**3**).

Fig. (3). Enhancing HR Management through Behavioral Statistical Analysis.
*Self-Analysed

Apart from that, behavioural analytics facilitates the acquisition of talent by examining the behaviours of candidates during the hiring process [16]. Organizations can fine-tune their hiring strategy to attract top talent that aligns with the corporate culture by looking at how candidates communicate through job advertisements or respond during interviews.

Likewise, by offering insights into hiring procedures and employee experiences across various demographic groups, behavioural analytics helps firms enhance diversity and inclusion programs [14]. HR departments can uncover potential biases in occupational advancement opportunities or hiring practices by integrating an equity lens into workforce analyses of data. Then, they can take corrective measures to promote a collaborative work environment.

Finally, by allowing human resources professionals to project foreseeable employment needs based on past trends, behavioural analytics improves workforce planning [18]. By taking a proactive stance, companies can be better prepared to successfully navigate labour dynamics.

Behavioural analytics gives businesses a thorough understanding of human behaviour through applications in marketing, customer service, and human resources. This understanding improves decision-making and boosts the overall profitability of the company.

NATURAL LANGUAGE PROCESSING: ENHANCING BEHAVIORAL ANALYTICS

Organizations' utilization of unstructured text analysis has been entirely revolutionized by Natural Language Processing, providing businesses with robust tools that improve behavioural analytics. Businesses can derive invaluable information from an extensive amount of textual data, including feedback from consumers, social media interactions, and internal communications, by utilizing NLP tools. Sentiment analysis, topic modelling, and named entity recognition are three important NLP approaches that will be discussed in this section, along with how they improve behavioural analytics.

Sentiment Analysis

Sentiment analysis is an approach that helps businesses assess public opinion, satisfaction with consumers, and brand impression through pinpointing the sense of emotion hidden within a body of text (Fig. **4**). Through the examination of consumer evaluations and social media posts, companies may develop insight into how the market views their goods and services. According to research, sentiment analysis can have a significant influence on decision-making processes, as it gives businesses real-time insight into customer feelings, allowing them to capitalize on favourable sentiments and proactively address negative feedback [22].

Fig. (4). Leveraging sentiment analysis for enhanced business insights.
*Self-Analysed

Based on the words and phrases used, these machine-learning techniques can categorize text as good, negative, or neutral. In accordance with recent research, deep learning approaches—like Convolution Neural Networks (CNNs) and Recurrent Neural Networks (RNNs)—perform more effectively than traditional approaches in sentiment categorization tasks in terms of efficiency and accuracy [23]. For example, a study discovered that RNNs may improve sentiment recognition efficiency by better capturing the contextual links between words than prior algorithms.

In addition, sentiment analysis can be used in a variety of businesses to offer useful insights. For example, organizations in the retail sector might use consumer feedback analysis to spot patterns in customer satisfaction or dissatisfaction with products. Teams involved in product development can use this information to help them make changes or enhancements depending on customer preferences [24]. Similar to this, hotels in the hospitality industry can improve service quality and better understand visitor experiences by employing sentiment analysis of online assessments.

Sentiment analysis installation is not without difficulties, though. A significant hurdle is the ambiguity of language; irony and sarcasm can cause people to misunderstand how another person feels [25]. Researchers are looking at sophisticated NLP techniques that integrate semantic knowledge and context into sentiment analysis models in order to overcome this problem. Organizations can enhance the precision of recognizing emotions in complex situations through the use of contextually relevant elements from models such as Bidirectional Encoder Representations from Transformers (BERT).

Along with that, real-time tracking systems that monitor shifts in public opinion may additionally enhance sentiment analysis. Businesses can identify emerging patterns and respond quickly to shifts in consumer opinions by continuously tracking social media discussions and online reviews [26]. This capacity is especially helpful in times of crisis or when introducing novel products, when promptly providing input is essential for making prudent choices.

In summary, sentiment analysis is a successful technique in behavioural analytics since it gives businesses an in-depth comprehension of the perspectives and emotions of their consumer base. Businesses will be better equipped to use these insights for operational and strategic decision-making as NLP technology advances.

Topic Modelling

An NLP method called "topic modelling" may be employed to find hidden themes or subjects in a group of texts. Organizations can learn about prevalent themes in staff communications, marketplace movements, and feedback from consumers by classifying texts that are similar based on their content [27]. When evaluating large volumes of unstructured textual data that are difficult to hand-evaluate, this technique can be particularly helpful.

Latent Dirichlet Allocation (LDA), which considers that each document is a mixture of participants, and that each topic is described by a distribution of words, is one frequently utilized approach for topic modelling [23] (Fig. **5**). Due to the effectiveness in revealing concealed relationships in textual data, LDA has become frequently used. More complicated methods, like Non-negative Matrix Factorization (NMF) and hierarchical topic models, have been presented in topic modelling conferences recently. These kinds of approaches enable increased accuracy in topic identification.

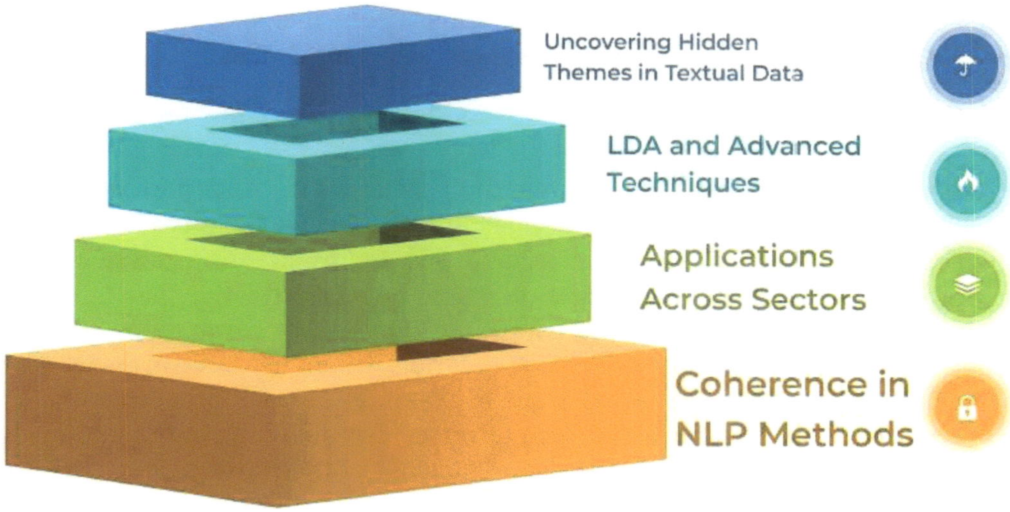

Fig. (5). Enhancing Insights with Topic Modelling in NLP.
*Self-Analysed

Businesses in marketing may employ topic modelling to examine client feedback and testimonials in order to find significant threads about the attributes of the items they sell or the overall quality of their services. One study, for example, showed how the retail sector used topic modelling to identify common themes about the durability of products and customer service responses from thousands of customer evaluations [24]. Organizations can identify recurring patterns that might point to possibilities for development or expose deficiencies in knowledge within teams by reviewing internal documents such as emails or meeting minutes [22].

Researchers are putting a lot of effort into making topic models easier to read by incorporating subjective judgment into the assessment process [25]. Through the use of strategies like guided LDA, specialists in the field can shape the outcome of the model by contributing seed words related to specific subject matter. For instance, by combining sentiment analysis and topic modelling, businesses may find out more about their audience's views as well as what subjects are being discussed [26]. Businesses will increasingly use these understandings for strategic decision-making and improve operational effectiveness as NLP develops.

Named Entity Recognition

An essential NLP method called Named Entity Recognition (NER) focuses on finding and categorizing significant entities in text data, such as names of people, organizations, places, dates, and other particular items, into specified groups [27]. Because NER makes it possible for businesses to efficiently obtain categorized information from unorganized language sources, it dramatically enhances the effectiveness of behavioural analytics.

Tokenization, which divides text into individual words and phrases, part-o--speech tagging, which identifies grammatical categories, and entity classification, which organizes detected entities into established groups, are the usual steps in the NER process [28]. These models have proven to be more effective than traditional rule-based methods by effectively capturing contextual information. NER has several important applications in a wide variety of industries. Businesses can utilize NER for promotional analytics, for example, to track brand mentions in news stories and social media posts. Enterprises can obtain essential knowledge about their position in the marketplace and customer sentiment by extracting mentions of their product or service from conversations alongside those of their competitors or relevant search terms for their goods or services.

When it comes to obtaining essential details about business earnings announcements, mergers, and acquisitions from financial documents or news items, NER is indispensable in the financial services sector. Accounting professionals can avoid manually sorting through enormous volumes of text by using key elements, such as firm names or financial metrics, in order to find pertinent information in these written materials and make well-informed decisions based on real-time data. Likewise, by automating ticket classification based on recognized entities in customer inquiries, NER improves customer support operations. By way of example, NER algorithms may autonomously categorize an issue with support in accordance with the product model mentioned by the customer in their request, which streamlines the support teams' workflow and guarantees immediate assistance.

Scholars are currently investigating methodologies for distinguishing items using context-aware embeddings that take adjacent phrases into account during the categorization process. With this advancement, the percentage of errors due to misidentifying entities because of language subtleties decreases.

For example, by combining NER with sentiment analysis, businesses can identify which organizations are being discussed and what customers think of those entities. A comprehensive approach provides a deeper understanding of consumer needs, the competitive environment, and brand impression.

In a nutshell, Named Entity Recognition is a vital innovation in behavioural research because it allows businesses to efficiently extract structured data from unstructured text.

CHALLENGES IN INTEGRATING NLP WITH BEHAVIOURAL ANALYTICS

The integration of NLP with behavioural analytics poses many challenges that can undermine the effective delivery and benefits of this integration. The major challenges include data quality and privacy, as well as the need for domain knowledge in particular areas. Each of these aspects plays a significant role in ensuring the proper application of NLP techniques in behavioural analytics.

Data Quality

Data quality is crucial for integrating NLP with behavioral analytics, as both system and information quality impact the accuracy of insights. Inaccurate or incomplete data reduces the value of analytics for decision-making. These challenges are amplified in big data analytics, where poor data quality can lead to false outcomes, affecting business value and performance. This is especially critical in fields like healthcare and finance, where flawed insights can have serious consequences.

Ensuring Data Integrity

Data quality is a critical concern in both NLP and behavioural analytics. Some common challenges in data quality are:

- **Inconsistent Data Sources:** Data inconsistencies arise when collecting information from multiple sources, often due to differences in format or structure. Without proper standardization, data scientists struggle to integrate and interpret the data accurately, leading to misleading conclusions.
- **Insufficient Training Data:** Insufficient training data is a major issue in machine learning. Small datasets can cause models to over-fit and perform poorly on new data. Ensuring diverse, representative data is essential for

building reliable and effective models.

- **Noisy Data:** Noisy data, containing irrelevant or incorrect information, significantly impacts machine learning effectiveness. It can stem from errors like data entry mistakes or sensor inaccuracies. Studies highlight that noisy data leads to biased predictions, emphasizing the importance of effective data cleaning [28].
- **Bias in Data:** Data bias, including selection and confirmation bias, can distort results and lead to unfair outcomes. Research shows that biased datasets may cause discrimination, but fair data collection and thorough bias evaluation help prevent these issues.
- **Data Sparsity:** Data scarcity occurs when certain categories or features have few data points, making model training and evaluation difficult, especially in collaborative filtering systems. Solutions include data augmentation or synthetic data generation to enhance dataset size and diversity.
- **Language Ambiguity:** Language ambiguity poses challenges for NLP, as words with multiple meanings, like homonyms and polysemy, can lead to misinterpretation. Even slight variations in context can cause analysis errors.

Awareness about the need for clean, anonymized data is increasing to ensure valid and ethical outputs. Studies highlight that data quality is closely tied to privacy and security, with poor-quality data raising the risk of breaches. Despite improvements, challenges like incomplete or inconsistent data persist, especially when applying NLP to behavioral analytics.

Privacy Concerns

Privacy is a key concern when combining NLP with behavioral analytics, as sensitive data is often involved. Research highlights that privacy protection measures are essential for building trust in analytics systems. For example, privacy-preserving measures in wearable technology are necessary to encourage user participation and acceptance of data analytics.

The importance of privacy in AI and big data analytics, particularly in building automation, where privacy challenges are significant, is also highlighted. It is noted that while privacy calculus models can predict user behavior regarding data sharing, effective privacy measures are inconsistently applied. This inconsistency may hinder NLP adoption, especially in sensitive areas like healthcare, where concerns about data misuse make individuals reluctant to share information.

Navigating Privacy Challenges

Privacy is a crucial barrier when integrating NLP with behavioural analytics, especially when dealing with personal or sensitive information:

- **Data Collection Ethics:** Collecting user behavior data often involves sensitive information, raising ethical concerns about consent and usage. Organizations must adhere to legal regulations when using NLP to extract insights from this data.
- **Anonymization Techniques:** Anonymization techniques protect privacy but can reduce data quality, complicating the extraction of accurate behavioral insights.
- **Consent Management:** Consent management is crucial for ethical data use. Users must be informed about data usage and able to opt out. Research highlights the importance of clear communication and user-friendly consent processes for trust and compliance.
- **Data Breach Risks:** Data breaches pose a serious privacy threat, as recent high-profile cases highlight the risks of weak security. Organizations must implement strong data protection strategies to effectively reduce these risks.
- **Ethical Dilemmas:** Ethical issues arise when the benefits of data analysis conflict with potential harm to individuals. This requires ongoing discussions about ethical standards and best practices to manage these complexities.

Although these challenges are widely recognized, there is still a need for strong frameworks that ensure privacy alongside strong data analytics capabilities. Future research must look at innovative privacy-preserving techniques that maintain data utility while ensuring that user confidentiality is maintained.

STRATEGIES FOR OVERCOMING INTEGRATION CHALLENGES

To address these challenges, organizations should adopt a comprehensive approach, focusing on data cleaning, privacy, domain knowledge, and interdisciplinary teamwork, as shown in Fig. (**6**).

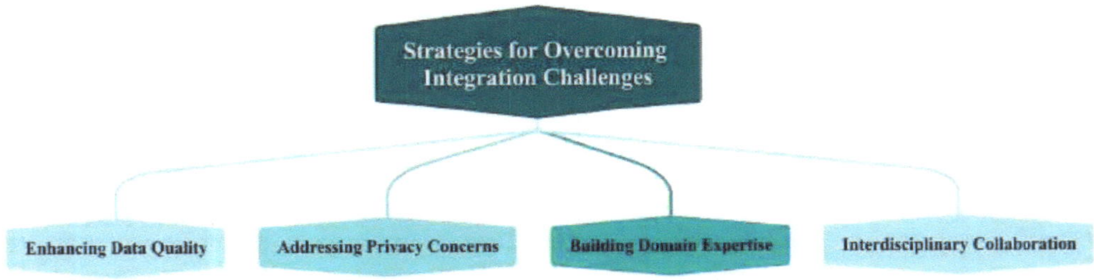

Fig. (6). Approaches to Tackle Integration Challenges.
*Self-Analysed

Enhancing Data Quality

Improved data quality is important for the successful integration of NLP with behavioural analytics. Key strategies include:

- **Implement Robust Data Cleaning Processes:** Thorough data cleaning ensures datasets are uniform and accurate, involving standardization, error correction, and duplicate removal. Organizations that prioritize data quality see significant improvements in analytical results, as reliable insights require clean data.
- **Applicability of Machine Learning Techniques:** Machine learning algorithms, such as anomaly detection and clustering, can identify and remove noise from datasets, enhancing data integrity. Research shows that machine learning pre-processing leads to more accurate predictive models by focusing only on relevant data.

Addressing Privacy Concerns

Privacy is a consideration when integrating NLP and behavioural analytics.

- **Develop Clear Privacy Policies:** Thorough data cleaning ensures datasets are uniform and accurate, involving standardization, error correction, and duplicate removal. Organizations that prioritize data quality see significant improvements in analytical results, as reliable insights require clean data.
- **Employ Anonymization Techniques:** Machine learning algorithms, such as anomaly detection and clustering, can identify and remove noise from datasets, enhancing data integrity. Research shows that machine learning preprocessing leads to more accurate predictive models by focusing only on relevant data.

Building Domain Expertise

Successful NLP integration into behavioral analytics requires domain knowledge to interpret nuances, context, and specialized terminology. This expertise helps tailor algorithms to specific fields, leading to more accurate insights and better decision-making.

- **Invest in Training Programs:** Companies should invest in training programs to educate employees on NLP technologies and their applications in the business. Research shows that continuous learning fosters innovation and helps organizations fully utilize new technologies.
- **Foster Partnerships with Domain Experts:** Collaborating with domain experts provides valuable insights into industry-specific terminology and practices. Research shows that combining technical skills with real-world expertise leads to stronger solutions.

Promoting Interdisciplinary Collaboration

It is important to foster interdisciplinary collaboration as it is vital for overcoming integration challenges.

- **Create Cross-Functional Teams:** Forming teams with diverse backgrounds in data science, behavioral analysis, and domain expertise fosters knowledge transfer and innovation. Research shows that interdisciplinary collaboration enhances creativity and produces holistic solutions by leveraging varied skill sets.
- **Encourage Regular Communication:** Collaborating with domain experts provides valuable insights into industry-specific terminology and practices. Research shows that combining technical skills with real-world expertise leads to stronger solutions.

So, by implementing these strategies, companies will be able to better overcome the hurdles of incorporating NLP into behavioural analytics and, in turn, gain greater insights and more efficient operations.

BENEFITS OF NLP-BASED BEHAVIOURAL ANALYTICS

NLP combined with behavioural analytics can offer a lot of benefits, which can significantly enhance the way an organization performs. That will then allow for better decision-making, a better customer experience, and greater operational efficiency. A more in-depth look at each benefit and the research behind it is as follows:

Improved Decision-Making

NLP enables organizations to analyze unstructured text data like customer reviews, social media posts, and support tickets, offering insights into customer behavior and preferences. Techniques such as sentiment analysis and topic modeling help uncover trends, allowing businesses to make data-driven decisions and adjust strategies based on feedback.

NLP also boosts predictive analytics by adding context to behavioral data. By combining text analysis with numerical data, companies gain clearer insights into future customer behavior, improving strategic planning and resource allocation.

Enhanced Customer Experience

NLP helps organizations understand customer sentiment by analyzing feedback across various channels, enabling personalized interactions and tailored recommendations. For example, online platforms can suggest products based on past behavior and reviews, enhancing the shopping experience.

NLP also supports real-time feedback analysis, allowing businesses to address customer concerns quickly and improve satisfaction. NLP-powered chatbots can interpret questions and provide instant, accurate responses, enhancing customer support.

Increased Operational Efficiency

NLP automates the extraction of insights from large datasets, streamlining processes and boosting efficiency. It eliminates the slow, labor-intensive task of manual text analysis, reducing time and minimizing human error.

This automation frees teams to focus on strategic initiatives. Instead of handling tedious tasks, they can engage in more valuable work, such as creative marketing and campaign development, while NLP tools manage data analysis.

RESULTS AND DISCUSSIONS

By using techniques like sentiment analysis, topic modeling, and NER to extract insights from unstructured text, NLP and behavioral analytics enhance decision-making. Sentiment analysis monitors consumer feelings, and sophisticated models increase precision. A retail firm improves satisfaction by 20% by addressing feedback, while topic modelling reveals issues affecting morale, increasing engagement by 15%. NER automates tasks like classifying service calls, cutting response times by 30%. Case studies show gains in NPS and customer satisfaction through NLP-driven insights.

NLP automation reduces manual work, speeds responses, and enhances service, but it requires high-quality data and privacy safeguards. Customizing models and adopting advanced techniques like contextual embeddings will further refine analysis, driving innovation in a data-driven world.

CONCLUSION

The future of Behavioral Analytics and NLP promises transformative growth, driven by technological advancements and the need for data-driven decisions. These technologies will expand across sectors like healthcare, finance, and education, extracting insights from unstructured data. In healthcare, NLP can analyze patient records to improve care, while in finance, behavioral analytics can predict trends and enhance fraud detection. Advancements in machine learning will boost predictive capabilities, helping businesses anticipate customer behavior, optimize resources, and improve satisfaction. Real-time analysis will become essential as companies react swiftly to market changes. However, ethical concerns about data privacy and security will require transparency and adherence to regulations like GDPR. Collaboration among data scientists, psychologists, and domain experts will lead to more targeted strategies. Organizations must invest in training, adopt advanced tools, and prioritize ethical data use. By embracing these technologies, businesses can integrate Behavioral Analytics and NLP into their strategic frameworks, gaining a competitive edge in a rapidly evolving market.

In order to extract more detailed behavioral insights from unstructured text, future research can focus on developing NLP techniques like transformer-based models and large language models. An all-encompassing understanding of human behavior may be achieved through the integration of multimodal data sources, such as audio, video, and sensor data. Studies conducted across industries and cultures may reveal adoption issues and domain-specific applications. For responsible implementation, it will be essential to address ethical issues like bias mitigation, data privacy, and transparency. Organizations can anticipate customer needs, optimize operations, and preserve a competitive edge in rapidly changing markets by utilizing real-time NLP-driven behavioral analytics to enhance personalization, predictive modeling, and strategic decision-making.

REFERENCES

[1] T. Kumar, T. Ganu, and S. Guha, "Document navigability: A need for print-impaired", Oct. 2022. [Online]. Available: https://arxiv.org/abs/2206.10253v1

[2] M. Myat, "Automated citation matching and relevancy score analysis for scientific papers", *Proc. Conf. Young Res. Electr. Electron. Eng. (ElCon),* 2024pp. 111-117 [http://dx.doi.org/10.1109/ElCon61730.2024.10468496]

[3] O. Olunuga, "Technology in marketing financial services, customer satisfaction and sustainability in banking sector", *Optimum. Econ. Stud.,* vol. 2, no. 112, pp. 177-192, 2023. [http://dx.doi.org/10.15290/oes.2023.02.112.10]

[4] A. Pan, Q. Sun, O.I. Okereke, K.M. Rexrode, and F.B. Hu, "Depression and risk of stroke morbidity and mortality: a meta-analysis and systematic review", *JAMA,* vol. 306, no. 11, pp. 1241-1249, 2011. [http://dx.doi.org/10.1001/jama.2011.1282] [PMID: 21934057]

[5] R. Anitha P. S. Adithyan V. A. Akshaya A. Bhuvanesh, "Enhancing customer analytics: A comprehensive framework for effective churn prediction", *International Journal of Advanced Research in Science, Communication and Technology,* no. Oct, pp. 406-410, 2024. [http://dx.doi.org/10.48175/IJARSCT-15770]

[6] A. Sathyanarayana, S. Joty, L. Fernandez-Luque, F. Ofli, J. Srivastava, A. Elmagarmid, T. Arora, and S. Taheri, "Correction of: Sleep quality prediction from wearable data using deep learning", *JMIR Mhealth Uhealth,* vol. 4, no. 4, p. e130, 2016. [http://dx.doi.org/10.2196/mhealth.6953] [PMID: 27885989]

[7] A. A. Varghese, M. Binoy, R. Jacob, A. Joseph, and A. Joseph, "Unleashing the power of data analytics: A pathway to insightful decision-making", *International journal of engineering technology and management sciences,* vol. 7, no. 4, pp. 433-437, 2023. [http://dx.doi.org/10.46647/ijetms.2023.v07i04.057]

[8] B. Goenandar, and M. Ariyanti, "Analysis of demography, psychograph and behavioral aspects of telecom customers using predictive analytics to increase voice package sales", *Journal of Consumer Sciences,* vol. 6, no. 1, pp. 1-19, 2021. [http://dx.doi.org/10.29244/jcs.6.1.1-19]

[9] B.J. McCloskey, P.M. LaCasse, and B.A. Cox, "Natural language processing analysis of online reviews for small business: extracting insight from small corpora", *Ann. Oper. Res.,* vol. 341, no. 1, pp. 295-312, 2024. [http://dx.doi.org/10.1007/s10479-023-05816-2]

[10] B. Liu, "Sentiment analysis and opinion mining", *Synthesis Lectures on Human Language Technologies,* vol. 5, no. 1, pp. 1-167, 2012. [http://dx.doi.org/10.2200/S00416ED1V01Y201204HLT016]

[11] C.C. Aggarwal, and C.X. Zhai, "Mining text data", *Mining Text Data,* vol. 9781461432234, pp. 1-522, 2013. [http://dx.doi.org/10.1007/978-1-4614-3223-4/COVER]

[12] C.H. Wang, and C.Y. Lien, "Combining design science with data analytics to forecast user intention to adopt customer relationship management systems", *Journal of Industrial and Production Engineering,* vol. 36, no. 4, pp. 193-204, 2019. [http://dx.doi.org/10.1080/21681015.2019.1645051]

[13] C. Srivastava, S. Kashmiri, and V. Mahajan, "Customer orientation and financial performance: Women in top management teams matter!", *J. Mark.,* vol. 87, no. 2, pp. 190-209, 2023.

[http://dx.doi.org/10.1177/00222429221120419]

[14] A. Al Mudaifer, "Intelligent course recommender for professional development", *Day 2 Tue,* vol. Mar. 14, 2023.
[http://dx.doi.org/10.2118/214116-MS]

[15] D. Gupta, B. Morris, T. Catapano, and G. Sautter, "A new approach towards bibliographic reference identification, parsing and inline citation matching", *Commun. Comput. Inf. Sci.,* vol. 40, pp. 93-102, 2009.
[http://dx.doi.org/10.1007/978-3-642-03547-0_10]

[16] E. Cambria, and B. White, "Jumping NLP curves: A review of natural language processing research", *IEEE Comput. Intell. Mag.,* vol. 9, no. 2, pp. 48-57, 2014.
[http://dx.doi.org/10.1109/MCI.2014.2307227]

[17] M.G. Younis, "Sentiment analysis and text mining for social media microblogs using open source tools: An empirical study", *Int. J. Comput. Appl.,* vol. 112, no. 5, pp. 44-48, 2015.
[http://dx.doi.org/10.5120/19665-1366]

[18] E. Musonda, and M.S. Bakr, "The singlet: Direct synthesis of pseudo-elliptic inline filters with frequency variant couplings", *IEEE Trans. Microw. Theory Tech.,* vol. 71, no. 11, pp. 4969-4981, 2023.
[http://dx.doi.org/10.1109/TMTT.2023.3269516]

[19] E.S. Jaya, L. Sekarasih, M.A. Shadiqi, and C.D.S. Riantoputra, "Editorial note: Makara human behavior studies in Asia's responds to political challenges in scientific publication", *Makara Human Behavior Studies in Asia,* vol. 26, no. 2, pp. 74-75, 2022.
[http://dx.doi.org/10.7454/hubs.asia.1110922]

[20] E. Yilmaz, and O. Can, "Unveiling shadows: Harnessing artificial intelligence for insider threat detection", *Engineering, Technology & Applied Science Research,* vol. 14, no. 2, pp. 13341-13346, 2024.
[http://dx.doi.org/10.48084/etasr.6911]

[21] F. Busquet, F. Efthymiou, and C. Hildebrand, "Voice analytics in the wild: Validity and predictive accuracy of common audio-recording devices", *Behav. Res. Methods,* vol. 56, no. 3, pp. 2114-2134, 2023.
[http://dx.doi.org/10.3758/s13428-023-02139-9] [PMID: 37253958]

[22] G. Mishra, B.K. Panda, W.A. Ramirez, H. Jung, C.B. Singh, S.H. Lee, and I. Lee, "Research advancements in optical imaging and spectroscopic techniques for nondestructive detection of mold infection and mycotoxins in cereal grains and nuts", *Compr. Rev. Food Sci. Food Saf.,* vol. 20, no. 5, pp. 4612-4651, 2021.
[http://dx.doi.org/10.1111/1541-4337.12801] [PMID: 34338431]

[23] H. Kjeldsen, P.F. Østergaard, H. Strauss, J. Nielsen, B. Tallawi, E. Georgin, P. Sabouroux, J.G. Nielsen, and J.O. Hougaard, "Calibration techniques for water content measurements in solid biofuels", *Energies,* vol. 17, no. 3, p. 635, 2024.
[http://dx.doi.org/10.3390/en17030635]

[24] H. Rizky, "The influence of B2B (business to business) and B2C (business to customer) marketing strategies on how to purchase lion group aircraft tickets in the public environment", *Journal of Social Research,* vol. 2, no. 8, pp. 2688-2697, 2023.
[http://dx.doi.org/10.55324/josr.v2i8.1324]

[25] J. Petch, J. Kempainnen, C. Pettengell, S. Aviv, B. Butler, G. Pond, A. Saha, J. Bogach, A. Allard-Coutu, P. Sztur, J. Ranisau, and M. Levine, "Developing a data and analytics platform to enable a breast cancer learning health system at a regional cancer center", *JCO Clin. Cancer Inform.,* vol. 7, no. 7, p. e2200182, 2023.
[http://dx.doi.org/10.1200/CCI.22.00182] [PMID: 37001040]

[26] S. Samuel, and C.P. Maheswaran, "Purchases insights using alteryx as self-service analytics", *Proc.*

8th Int. Conf. Commun. Electron. Syst. (ICCES), 2023pp. 1644-1648 [http://dx.doi.org/10.1109/ICCES57224.2023.10192692]

[27] J. Samuel, M. Brennan-Tonetta, Y. Samuel, P. Subedi, and J. Smith, "Strategies for democratization of supercomputing: Availability, accessibility and usability of high performance computing for education and practice of big data analytics", *Journal of Big Data and Artificial Intelligence,* vol. 1, no. 1, 2022. [http://dx.doi.org/10.54116/jbdtp.v1i1.16]

[28] K. Lo, L.L. Wang, M. Neumann, R. Kinney, and D.S. Weld, "S2ORC: The semantic scholar open research corpus", *Proc. Annu. Meet. Assoc. Comput. Linguist,* pp. 4969-4983, 2019. [http://dx.doi.org/10.18653/v1/2020.acl-main.447]

CHAPTER 8

The Dawn of A New Era: Digital Currency and its Impact on Banking

Sayangshree Panda[1], **Nandinee Anand**[1], **Ritik Kumar Sahoo**[1] and **Swapnamoyee Palit**[2,*]

[1] *School of Computer Engineering, KIIT Deemed to be University, Bhubaneswar, Odisha, India*

[2] *School of Economics & Commerce, Kalinga Institute of Industrial Technology DU, Bhubaneswar, Odisha, India*

Abstract: In recent times, banks and other sectors have implemented substantial innovations in modern electronic payment systems. The Reserve Bank's initiative to foster a less-cash society has led to widespread adoption of digital payment methods in the country. Amidst the surge in electronic payment systems, digital banking stands out as a significant milestone in banking history. In today's landscape, banks are exploring innovative ways to differentiate their services. Considering this evolution in banking practices, the introduction of digital currency by banks as a mainstream alternative to physical currency could have far-reaching implications. This paper delves into the potential consequences of integrating digital currency as a standard form of currency alongside physical cash in banking and various transactions. It explores the implications of incorporating digital currency into everyday e-payment practices within the framework of digital banking. Furthermore, it investigates the effects of digital currency on the broader economy, questioning whether its adoption would be advantageous or detrimental to society. Additionally, the study examines how this technological shift in monetary transactions would impact the general public. The survey shows high familiarity with e-payment options, with 91.1% using them, 7.3% avoiding them, and 1.6% relying on others. Awareness ratings were 26.6% excellent, 62.1% good, and 8.9% fair. While 71.8% were aware of digital currency, only 39.5% understood it fully, 36.3% partially, and 24.2% not at all. In terms of investment, 23.4% had invested, 46% had not, 26.6% planned future investment, and 4% were unaware. Advantages were acknowledged by 64.5%, while 35.5% disagreed. Acceptance stood at 38.7% outright, 16.9% in disagreement, and 44.4% conditional on centralized assurance. Regarding economic impact, 44.5% were positive, 15.3% were negative, and 41.2% were uncertain.

Keywords: Bank, Bitcoin, Digital currency, E-payment systems.

* **Corresponding author Swapnamoyee Palit:** School of Economics & Commerce, Kalinga Institute of Industrial Technology DU, Bhubaneswar, Odisha, India; E-mail: swapnamoyee.palit@gmail.com

Shradhanjali Panda, Leena Priyadarshini Singh, V. Ramasamy & S. Balamurugan (Eds.)

INTRODUCTION

Every country's banking sector serves as its economy's backbone, regardless of its development status. It strategizes and implements various monetary policies that shape the economic landscape. Any alterations or advancements in this domain, particularly through the adoption of technological innovations, can profoundly impact economic growth.

The Reserve Bank's initiative to foster a less-cash society has led to widespread adoption of digital payment methods in the country. Amidst the surge in electronic payment systems, digital banking stands out as a significant milestone in banking history. Despite the numerous benefits it offers to customers, online banking also presents several key challenges for marketers in the sector, prompting banks to prioritize the security of e-transactions. Consequently, efforts have been directed towards building a robust technological infrastructure to ensure the smooth functioning of essential payment and settlement systems nationwide.

In today's landscape, banks are exploring innovative ways to differentiate their services. Considering this evolution in banking practices, the introduction of digital currency by banks as a mainstream alternative to physical currency could have far-reaching implications [1].

As digitalization progresses, there has been a rise in privately issued digital currencies, lacking physical counterparts. It is crucial to differentiate between these private digital currencies and the digitalization of fiat money. Currently, there is no authorized entity with complete control over existing digital currencies in India, although the concept of digital currency remains a prominent topic in the economy. Therefore, by analyzing this trend and leveraging its positive impact on the economy, it may be possible to introduce digital currency in a centralized manner with regulatory oversight from the Reserve Bank of India.

ABOUT DIGITAL CURRENCY

Digital currency, also known as cybercash, electronic currency, or electronic money, refers to currency that exists exclusively in electronic or digital form. Transactions involving digital currency are conducted through computers or electronic wallets connected to the internet or specific networks. Unlike traditional currencies, digital currencies often do not require intermediaries, making them a cost-effective means of trading currencies. They offer seamless value transfer and reduce transaction costs.

At the heart of digital currencies lies their blockchain network, which serves as a public ledger recording all transactions. Built on blockchain technology, digital currencies rely on this protocol for their creation and use as a viable form of money. The blockchain network maintains a record of all transactions, with new transactions grouped into blocks. These blocks undergo validation by multiple users across the network before being added to the chain. Miners play a crucial role in confirming transactions within new blocks by competing to generate unique cryptographic sequences called "hashes." Once a miner successfully completes a hash, the new block is confirmed, and the hash is stored alongside it. The blockchain protocol regulates the currency supply and controls inflation by adjusting mining difficulty and governing the issuance of new coins, ensuring that new blocks are added at a predictable rate as network hash power increases [2].

Digital currencies are stored in digital wallets when mined or transferred among users, where they remain until their new owner decides to use them. Digital currencies can be stored in these wallets securely for an indefinite period.

Advantages of Digital Currency

- *Faster Transactions:* Digital currencies often settle transactions much faster than traditional methods like ACH or wire transfers, which can take days. This means faster access to your funds and quicker completion of purchases.
- *Lower Fees:* Transactions involving digital currencies often have lower fees compared to traditional financial institutions, especially for international transfers. This eliminates the need for intermediary fees and saves you money.
- *Accessibility:* Anyone with an internet connection and a digital wallet can access and use digital currencies. Thus, financial inclusion is promoted by opening up these financial services to unbanked and underbanked individuals.
- *Security:* Digital currencies like Bitcoin utilize blockchain technology, offering a high level of security and transparency. Transactions are encrypted and publicly recorded, making them resistant to fraud and counterfeiting.
- *24/7 Availability:* Digital currency markets operate 24/7, unlike traditional banks. This allows for instant transactions and greater flexibility in managing your finances.

Disadvantages of Digital Currency

However, in spite of its tremendous benefits, there are several issues that raise serious concerns and need to be adequately addressed to ensure the safety and security of the stakeholders' investments. These are shown in Fig. (**1**). Among all the disadvantages, the prime concerns are the high risk involved in digital currency transactions, the security of investors' money, and the sheer unpredictability of the system's smooth functioning, given exposure to a variety of rules and regulations with no uniformity.

Fig. (1). The disadvantages of digital currency.
Source: Authors' own

DIGITAL CURRENCY IN INDIA

The rise of digital currencies presents a transformative shift in the financial landscape, potentially impacting both the financial system and banking practices. Despite India's reliance on physical currency, digital transactions are increasingly prevalent through e-payment methods and digital banking. However, the decentralized nature of current digital currencies raises security concerns, prompting consideration of centralization under the control of central banks or government bodies.

Central Bank Digital Currencies (CBDCs) are emerging as a solution, representing digital forms of legal tender issued by central banks. These sovereign currencies would be equivalent to fiat cash but in electronic form, potentially exchangeable for physical currency. Central banks globally are actively exploring CBDCs, with many conducting research, experimenting with technology, and even launching trial projects.

The Bank for International Settlements (BIS) reported that 86% of central banks were researching CBDCs in 2021, with over 90 countries, representing a significant portion of the world's GDP, actively developing their own centralized digital currencies. In India, the central bank spearheaded the development of a digital currency expected to launch in early 2023. This digital currency will resemble existing electronic wallets, but with the distinction of being a sovereign facility [2, 3].

LITERATURE REVIEW

Numerous articles have explored digital currencies, discussing their functionalities, advantages, and associated risks and security issues on a global scale. Recent trends indicate a higher percentage of users opting for digital banking over traditional banking methods. Studies highlight a significant transformation in banking culture following the introduction of digital banking concepts. For instance, data from the Ministry of Electronics and IT revealed a 33% year-on-year increase in digital transactions in India during the 2021-22 financial year, totaling over 35 billion transactions worth Rs. 7,422 crores.

Digital currency has emerged as a prominent topic in the current financial market, albeit accompanied by concerns about risks and security [4]. Centralized control over digital currency could potentially have a significant impact on the economy. In line with this, the Indian government announced plans to launch a central bank-backed 'digital rupee,' as stated by Finance Minister Nirmala Sitharaman in the 2022–23 budget speech. The Reserve Bank of India (RBI) publicly proposed adopting digital currency in stages, with Deputy Governor T. Rabi Sankar noting progress on the wholesale component of the Central Bank Digital Currency (CBDC) in December. The digital rupee, based on blockchain technology, aims to reduce currency maintenance costs and decrease the production of physical notes. Its digital nature extends its lifespan, as digital forms cannot be lost or destroyed [5, 6].

PROBLEM STATEMENT

The adoption of digital currency in the banking industry has the potential to accelerate both domestic and cross-border transactions while reducing transaction costs. Moreover, it could serve to enhance financial inclusion by providing rural households with broader access to the financial system. However, the consequences of the banking sector introducing digital currency, its impact on the economy, and its acceptance by the general public need to be examined.

- Could the normalization of digital currency have adverse effects on the economy?
- Does digital currency serve as a favorable e-payment option offered by banks?
- Is digital currency genuinely beneficial for the general public within the country?
- What risks are associated with the use of digital currency?
- Can the government adequately meet the public's needs through the issuance of a Central Bank Digital Currency (CBDC)?

OBJECTIVE OF THE STUDY

- To investigate public awareness regarding digital currency.
- To understand public opinions regarding the potential normalization of digital currency by centralized authorities, similar to physical currency.
- To analyze the impact on economic conditions.
- To analyze the role of banking institutions in facilitating the normalization of digital currency.
- To examine the government's stance and actions concerning the implementation of a Central Bank Digital Currency.

RESEARCH METHODOLOGY

The research methodology employs a descriptive research design to delve deeply into the understanding of public awareness regarding practices involving digital currency and e-payment in banking, based on both secondary and primary data. Collection of primary data is through applied research methods, and secondary data are gathered through exploratory means. This approach lends realism and practicality to the study, capturing the current perspectives of respondents towards digital currency.

- **Sampling Technique:** It involves simple random sampling, in which samples are randomly drawn from a suitable population. The population under study predominantly consists of different age groups within the younger generation.
- **Sources of Data:** They include both primary and secondary sources. Primary data is collected electronically through Google Forms, utilizing a set of questionnaires to gather responses directly from the target population. Secondary data comprises various articles, books, and online resources related to the topic.

DATA ANALYSIS

Due to time constraints, field research was not feasible, so relevant data was collected digitally. A total of 124 accurate respondents participated, providing insights into their opinions.

Respondent Profile

The target population primarily comprises individuals with a basic understanding of digital currency, categorized by age, location, and educational and employment backgrounds. Among the respondents, 71.8% fall within the 18-25 age bracket, 24.2% are aged 26-35, and the remaining 4.0% are aged 36 or older (Fig. **2**). In terms of education, 52.4% hold a graduate degree, 35.5% have postgraduate qualifications, 8.1% have completed 10+2 or diplomas, and 3.2% possess advanced degrees such as PhDs or CAs (Fig. **3**).

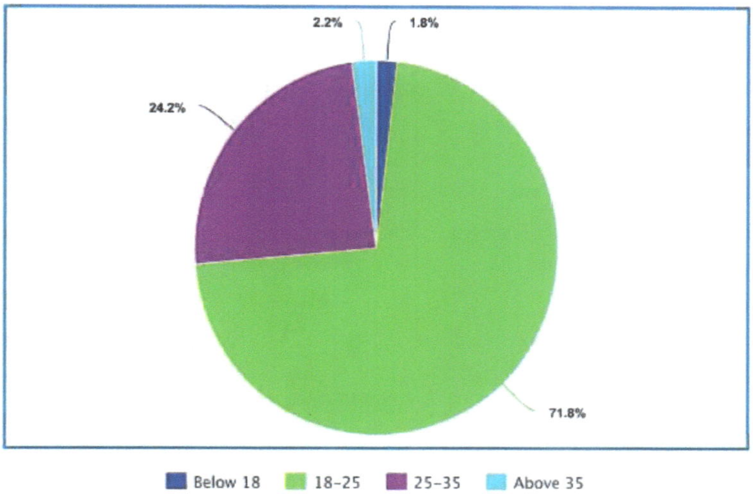

Fig. (2). Age Profile of the Respondents.
[Source: Authors' own from the data collected]

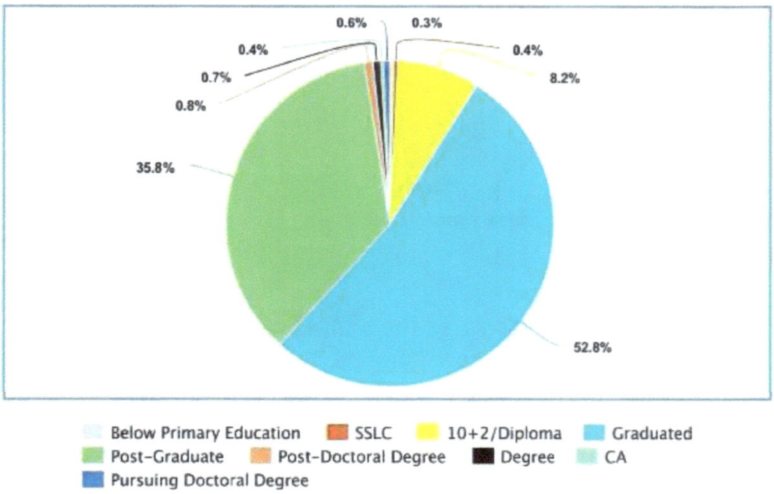

Fig. (3). Educational Profile of the Respondents.
[Source: Authors' own from the data collected]

FINDINGS OF THE STUDY

The survey reveals that 91.1% of respondents use e-payments, 71.8% are aware of digital currency, but only 39.5% have a full understanding of it. Investment remains limited at 23.4%, though 64.5% recognize its advantages and 44.5% anticipate a positive economic impact. Respondents emphasize the need for centralized trust from institutions, gradual integration alongside cash, improved public awareness, and inclusive access. While most are comfortable with digital banking, concerns about security, legitimacy, and usability persist. The findings largely reflect younger generations' perspectives, indicating greater openness to technological change and innovation compared to other demographic groups. According to the study, centralized trust is essential. The majority of respondents expressed concerns about security and legitimacy and sought strong support from organizations such as governments or banks before fully adopting digital currencies. There are still large knowledge gaps, which emphasize the need for easily understandable instruction on digital currencies and their applications. In order to prevent possible economic and social upheavals, people prefer the gradual integration of digital currencies alongside cash, even though they are generally comfortable with digital banking. There are still accessibility issues because some groups may have trouble using the site. The results may be skewed toward greater openness to technological change and innovation because they largely represent the viewpoints of younger generations.

SUGGESTIONS

- *Prioritize public education:* Centralized authorities, like banks and government agencies, should prioritize nationwide awareness campaigns to educate the public about digital currencies. This will dispel misconceptions, build trust, and encourage adoption.
- *Emphasize security:* Implementing robust security measures and highlighting them effectively will be crucial for gaining public confidence and widespread acceptance of digital currencies.
- *Phased implementation:* Advocating for a gradual, step-by-step rollout of digital currency, with ongoing evaluation of its success and impact, will mitigate risks and ensure a smoother transition.
- *Offer choice and flexibility:* Introducing digital currency as an optional addition to existing physical cash allows individuals to choose based on their comfort and understanding, promoting broader adoption without forcing a complete shift.
- *Data-driven approach:* Conducting thorough economic studies and collaborating with economists will be essential for designing and implementing a digital currency system that aligns with India's specific economic context and minimizes potential disruptions.

CONCLUSION

The integration of digital currency within the banking sector holds promise for enhancing the efficiency of both domestic and international transactions, offering potential reductions in transaction expenses, and extending financial services to previously underserved rural communities [7, 8]. However, this technological advancement also brings with it the risk of destabilizing financial markets and increasing the potential for contagion across markets. Thus, it is imperative to conduct comprehensive studies to understand the multifaceted impacts of digital currency adoption before proceeding further with its implementation. Such studies should encompass analyses of its effects on market dynamics, regulatory frameworks, and systemic risks, allowing policymakers and industry stakeholders to develop appropriate strategies and safeguards to navigate the complexities associated with this innovation responsibly.

By approaching the integration of digital currency with careful consideration and thorough examination, stakeholders can maximize its benefits while minimizing potential adverse consequences for the stability and integrity of the financial system. The long-term effects of integrating digital currency with current banking systems on the economy, society, and regulations can be investigated in future studies. In order to guarantee accessibility, inclusivity, and stability in the shift to a hybrid cash–digital currency economy, studies may look at adoption barriers, security concerns, demographic differences, and trust-building techniques in addition to assessing technological advancements.

REFERENCES

[1] R. Ali, J. Barrdear, R. Clews, and J. Southgate, "Innovations in payment technologies and the emergence of digital currencies", *Bank of England Quarterly Bulletin*. vol. 2014 Q3, Sep. 2014. [Online]. Available: https://ssrn.com/abstract=2499397

[2] M.B. East Shaik, "M. K., T. Jaggaiah, and M. Khizerulla, "Literacy and investment behaviour of IT professionals in India,"", *Asian J. Multidiscip. Res.*, vol. 1, no. 5, pp. 777-788, 2022. [http://dx.doi.org/10.55927/eajmr.v1i5.514]

[3] E.S. Prasad, *The Future of Money: How the Digital Revolution Is Transforming Currencies and Finance*. 2021. [Online]. Available: https://www.futureofmoneybook.com/

[4] J.S. Gans, and H. Halaburda, "Some economics of private digital currency", *NBER Chapters*. p. 1956. [Online]. Available: http://www.nber.org/chapters/c1299

[5] P. Revathi, "Digital banking challenges and opportunities in India", *EPRA Int. J. Econ. Bus. Rev*. vol. 7, no. 12, 2019. [Online]. Available: https://www.researchgate.net/publication/338139871

[6] S. Gilbert, and H. Loi, "Digital currency risk", *Int. J. Econ. Finance,* vol. 10, no. 2, p. 108, 2018. [http://dx.doi.org/10.5539/ijef.v10n2p108]

[7] M.B. Shaik, M. Kethan, I. Rani, U. Mahesh, C.S. Harsha, M.K. Navya, and D. Sravani, "Which determinants matter for capital structure? An empirical study on NBFCs in India", *Int. J. Entrepreneurship,* vol. 26, pp. 1-9, 2022. [Online]. [Available: https://www.abacademies.org/

articles/which-determinants-matter-for-capital-structure-an-empirical-study-on-nbfcs-in-india.pdf].

[8] T. Keister, and D. Sanches, "Should central banks issue digital currency?", *Federal Reserve Bank of Philadelphia*. Working Paper No. 21-37, 2021.
[http://dx.doi.org/10.21799/frbp.wp]

CHAPTER 9

Exploring the Role of AI in Enhancing Academic Performance: A Study on Management Students of Odisha

Swati Mishra[1,*]

[1] *Department of MBA, Institute of Management and Information Technology, Cuttack-753008, Odisha, India*

Abstract: In today's world, Artificial Intelligence has become extremely important, as it has the power to revolutionize many industries, including the educational sector. Student feedback on educational services is crucial since they are the ones who will ultimately benefit from it. Improved student accomplishment, attitudes towards learning, study motivation, and learning methodologies are some of the aspects that are focused on in this investigation of the link between AI and students' academic performance. It also aims to evaluate and investigate how Artificial Intelligence enhances students' ideas and creative thinking. Snowball sampling was used to select 104 respondents, based on preset parameters. The results imply that almost all identified variables are positively related, and that AI successfully meets the unique learning needs of students, resulting in more thorough and improved educational experiences. AI identifies students with academic difficulties and provides them with the support and treatment they need to improve. Furthermore, AI offers accurate assessments and enhancements for students' attitudes towards learning, leading to a more comprehensive comprehension of the learning process. Additionally, it boosts students' enthusiasm for learning and their study habits. AI's adaptive learning techniques provide students with insightful feedback and guidance for their learning. Moreover, the adaptive learning features of AI provide valuable feedback and guide students on their learning journeys.

Keywords: Artificial intelligence, Academic process, Educational sector.

INTRODUCTION

With major improvements in "computing power, increasingly sophisticated algorithms, and the ability to process enormous volumes of data, artificial intelligence represents a new level of scientific and technological development

* **Corresponding author Swati Mishra:** Department of MBA, Institute of Management and Information Technology, Cuttack-753008, Odisha, India; E-mail: swatimishra0674@gmail.com

Shradhanjali Panda, Leena Priyadarshini Singh, V. Ramasamy & S. Balamurugan (Eds.)

that will fundamentally change how the world functions as we know it" [1]. In the current situation, the application of Artificial Intelligence in the educational sector is becoming more receptive and flexible in creating a learning climate that improves students' learning and fulfills their requirements. Artificial Intelligence deals with robotic technologies that combine cognitive functions with human intelligence. Education is one of the numerous sectors that artificial intelligence has impacted. The higher education department is also affected by it, since "universities are the main producers of highly trained labour and knowledge and are vital in the development of societies and economies based on knowledge" [2]. Students should be placed at the core of a value creation process as active participants and co-creators of services, according to the service-dominant logic and co-creation; they can even be viewed as customers.

In order to make the use of AI in education simpler and more student-centered, it is important to understand students' characteristics. This is because AI technology has the ability to impact the student experience. Artificial intelligence technologies may one day make it easier to tailor lessons and course materials to each student. Students' diverse backgrounds necessitate a deeper comprehension of their learning requirements, which means that instructional materials must be tailored to meet those needs [3]. With an emphasis on the educational process, some researchers have examined artificial intelligence from the viewpoint of the students. Several studies looked at how students felt about artificial intelligence in the classroom. According to the results of these research studies, most people think AI will be a good thing for schools. Furthermore, the perceived advantages and disadvantages of AI in the classroom were also investigated. Regarding the learning experience, students mainly appreciated the presence of the virtual assistant. When considering learning itself, the key benefit recognized was universal access, whereas, in terms of the assessment process, many students pointed out continuous feedback as the principal advantage. One of the main limitations of AI is the decrease in interaction between teachers and students.

LITERATURE REVIEW

Artificial Intelligence in Education

The term "Artificial Intelligence" is often thought of in conjunction with computing devices. An analysis of different articles, particularly those focusing on education, indicates that while computers have played a crucial role in AI development, it is more than just hardware, software, or technology. "The advent of embedded computers, sensors, and other emerging technologies has facilitated the incorporation of artificial intelligence into machines and various entities, including structures and robots, which together provide a dual definition and characterization of AI" [4]. "Artificial Intelligence (AI) is a branch of computer science dedicated to tackling various cognitive challenges generally associated with human intelligence, such as learning, problem-solving, and pattern recognition, while also enabling adaptation". "As a theoretical framework, AI guides the creation and use of computer systems that exhibit human-like abilities, particularly intelligence and the capability to perform tasks that require human intelligence, including visual perception, speech recognition, decision-making, and language translation" [4].

Artificial Intelligence in Higher Education

From various research studies, it is clearly evident that AI tools and techniques improve writing quality and students' academic performance. Several studies have brought attention to the significance of AI writing tools for universities. The impacts of Grammarly, an AI-based grammar and style checking tool, on the writing abilities of undergraduate students were studied by several studies [5, 6]. The results showed that compared to the control group, students whose assignments included Grammarly had more grammatical correctness and higher-quality writing. Researchers have looked at how well AI language models, such as ChatGPT, can guide students as they write [7, 8]. Studies have found that graduate students used ChatGPT to help them draft their research proposals. The results showed that AI-generated content was useful for generating initial ideas and organizing suggestions; however, students needed to refine and elaborate on the material produced. Researchers [9, 10]surveyed students to find out what they thought about AI tools and how they understood how to utilize AI-generated material correctly. The results underscored the necessity for adequate teaching and instruction on the utilization of AI tools to prevent plagiarism and uphold academic integrity.

Effect of AI on Students' Thought Process

Education is only one of several areas where Artificial Intelligence (AI) is having an enormous effect. As AI becomes increasingly integrated into the academic landscape, it is profoundly influencing how students think, learn, and approach problem-solving. One of the most significant ways AI affects students is by enhancing access to information. With AI-powered tools like search engines, virtual tutors, and personalized learning platforms, students can quickly retrieve vast amounts of data and receive immediate feedback. This speeds up the learning process, but it can also make students more reliant on AI for answers, potentially reducing their willingness to engage in deep, critical thinking. When information is readily available, the temptation to seek quick solutions might discourage the kind of curiosity and problem-solving skills that come from struggling with complex issues [11].

RESEARCH METHODOLOGY

This study was structured as a quantitative research endeavour. The researcher used a snowball sampling method to distribute an online survey using Google Forms. To better understand the students' thoughts and feelings, the researcher interviewed them. Using this method, we asked students how they felt about the potential use of AI in developing original ideas and research papers. The goal of this study is to better understand why students choose to utilize or not use AI in their academic work by collecting their thoughts on the matter. The research also emphasizes the most popular AI apps used by students.

A subset of the Management students at Odisha's Biju Pattnaik University of Technology was given the link to the Google Forms survey. The researcher sought assistance from her networks, especially from those now employed in educational institutions. The poll link was shared with potential participants *via* several platforms, including WhatsApp groups and Facebook pages. The Statistical Package for the Social Sciences, version 26, was used for data analysis. The researcher started by cleaning and reviewing the data in Microsoft Excel after importing it from Google Forms to make sure it was accurate. Next, SPSS was used to import the data and code it for analysis. A Cronbach's alpha score of 0.94 was obtained from an internal reliability analysis, indicating that all 104 survey questions had a high level of internal consistency. Quantitative data addressing the study objectives and providing insights into students' perspectives on AI applications in academic success were obtained *via* the use of descriptive statistics.

RESULTS AND DISCUSSION

From the data in Table **1**, we can deduce that there are 57 male students (54.80%) and 47 female students (45.2%) out of a total of 104 students.

Table 1. Gender.

-		**Frequency**	**Percent**	**Valid Percent**	**Cumulative Percent**
Valid	Male	57	54.8	54.8	54.8
	Female	47	45.2	45.2	100.0
	Total	**104**	**100.0**	**100.0**	-

*Self-Computed

It is apparent from the data in Table **2** that, among a sample of 104 students, the largest proportion of students (33) spend 3–4 hours (equivalent to 33%) and the smallest proportion (8) spend less than an hour (equivalent to 7.7%).

Table 2. Hours spent on the study.

-		Frequency	Percent	Valid Percent	Cumulative Percent
Valid	Less than 1 hrs	8	7.7	7.7	7.7
	1-2 hrs	32	30.8	30.8	38.5
	2-3 hrs	31	29.8	29.8	68.3
	3-4 hrs	33	31.7	31.7	100.0
	Total	**104**	**100.0**	**100.0**	-

*Self-Computed

Table **3** shows that out of 104 students surveyed, the majority believe that AI will have the greatest impact in the scientific community (40 students, or 38.5% of the total) and the least in the fields of PE and social studies (two students, or 1.9% of the total).

Table 3. Subjects that can benefit the most from Artificial Intelligence.

-		Frequency	Percent	Valid Percent	Cumulative Percent
Valid	Math	25	24.0	24.0	24.0
	Science	40	38.5	38.5	62.5
	Language	26	25.0	25.0	87.5
	Art	9	8.7	8.7	96.2
	Social Science	2	1.9	1.9	98.1
	Phy Education	2	1.9	1.9	100.0
	Total	**100**	**100.0**	**100.0**	-

*Self-Computed

Table **4** shows that out of 104 students surveyed, the majority believe that AI can boost students' grades in the following areas: problem-solving, critical thinking, creativity, collaboration, personalized learning, and data analysis (24 students, or 23.1% of the total). In contrast, the lowest response is recorded for problem-solving, critical thinking, and personalized learning alone, selected by only 1 student (1%).

Table 4. Frequency and percentage measures of academic performance of students.

	-	Frequency	Percent	Valid Percent	Cumulative Percent
Valid	collaboration	1	1.0	1.0	1.0
	Creativity	8	7.7	7.7	8.7
	Creativity, Collaboration, Data analysis	1	1.0	1.0	9.6
	Creativity, Data analysis	1	1.0	1.0	10.6
	Creativity, Personalized learning	2	1.9	1.9	12.5
	Critical thinking	1	1.0	1.0	13.5
	Critical thinking, Creativity	2	1.9	1.9	15.4
	Critical thinking, Creativity, Collaboration	2	1.9	1.9	17.3
	Critical thinking, Creativity, Data analysis	1	1.0	1.0	18.3
	Critical thinking, Creativity, Personalized learning	3	2.9	2.9	21.2
	Critical thinking, Creativity, Personalized learning, Data analysis	2	1.9	1.9	23.1
	Critical thinking, Personalized learning, Data analysis	1	1.0	1.0	24.0
	Data analysis	2	1.9	1.9	26.0
	Personalized learning	7	6.7	6.7	32.7
	Problem-solving	6	5.8	5.8	38.5
	Problem-solving, Collaboration, Data analysis	1	1.0	1.0	39.4
	Problem-solving, Creativity	2	1.9	1.9	41.3
	Problem-solving, Creativity, Data analysis	3	2.9	2.9	44.2
	Problem-solving, Creativity, Personalized learning	1	1.0	1.0	45.2

(Table 4) cont.....

Valid	Problem-solving, Creativity, Personalized learning, Data analysis	3	2.9	2.9	48.1
	Problem-solving, Critical thinking, Collaboration, Personalized learning, Data analysis	1	1.0	1.0	49.0
	Problem-solving, Critical thinking, Creativity	1	1.0	1.0	50.0
	Problem-solving, Critical thinking, Creativity, Collaboration, Personalized learning, Data analysis	24	23.1	23.1	73.1
	Problem-solving, Critical thinking, Creativity, Data analysis	6	5.8	5.8	78.8
	Problem-solving, Critical thinking, Creativity, Personalized learning	1	1.0	1.0	79.8
	Problem-solving, Critical thinking, Creativity, Personalized learning, Data analysis	6	5.8	5.8	85.6
	Problem-solving, Critical thinking, Data analysis	1	1.0	1.0	86.5
	Problem-solving, Critical thinking, Personalized learning	1	1.0	1.0	87.5
	Problem-solving, Critical thinking, Personalized learning, Data analysis	2	1.9	1.9	89.4
	Problem-solving, Data analysis	2	1.9	1.9	91.3
	Problem-solving, Personalized learning	2	1.9	1.9	93.3
	Problem-solving, Personalized learning, Data analysis	7	6.7	6.7	100.0
	Total	**104**	**100.0**	**100.0**	-

*Self-Computed

Table 5. Innovative thinking.

-		Frequency	Percent	Valid Percent	Cumulative Percent
Valid	Yes	72	69.2	69.2	69.2
	No	13	12.5	12.5	81.7
	Note Sure	19	18.3	18.3	100.0
	Total	**104**	**100.0**	**100.0**	-

*Self-Computed

Based on the data presented in Table **5**, it is clear that out of a sample of 104 students, 72 students (69.2%) believe that Artificial Intelligence can enhance innovative thinking. In contrast, 13 students (12.5%) do not think that AI will enhance innovative thinking, while 19 (18.3%) are unsure.

Based on the data presented in Table **6**, it is clear that out of a sample of 104 students, 19 students (18.3%) are very familiar with Artificial Intelligence, 79 students (76%) are somewhat familiar with AI, and 6 students (5.8%) are unfamiliar with it.

Based on the data presented in Table **7** , out of the 104 students surveyed, 17 students (16.3%) indicate a preference for an AI tutor over a human tutor. Additionally, 50 students (48.1%) report that their preference for an AI tutor depends on the subject. In contrast, 37 students (35.6%) state that they do not prefer an AI tutor over a human tutor.

Table 6. Familiarity with AI.

-		Frequency	Percent	Valid Percent	Cumulative Percent
Valid	Very Familiar	19	18.3	18.3	18.3
	Some What Familiar	79	76.0	76.0	94.2
	Not Familiar at all	6	5.8	5.8	100.0
	Total	**104**	**100.0**	**100.0**	-

*Self-Computed

Table 7. Preference for AI tutor.

-		Frequency	Percent	Valid Percent	Cumulative Percent
Valid	Yes	17	16.3	16.3	16.3
	No	37	35.6	35.6	51.9
	Depend on the Subject	50	48.1	48.1	100.0
	Total	104	100.0	100.0	-

*Self-Computed

Table **8** shows that, out of 104 students surveyed, the majority believe that AI can boost students' grades in machine learning (20.1% of the total), with the least in natural language processing, virtual reality, and augmented reality (1% of the total).

It is evident from the data in Table **9** that, of a sample of 104 students, the majority (81.7%) are currently using AI tools or platforms to support their learning in 85 areas, while 19 students (18.3%) are not currently using any AI tools or platforms to support their learning.

According to the data in Table **10**, 42 out of 104 students in the sample are very comfortable (40.4%) with incorporating AI into their learning process, 58 are somewhat comfortable (55.8%), and 4 are not comfortable (3.8%).

Table 8. AI technology.

-		Frequency	Percent	Valid Percent	Cumulative Percent
Valid	Augmented reality	1	1.0	1.0	1.0
	chatbot	11	10.6	10.6	11.5
	Chatbots, Virtual reality	2	1.9	1.9	13.5
	Chatbots, Virtual reality, Augmented reality	3	2.9	2.9	16.3
	Machine learning	21	20.2	20.2	36.5
	Machine learning, Augmented reality	2	1.9	1.9	38.5
	Machine learning, Chatbots	6	5.8	5.8	44.2
	Machine learning, Chatbots, Virtual reality	5	4.8	4.8	49.0
	Machine learning, Chatbots, Virtual reality, Augmented reality	1	1.0	1.0	50.0
	Machine learning, Natural language processing	1	1.0	1.0	51.0
	Machine learning, Natural language processing, Chatbots	9	8.7	8.7	59.6
	Machine learning, Natural language processing, Chatbots, Virtual reality	1	1.0	1.0	60.6
	Machine learning, Natural language processing, Chatbots, Virtual reality, Augmented reality	15	14.4	14.4	75.0

(Table 8) cont.....

-		Frequency	Percent	Valid Percent	Cumulative Percent
Valid	Machine learning, Natural language processing, Virtual reality	1	1.0	1.0	76.0
	Machine learning, Natural language processing, Virtual reality, Augmented reality	1	1.0	1.0	76.9
	Machine learning, Virtual reality	1	1.0	1.0	77.9
	Machine learning, Virtual reality, Augmented reality	4	3.8	3.8	81.7
	Natural language processing	6	5.8	5.8	87.5
	Natural language processing, Chatbots	1	1.0	1.0	88.5
	Natural language processing, Chatbots, Augmented reality	1	1.0	1.0	89.4
	Natural language processing, Chatbots, Virtual reality	3	2.9	2.9	92.3
	Natural language processing, Virtual reality, Augmented reality	1	1.0	1.0	93.3
	Virtual reality	5	4.8	4.8	98.1
	Virtual reality, Augmented reality	2	1.9	1.9	100.0
	Total	104	100.0	100.0	-

*Self-Computed

Table 9. Using AI tools.

-		Frequency	Percent	Valid Percent	Cumulative Percent
Valid	Yes	85	81.7	81.7	81.7
	No	19	18.3	18.3	100.0
	Total	**104**	**100.0**	**100.0**	-

*Self-Computed

Table 10. Comfortable using AI.

-		Frequency	Percent	Valid Percent	Cumulative Percent
Valid	Very Comfortable	42	40.4	40.4	40.4
	Somewhat Comfortable	58	55.8	55.8	96.2
	Not Comfortable	4	3.8	3.8	100.0
	Total	**104**	**100.0**	**100.0**	-

*Self-Computed

Based on the information presented in Table **11**, it is clear that out of a sample of 104 students, 69 students (66.3%) believe that AI can help in identifying and addressing students' individual learning needs, 26 students (25%) state that AI cannot help in identifying and addressing students' individual learning needs, *i.e.*, they are somewhat comfortable using AI, and 9 (8.7%) are not sure.

Table 11. Learning needs.

-		Frequency	Percent	Valid Percent	Cumulative Percent
Valid	Yes	69	66.3	66.3	66.3
	No	9	8.7	8.7	75.0
	Not Sure	29	25.0	25.0	100.0
	Total	**104**	**100.0**	**100.0**	-

*Self-Computed

Based on the information presented, it is clear that out of a sample of 104 students, 24 of the students think that their academic life can be improved with the help of AI, which is equal to 23.1%, while the lowest response is recorded for test preparation, sssay writing, time management, revision, and review (1), selected by only 1% of the students.

Based on the information presented in Table **12**, it is clear that out of a sample of 104 students, 98 students have experienced benefits from using AI tools or platforms for studying, which is equal to 94.2%, and 6 students said that they have not experienced any benefits from using AI tools or platforms for studying, which is equal to 5.9%.

Table 12. Benefits of using AI.

-		Frequency	Percent	Valid Percent	Cumulative Percent
Valid	Yes	98	94.2	94.2	94.2
	No	6	5.8	5.8	100.0
	Total	**104**	**100.0**	**100.0**	-

*Self-Computed

Based on the data presented in Table **13**, it is clear that out of a sample of 104 students, 13 students (12.4%) think that AI can replace human interaction and support in education, 40 students (38.1%) said that AI cannot replace human interaction and support in education, and 51 students (48.6%) said that it depends on the context.

Table 13. Replacing human interaction.

-		Frequency	Percent	Valid Percent	Cumulative Percent
Valid	Yes	13	12.4	12.5	12.5
	No	40	38.1	38.5	51.0
	Depends on Context	51	48.6	49.0	100.0
	Total	104	99.0	100.0	-
Missing	System	1	1.0	-	-
Total		**105**	**100.0**	-	-

*Self-Computed

Based on the data presented in Table **14**, it is clear that out of a sample of 104 students, 68 students (64.8%) said that they will be interested in participating in research projects that explore the effectiveness of AI in education, 3 students (2.9%) said that they will not be interested, and 33 students (31.4%) said that it depends on the situation.

Table 14. Interested in participation.

-		Frequency	Percent	Valid Percent	Cumulative Percent
	Yes	68	64.8	65.4	65.4
	No	3	2.9	2.9	68.3
	May be	33	31.4	31.7	100.0
Valid	Total	104	99.0	100.0	-
Missing	System	1	1.0	-	-
Total	-	**105**	**100.0**	-	-

*Self-Computed

Based on the data presented in Table **15** , out of the 104 students surveyed, 46 students (43.8%) indicate that they are likely to recommend AI-powered educational tools to other students. Additionally, 27 students (25.7%) express a neutral stance, while 29 students (27.6%) report that they are very likely to recommend such tools.

Table 15. Recommend AI-powered educational tools to other students.

-		Frequency	Percent	Valid Percent	Cumulative Percent
Valid	Likely	46	43.8	43.8	43.8
	Neutral	27	25.7	25.7	69.5
	Very Likely	29	27.6	27.6	97.1
	Unlikely	3	2.9	2.9	100.0
	Total	**105**	**100.0**	**100.0**	-

*Self-Computed

CONCLUSION

The use of artificial intelligence systems in the classroom requires extreme caution due to the delicate nature of the subject matter. The field of education stands to benefit greatly from the many opportunities and benefits offered by artificial intelligence technology. To improve learning, AI-powered tutoring applications may provide personalized feedback and recommendations [12, 13]. Educators need to change the way they teach, the content they cover, and the spaces their students study in if they want to keep up with the ever-changing workforce and thrive in a world driven by artificial intelligence [14]. According to the findings, every dimension had a favourable and significant impact on the students' use of AI. The domains of problem-solving, critical thinking, creativity, collaboration, personalised learning, inventive thinking, and data analysis that are enabled by AI were therefore very important to students. It offers a forum for discussions, policy development, and tactical planning to fully realise AI's potential while preserving high standards of instruction and human interaction in learning settings.

Future studies can investigate the broader ramifications of AI in education by examining how it affects the academic performance, creativity, and critical thinking of diverse student populations over the long term. Studies comparing AI-assisted and conventional learning techniques may demonstrate their efficacy and scalability. Deeper insights can be gained by looking into AI's role in adaptive curriculum design, early learning challenge identification, and personalized learning pathways. Additionally, research can address potential biases in AI-driven educational tools, data privacy, and ethical issues. Furthermore, examining how AI is incorporated with cutting-edge technologies like virtual reality may uncover creative ways to improve motivation, engagement, and overall learning outcomes.

REFERENCES

[1] N. Almusharraf, and H. Alotaibi, "An error-analysis study from an EFL writing context: Human and Automated Essay Scoring Approaches", *Technology, Knowledge and Learning,* vol. 28, no. 3, pp. 1015-1031, 2023.
[http://dx.doi.org/10.1007/s10758-022-09592-z]

[2] A. Bhutoria, "Personalized education and Artificial Intelligence in the United States, China, and India: A systematic review using a Human-In-The-Loop model", *Computers and Education: Artificial Intelligence,* vol. 3, p. 100068, 2022.
[http://dx.doi.org/10.1016/j.caeai.2022.100068]

[3] J.L.H. Bowden, "Engaging the student as a customer: A relationship marketing approach", *Mark. Educ. Rev.,* vol. 21, no. 3, pp. 211-228, 2011.
[http://dx.doi.org/10.2753/MER1052-8008210302]

[4] M. Chassignol, A. Khoroshavin, A. Klimova, and A. Bilyatdinova, "Artificial Intelligence trends in education: a narrative overview", *Procedia Comput. Sci.,* vol. 136, pp. 16-24, 2018.
[http://dx.doi.org/10.1016/j.procs.2018.08.233]

[5] I.S. Chaudhry, S.A.M. Sarwary, G.A. El Refae, and H. Chabchoub, "Time to revisit existing student's performance evaluation approach in higher education sector in a new era of ChatGPT — A case study", *Cogent Education,* vol. 10, no. 1, p. 2210461, 2023.
[http://dx.doi.org/10.1080/2331186X.2023.2210461]

[6] D.R.E. Cotton, P.A. Cotton, and J.R. Shipway, "Chatting and cheating: Ensuring academic integrity in the era of ChatGPT", *Innov. Educ. Teach. Int.,* pp. 1-12, 2023.
[http://dx.doi.org/10.1080/14703297.2023.2190148]

[7] V. Dinu, "The knowledge-based economy: implications for higher education in economics and business", *Amfiteatru Econ. J.,* vol. 13, no. 30, pp. 343-344, 2011.

[8] M. Farrokhnia, S.K. Banihashem, O. Noroozi, and A. Wals, "A SWOT analysis of ChatGPT: Implications for educational practice and research", *Innov. Educ. Teach. Int.,* vol. 61, no. 3, pp. 460-474, 2024.
[http://dx.doi.org/10.1080/14703297.2023.2195846]

[9] G. Gasmi, and D. Prlja, "Ugrožavanje ljudskih prava I veštačka inteligencija", *ZbornikradovaKopaoničkeškoleprirodnogprava – Slobodan Perović,* pp. 323-335, 2021.

[10] W. Holmes, and I. Tuomi, "State of the art and practice in AI in education", *Eur. J. Educ.,* vol. 57, no. 4, pp. 542-570, 2022.
[http://dx.doi.org/10.1111/ejed.12533]

[11] A.C. Klassen, J. Creswell, V.L. Plano Clark, K.C. Smith, and H.I. Meissner, "Best practices in mixed methods for quality of life research", *Qual. Life Res.,* vol. 21, no. 3, pp. 377-380, 2012.
[http://dx.doi.org/10.1007/s11136-012-0122-x] [PMID: 22311251]

[12] S. Kreps, R.M. McCain, and M. Brundage, "All the news that's fit to fabricate: AI-generated text as a tool of media misinformation", *J. Exp. Political Sci.,* vol. 9, no. 1, pp. 104-117, 2022.
[http://dx.doi.org/10.1017/XPS.2020.37]

[13] D. Miranty, U. Widiati, B.Y. Cahyono, and T.I.S.T. Sharif, "The effectiveness of using Grammarly in teaching writing among Indonesian undergraduate EFL students", *Proc. Int. Seminar Lang., Educ., Cult. (ISoLEC 2021),* pp. 41-45, 2021.
[http://dx.doi.org/10.2991/assehr.k.211212.008]

[14] P. Rospigliosi, "Artificial intelligence in teaching and learning: what questions should we ask of ChatGPT?", *Interact. Learn. Environ.,* vol. 31, no. 1, pp. 1-3, 2023.
[http://dx.doi.org/10.1080/10494820.2023.2180191]

CHAPTER 10

Balancing Transparency and Ethics in Behavioural Analytics for Business Insights

Tamanna Mohapatra[1,*]

[1] *Department of Business Administration, National Law University, Cuttack, Odisha, India*

Abstract: Businesses may improve operations, tailor consumer experiences, and hone their strategy by analysing enormous volumes of data. But there are serious ethical questions raised by the growing use of behavioural analytics, especially regarding consent, privacy, and the potential for manipulation. This chapter explores the delicate balance between leveraging data for valuable business insights and maintaining ethical standards, with a focus on transparency. The chapter outlines strategies for transparency in data practices, emphasizing clear communication on data collection, usage purposes, and safeguards to protect consumer information. Additionally, it addresses the need for businesses to be accountable and to adopt practices that prioritize consumer welfare alongside business objectives. The chapter also discusses regulatory frameworks that govern data use, such as the General Data Protection Regulation (GDPR) and the California Consumer Privacy Act (CCPA), and their implications for businesses that employ behavioural analytics. The findings reveal that ethical behavioural analytics fosters trust, strengthens brand loyalty, and supports sustainable growth. Balancing data-driven insights with privacy protection encourages consumer partnership, enhances transparency, and aligns corporate values with societal expectations, ensuring innovation while safeguarding individual rights in an increasingly data-dependent business environment. It concludes that businesses should integrate ethics into their behavioural analytics strategies, balancing insights with ethical practices to achieve objectives while fostering trust-based, long-term customer relationships.

Keywords: Behavioural analytics, Business insights, CCPA, Data ethics, Data regulation, Ethical data practices, GDPR, Transparency.

INTRODUCTION

In today's commercial world, behavioural analytics is a powerful tool that involves gathering, analysing, and interpreting data on the interactions, behaviour,

* **Corresponding author Tamanna Mohapatra:** Department of Business Administration, National Law University, Cuttack, Odisha, India; E-mail: tamanna.1710@gmail.com

and patterns of customers. Extraction of actionable insights that can inform company decisions and enhance customer engagement, retention, and overall business success is the main objective of behavioural analytics [1, 2]. Businesses can better understand client preferences, forecast future behaviour, and adjust their tactics to better suit the demands of their target audiences by analysing vast, diverse data.

Many different sources of data are employed in behavioural analytics, which enables the creation of a full picture of client behaviour. Usually, these sources consist of online activity, wherein information about page views, click-through rates, and duration spent on particular pages is examined to ascertain the elements of a website that captivate users. Through likes, shares, comments, and total follower growth, social media interactions also reflect trends in customer sentiment, engagement levels, and brand perception. Additionally, companies can monitor consumer preferences and loyalty over time by tracking purchasing habits such as transaction history, frequency of transactions, and average order value [3]. Chat logs, call centre transcripts, and feedback forms are examples of customer service interactions that offer valuable insights into consumer satisfaction levels and point out areas where organizations can enhance their service offerings.

The capacity of behavioural analytics to handle and interpret massive amounts of data utilizing cutting-edge technologies like big data analytics, Artificial Intelligence, and machine learning is one of its main advantages [4, 5]. In today's digital age, where vast and increasingly complex amounts of data are generated daily, these technologies have become indispensable. In data, machine learning algorithms can automatically spot correlations and patterns that human analysts might not notice right away. This makes it possible to continuously improve business plans based on current information.

Machine learning algorithms, for instance, can provide personalized product suggestions for businesses by analysing client purchasing behaviour to forecast what a customer is likely to buy next. By automating decision-making based on these data, AI further improves this process and enables businesses to respond swiftly to the demands and preferences of their customers. Big data analytics is essential because it helps companies handle, store, and analyse massive volumes of data from many sources in an effective and scalable manner.

For firms, behavioural analytics offers several important advantages. Firstly, it gives businesses a comprehensive grasp of customer preferences, allowing them to tailor their advertising efforts, product lines, and clientele. Secondly, it assists companies in recognizing patterns in consumer behaviour, which enables them to predict future demands and changes in the market and maintain an advantage over rivals [6]. Thirdly, by detecting inefficiencies or bottlenecks in the client journey, it helps companies optimize their operations. In the long run, behavioural analytics gives companies the ability to make data-driven decisions that improve customer satisfaction and boost overall company performance, resulting in an operations strategy that is more specialized, effective, and customer-focused.

The study can be divided into 3 segments. The first part deals with highlighting the importance of modern business and behavioural analytics. The second part deals with focusing on challenges faced by citing selected case studies. The third part deals with the regulatory environment and concludes the strategies that help in strengthening customer-preferred relationships. A wide range of literature related to the theme of the paper is discussed and cited in the appropriate places.

IMPORTANCE IN MODERN BUSINESS

Success in the fiercely competitive corporate world of today depends on having a solid understanding of consumer behaviour. In order to better retain customers, customize consumer experiences, and provide goods and services that cater to particular demands, behavioural analytics is essential for businesses. Predicting consumer trends and industry shifts helps businesses to drive innovation, optimize marketing campaigns, and streamline operations. Furthermore, behavioural analytics improves decision-making by offering data-driven insights, which are critical for maintaining competitiveness and agility in a market that is rapidly changing. Businesses that successfully apply behavioural analytics frequently observe increases in profitability, operational effectiveness, and customer happiness [7, 8].

Understanding consumer behaviour has become essential for achieving success and preserving a competitive edge in the fast-paced, fiercely competitive commercial world of today. Businesses today have access to previously unheard-of volumes of data due to the growing digitization of consumer interactions. Proper analysis of this data can provide profound insights into the preferences, habits, and decision-making processes of customers. At the forefront of this change is behavioural analytics, which is essential to an organization's ability to tailor its offerings, adjust to the demands of its clients, and make wise strategic choices.

One of the primary benefits of behavioural analytics in modern business is its ability to personalize customer experiences. Businesses that employ behavioural analytics can use information from online activity, buying patterns, and customer feedback to give individualized recommendations, offers, and messages in a market where consumers demand highly customized interactions. To boost engagement and consumer satisfaction, businesses such as Amazon and Netflix employ behavioural analytics to suggest products or content based on user preferences [9, 10]. By making interactions more relevant, personalization helps organizations form closer bonds with their clients, which in turn promotes repeat business and loyalty.

Another key advantage of behavioural analytics is its ability to improve customer retention. Businesses can spot early warning signs of disengagement and take proactive steps to retain clients by examining trends like churn rates, frequency of customer contacts, and satisfaction levels. Businesses can use this information to provide customized incentives, address problems, or modify their services to better suit the needs of the client, for instance, if the consumer has ceased using a service or is showing signs of dissatisfaction. In addition to improving retention rates, this capacity to anticipate and manage customer attrition lowers the expenses related to bringing on new clients.

In addition to enhancing personalization and retention, behavioural analytics helps businesses design products and services that more accurately align with customer needs and preferences. Businesses can find gaps in their offerings and create new products or services that satisfy changing consumer needs by examining usage trends and customer feedback. For instance, a software business may monitor which of its platform's functions are most and least utilized. The company's offers will be more likely to succeed in the market if this data is used to inform future product upgrades or new developments that are in line with user preferences.

Beyond customer experience, marketing optimization is another area where behavioural analytics offers significant advantages. Conventional marketing strategies frequently depend on general demographics and presumptions on consumer preferences. Businesses can more successfully customize their messaging and targeting strategies by using behavioural analytics, which offers detailed data on how various client segments react to marketing efforts. Businesses can develop more targeted campaigns, increase conversion rates, and improve the efficiency of their marketing expenditures by knowing which messages appeal to particular demographics.

Moreover, behavioural analytics supports the streamlining of operations. Businesses can find areas for improvement and streamline their operations by examining statistics on operational efficiency, such as employee productivity, supply chain performance, and customer service response times. This results in better client happiness, lower operating costs, and quicker service delivery. For example, a retail business may use supply chain data analysis to pinpoint bottlenecks and implement data-driven changes that shorten wait times and increase product availability.

Driving innovation is another critical benefit of behavioural analytics. By predicting consumer trends and anticipating shifts in the market, companies can stay ahead of their competitors. Behavioural analytics allows businesses to identify emerging patterns and preferences, enabling them to innovate in areas such as product development, customer engagement strategies, and even business models. This forward-looking approach helps companies remain agile and responsive in a rapidly changing market landscape.

Finally, the role of behavioural analytics in enhancing decision-making processes cannot be overstated. In an era where agility is paramount, businesses must rely on data-driven insights to make informed decisions quickly and accurately. Behavioural analytics provides real-time information that helps companies make strategic choices with confidence, whether it is adjusting pricing strategies, launching new products, or entering new markets. Businesses that integrate behavioural insights into their decision-making processes are better positioned to respond to market changes, mitigate risks, and capitalize on opportunities.

In summary, behavioural analytics is indispensable in modern business, offering a wide range of benefits that include personalizing customer experiences, improving retention, optimizing marketing efforts, and streamlining operations. Companies that effectively leverage behavioural analytics often see marked improvements in customer satisfaction, operational efficiency, and profitability, positioning them for long-term success in an increasingly competitive and dynamic business environment [11 - 13].

CASE STUDIES OF BEHAVIOURAL ANALYTICS IN ACTION

Amazon: Behavioural Analytics in Recommendations

One of the best examples of behavioural analytics in action is Amazon's recommendation engine. Amazon customizes product recommendations for each user based on their browsing history, purchase history, and interactions on the website. This method makes use of collaborative filtering, which finds patterns in customers' actions and uses that data to suggest items that other users similar to them have either viewed or bought. By using machine learning algorithms, Amazon is able to continuously improve these suggestions, resulting in more individualized shopping experiences that are relevant and easy to use. This improves customer satisfaction and increases sales [14, 15].

Netflix: Personalizing Content Through Behavioural Data

Netflix creates a highly customized viewing experience for its viewers by utilizing behavioural data. Netflix generates personalized content recommendations by monitoring and evaluating a wide range of user activities, including watching history, time spent on particular episodes, ratings, and even pause patterns. By finding similarities in user interests and recommending TV series or films based on what comparable users have seen, its machine learning algorithms further improve suggestions. Because it helps users find information that better suits their interests, this tailored content curation has been essential in increasing user engagement and retention rates, which in turn keep users on the site longer [8, 9].

Starbucks: Loyalty Programs and Personalized Offers

Starbucks creates highly customized promotions and offers by utilizing behavioural data from its mobile app and loyalty program. Starbucks customizes discounts, rewards, and incentives for each consumer by looking at their purchase history, preferences, and trends. For example, a regular consumer of a certain kind of coffee may be offered discounts on related or complimentary goods. Because each user has a personalized experience, this data-driven customisation increases consumer loyalty. By enticing users to use the app frequently and providing prompt incentives that boost user happiness and brand loyalty, it also promotes repeat business [8, 15].

ETHICAL CONSIDERATIONS IN BEHAVIOURAL ANALYTICS

Privacy Concerns and Data Sensitivity

Privacy concerns are paramount in the realm of behavioural analytics because the data collected is often deeply personal, including browsing habits, purchase behaviours, location data, and even emotional responses. Businesses use this data to create detailed consumer profiles, which can lead to highly targeted marketing and personalized experiences. However, the sensitivity of this data raises significant privacy issues.

- ***Data Sensitivity:*** Behavioural data often contains sensitive information, such as health-related behaviours, financial activity, or personal preferences, which, if mishandled, can expose individuals to risks like identity theft or unauthorized surveillance. The more granular the data, the greater the risk of identifying individuals, even if the data is anonymized.
- ***Data Security:*** Ensuring robust protection of behavioural data is crucial. Data

breaches can result in massive losses of customer trust and lead to financial and legal repercussions for businesses. Organizations must employ stringent data security measures to safeguard against hacking or unauthorized access.

- ***Privacy as a Right:*** In many jurisdictions, privacy is seen as a fundamental right. Behavioural analytics must respect this right by limiting data collection to what is necessary for business operations, ensuring that data is stored and processed responsibly [3, 4].

The Challenge of Informed Consent

Informed consent is a critical ethical and legal requirement when collecting and processing behavioural data. However, in practice, obtaining truly informed consent is challenging for several reasons:

- ***Complexity of Data Collection:*** Many users remain unaware of how their data is collected, especially when it is done passively. Behavioural data is often collected through cookies, website tracking, and mobile apps that monitor interactions without direct user engagement. For instance:
- ***Tracking with Cookies:*** Websites often collect browsing behaviour data through cookies, but users may only receive vague descriptions in the "cookie consent" banner, typically agreeing without reading the details. This consent often includes terms that allow extensive data sharing across multiple websites and partners. Facebook, for example, collects vast amounts of user data through cookies and third-party plugins across other websites, giving the company insights even when users aren't on Facebook's site [8, 9].
- ***Mobile App Permissions:*** Apps may ask for permission to access location data, contacts, or camera, but users may not fully understand how this data will be used. In 2020, Google settled a lawsuit regarding claims that it tracked users' locations even after users had turned location history off, raising questions about what "consent" meant in such cases [1, 15].

Transparency and Clarity: For consent to be valid, it must be obtained in a transparent, accessible way. However, companies often present lengthy and complex Terms Of Service (TOS) agreements that few users read or understand. Simplifying these terms and creating clear, easy-to-navigate consent forms can help users make informed choices. Examples include:

- Simplified Consent Forms: Some companies, like Apple, have begun using simplified data collection statements, explaining exactly what data is collected and how it is used, often directly on their privacy pages and consent banners. By clearly stating purposes such as "improving user experience" or "providing personalized recommendations," Apple attempts to ensure users are aware of the implications [6, 8].

- Unclear Use in Third-Party Sharing: In contrast, some companies continue to use vague language to justify third-party data sharing, making it difficult for users to understand that their data might be used in ways they did not expect. For example, Spotify has faced criticism for its broad data-sharing agreements with third-party advertisers, which led to backlash from users who were uncomfortable with their listening data being used for targeted advertising [6, 9].

Consent *vs.* Coercion: Sometimes, users feel pressured to give consent to access core features or services, creating a "take-it-or-leave-it" scenario. This issue raises ethical concerns about whether such consent is truly voluntary. Examples include:

- Social Media Platforms: Facebook and Instagram require consent for extensive data collection as a condition of using their services, leaving users with limited control over data privacy. In 2019, Germany's competition watchdog ruled that Facebook's data practices exploited users by forcing them to consent to the integration of data across multiple apps without a true opt-out option [8, 15].
- Freemium Apps and Ad-Tracking: Many Freemium apps provide an "ad-free" version only if users pay for a premium upgrade; otherwise, they must agree to extensive data collection for ad personalization. While users technically have a choice, this approach may feel coercive to some, as they must either pay or forfeit their data privacy [6, 15].

Potential for Manipulation and Exploitation

Behavioural analytics allows businesses to understand and anticipate consumer actions, but this insight can also lead to ethical concerns, especially when data is used to manipulate or exploit vulnerable individuals.

Targeted Manipulation

Businesses may use behavioural data to push consumers toward certain choices, and this can become manipulative when it exploits vulnerabilities.

- **Gambling and Addictive Behaviours:** Online gaming and gambling companies, for instance, use behavioural data to encourage more frequent play, targeting users identified as high spenders or those with gambling tendencies. In one case, UK-based gambling companies were found to use behavioural data to identify individuals likely to spend more and sent them personalized offers, like free credits, to encourage gambling, contributing to problematic gambling behaviours [8, 15].

- **Food Delivery and Promotions:** Food delivery apps, such as UberEATS and DoorDash, track browsing and purchase history to promote specific deals to users, potentially increasing impulsive food purchases. By targeting individuals with offers like free delivery for high-calorie foods or late-night deals, these platforms may be exploiting those struggling with dietary issues or food addictions [6, 15].

Dark Patterns

"Dark patterns" refer to design strategies that subtly influence users to make choices they might not otherwise make, often without being fully aware.

- **Subscription Traps:** Some companies make it difficult to cancel subscriptions by burying the cancellation option in complex menus or using confusing language. For example, Amazon has been criticized for making it difficult to cancel Prime memberships, a process that involves navigating multiple steps, potentially discouraging cancellations [8, 9].
- **Excessive Data Sharing:** Some online services use pop-ups and nudges to encourage users to share more data than they might prefer. LinkedIn, for example, nudges users into uploading their entire contact list to grow their network, which also benefits LinkedIn by expanding its own database and reach [6, 8].

Exploitation of Vulnerable Groups

Behavioural data can reveal insights about vulnerable individuals, including children, elderly users, and those with mental health concerns, potentially opening doors for exploitation.

- Marketing to Children: Children's online behaviour is closely monitored on platforms like YouTube, where algorithms promote content based on viewing patterns. Although the platform has taken steps to limit data collection, YouTube faced a record $170 million fine in 2019 for violating the Children's Online Privacy Protection Act (COPPA). The platform's algorithmic recommendations had exposed children to targeted ads and content, raising concerns about data-driven exploitation [15].
- Targeting the Elderly: Elderly individuals are often targeted with certain types of

advertising, such as health products, insurance, or financial schemes, based on their browsing patterns and search history. Studies show that older users are more likely to be impacted by ads for financial products with high fees or misleading terms. AARP has noted the frequent targeting of the elderly for products like reverse mortgages, which can be complex and risky for uninformed buyers.

The ethical challenges associated with informed consent, as well as the potential for manipulation and exploitation, underscore the need for responsible use of behavioural data. Examples from companies across sectors illustrate how easily consent can become unclear and how behavioural insights can be used to push the boundaries of consumer influence. By ensuring clarity in consent and avoiding exploitative practices, companies can use behavioural analytics to improve user experience while respecting ethical principles and maintaining consumer trust.

THE ROLE OF TRANSPARENCY IN ETHICAL DATA USE

Transparency in data practices is a cornerstone of ethical data use, ensuring that consumers are informed about how their data is collected, stored, processed, and used. Transparent practices build trust, empower consumers to make informed choices, and help companies avoid legal and ethical pitfalls. This section breaks down the role of transparency, focusing on its definition, strategies for ensuring it, and ways to communicate data practices effectively to consumers.

Defining Transparency in Data Practices

Transparency in data practices refers to the clear, open, and honest disclosure of information to consumers about the data life cycle. This involves making sure that consumers understand:

- **What Data is Collected:** Companies should specify what types of data are being collected—whether it is personal data (*e.g.*, age, location) or behavioural data (*e.g.*, browsing history, purchase patterns).
- **Why the Data is Collected:** Clearly stating the purpose behind data collection is key. For instance, data may be gathered to personalize user experiences, improve product recommendations, or develop new features.
- **How the Data is Used and Shared:** Transparency also means informing consumers if their data will be shared with third parties, such as advertisers or analytics partners, and how it will be processed within the company.
- **How Long Data is Retained:** Data retention policies should be made clear,

allowing users to understand how long their information will be stored and when it will be deleted or anonymized.

By defining transparency in these specific areas, companies set a clear framework that respects users' right to know about their data and its purpose within the organization. These are a few definitions that generally focus on openness, accessibility, and clarity in how data is collected, used, and shared with consumers.

- Transparency is one of the key principles of the General Data Protection Regulation (GDPR), which mandates that businesses give clear, easily comprehensible information about the acquisition, processing, and retention of data. The goal of the GDPR's transparency rules is to give data subjects the ability to comprehend and manage their data [5].
- Transparency, according to Luciano Floridi, is the display of data practices in a way that is easy to comprehend, accessible, and essential to ethical data governance. In order to empower consumers to make knowledgeable decisions regarding their data, Floridi promotes openness [6].
- Richards and King talk about reducing the "black box" impact of data analytics by being transparent. To provide informed consent and accountability, they propose that openness entails disclosing algorithmic procedures and data sources [13].
- Nissenbaum highlights transparency as a fundamental aspect of privacy, emphasizing the necessity of providing unambiguous justifications for data flows and goals. She contends that openness should guarantee that people are aware of the data being gathered and how it conforms to social norms [10].

Strategies for Ensuring Transparency

To achieve meaningful transparency, organizations can implement various strategies that prioritize openness and accountability in data practices.

Clear and Simple Privacy Policies: Often, privacy policies are long, legalistic, and difficult for the typical user to comprehend. Transparency can be greatly increased by developing a privacy policy that is precise, succinct, and devoid of jargon. For example, businesses like Apple and Mozilla have streamlined their privacy policies, emphasizing clear language and visual aids to help customers grasp important information [6, 8].

Granular Consent Options: Giving consumers fine-grained control over the information they divulge enables them to customize their privacy settings according to their needs and comfort levels. For example, companies can allow consumers to opt in or out of particular data uses, such as location tracking or targeted advertising, as an alternative to requiring their consent. Platforms like Google frequently employ this strategy, which enables consumers to personalize their data-sharing settings [1, 6].

Periodic Privacy Notices: A proactive approach to transparency is developed by routinely updating users on changes to privacy rules or data practices. Businesses should promptly advise users of any changes to rules or procedures and provide a summary of the most important developments. For example, anytime Facebook makes major changes to its data practices, pop-up notifications appear within the app [8, 9].

***Data Access and Portability*:** More transparency and ownership are made possible by letting people see and download their data. Users are entitled to data portability under laws like the GDPR, which enables them to access and transfer their data between providers. Businesses assist users in gaining control and visibility into their data by implementing simple download capabilities, like those seen on LinkedIn and Twitter [4, 5].

***Audit and Compliance Checks*:** The actual enforcement of transparency policies is ensured by routine audits of data practices. Verifying that data is gathered, used, and shared in accordance with policy can be achieved through internal audits or third-party reviews. For example, in order to make sure they comply with both corporate norms and legal frameworks, businesses may hire external compliance services to perform privacy impact studies [4, 9].

Communicating Data Practices to Consumers

Effectively communicating data practices involves more than just posting a privacy policy. Companies must find ways to share information about their data practices in an accessible and engaging way to empower consumers with the knowledge needed to make informed choices.

- ***Interactive Privacy Dashboards*:** Privacy dashboards allow users to visualize and manage their data permissions easily. By giving users a centralized place to view and adjust their data settings, companies like Microsoft help users understand their data at a glance, enabling more informed decisions. Dashboards also provide real-time information on data use, making transparency a continuous part of the user experience.
- ***Consent Pop-Ups and Inline Notices*:** When collecting data for a specific

purpose, companies should use consent pop-ups or inline notifications to explain why the data is needed and how it will be used. For instance, many websites display cookie consent banners to explain tracking practices, giving users the option to manage or deny specific types of data collection. Google's cookie banner, for example, provides links to learn more about cookies and customize settings before users agree.

- ***Education Initiatives and FAQs***: Educating users on data practices through FAQs, videos, or blog posts can demystify data processes. Some companies provide resources that explain, in simple terms, how data supports their services, the user's rights, and why specific permissions are requested. For example, LinkedIn and Amazon frequently use help sections and FAQ pages to explain their data practices in detail.
- ***Multi-Channel Communication***: Communicating data practices through emails, app notifications, and social media allows companies to reach users where they are most likely to engage. For instance, when privacy policies are updated, companies like WhatsApp send direct in-app messages to ensure users are aware of new terms and any potential implications for their data use.
- ***Regular Transparency Reports***: Publishing periodic transparency reports allows companies to provide a comprehensive overview of their data handling practices, including metrics on data requests from governments or third-party agencies. Companies such as Apple, Google, and Twitter release regular transparency reports detailing their data practices and the number of information requests they receive from authorities. This practice demonstrates accountability and allows users to stay informed about external factors influencing data use.

In order to establish a foundation of trust between businesses and their users, ethical behavioral analytics requires transparency in data practices. Businesses can navigate the complexities of data ethics and make sure that their operations meet both legal requirements and customer expectations by establishing a clear definition of transparency, implementing workable enforcement tactics, and communicating with users in an effective manner. Businesses may cultivate a more knowledgeable, capable, and trustworthy clientele by being transparent.

REGULATORY FRAMEWORKS GOVERNING BEHAVIOURAL ANALYTICS

Regulatory frameworks are essential for protecting users' rights and establishing moral guidelines for data use, especially as companies depend more and more on behavioural analytics to understand customer behaviour. Important laws like the California Consumer Privacy Act (CCPA) and the General Data Protection Regulation (GDPR) set rules for data collecting, processing, and security, influencing how companies manage behavioural data. This section examines important rules, the difficulties in complying with them, and how they support moral behaviour in behavioural analytics.

Overview of Key Regulations (GDPR, CCPA)

The General Data Protection Regulation (GDPR) and the California Consumer Privacy Act (CCPA) are two of the most comprehensive data privacy laws, setting global standards for data protection and user rights.

General Data Protection Regulation (GDPR): Enforced in the European Union, GDPR is one of the world's most stringent data protection regulations. It mandates that companies obtain explicit consent from users before collecting their personal data, clearly define the purpose of data collection, and limit data processing to that purpose. Key GDPR principles include:

- **Right to Access:** Individuals have the right to access their data and understand how it's being used.
- **Right to Erasure:** Also known as the "right to be forgotten," users can request that their data be deleted under certain conditions.
- **Data Portability:** Users have the right to request a copy of their data in a structured format.
- **Data Minimization**: Only data necessary for specific purposes should be collected and stored.

GDPR has an extraterritorial impact, meaning non-EU businesses handling EU residents' data must also comply. For example, Facebook and Google, though headquartered in the U.S., are required to follow GDPR principles when dealing with European users.

California Consumer Privacy Act (CCPA): The CCPA, effective in California since 2020, grants consumers greater control over their personal data. Like GDPR, it mandates transparency, requiring companies to inform users about what data is collected and how it's used. Key elements of the CCPA include:

- **Right to Know:** Consumers can request to know what personal information is being collected and shared, and with whom.
- **Right to Delete**: Similar to GDPR's erasure provision, consumers can request deletion of their personal data.
- **Right to Opt-Out:** Users can choose to opt out of data sales, which is particularly important for digital advertisers.

Only companies that meet specific requirements—such as generating more than $25 million in revenue annually or gathering data from more than 50,000 Californians—are subject to the CCPA. Through the California Privacy Rights Act (CPRA), which strengthens the CCPA's obligations, California has increased data protection measures since the CCPA's inception [3].

Compliance Challenges for Businesses

Adhering to GDPR and CCPA standards can be challenging for businesses, particularly those heavily reliant on behavioural analytics for targeted advertising and user insights.

Complex Data Mapping: Organizations must map data sources, comprehend data flows, and record processing operations in order to comply with the CCPA and GDPR. Finding all data sources and making sure they comply with these rules is a difficult, resource-intensive undertaking for businesses with extensive data operations, especially international corporations.

Consent Management: Under GDPR, gaining and maintaining user consent is difficult. Companies must design easily navigable permission forms and offer unambiguous choices for opting in or out of data sharing. Cross-platform implementation can be challenging, and if done poorly, it may cause user annoyance. To handle consent, for example, many businesses utilize cookie banners; nevertheless, in order to avoid legal repercussions, these must be transparent and compliant.

Data Security Measures: The CCPA and GDPR require companies to implement measures to prevent misuse, unauthorized access, and data breaches. However, it can be expensive and logistically difficult for companies of all sizes to maintain high data security standards across all platforms, particularly when third-party interfaces are involved.

Frequent Policy Updates and Legal Compliance: Both the CCPA and GDPR are subject to frequent revisions, so companies must keep up with the most recent rules and modify their operations accordingly. Retraining employees, updating privacy policies, and consulting with lawyers are frequently necessary for compliance. For example, businesses are required to guarantee adherence to even more stringent rules on data sharing and user rights under the most recent revisions to the CCPA (CPRA).

Cross-Border Data Transfers: The GDPR's restrictions on data transfers pose further difficulties for businesses that operate globally. Businesses transferring data across borders now face uncertainty as a result of the Schrems II verdict, which declared the Privacy Shield data transfer framework between the EU and the U.S. illegal. Nowadays, companies must rely on Standard Contractual Clauses (SCCs), which makes doing business internationally more difficult.

The Role of Regulation in Promoting Ethics

Regulations like GDPR and CCPA serve as ethical guardrails, ensuring that companies use behavioural analytics responsibly and prioritize user rights.

- ***Encouraging Ethical Data Collection*:** These regulations require organizations to obtain explicit consent before collecting data and encourage them to carefully evaluate the information they gather, ensuring that it is necessary, relevant, and appropriate for their intended purpose. These methods incorporate ethical concerns by ensuring companies acquire only the necessary data, avoiding over-collection that can compromise customer privacy.
- ***Promoting Transparency and Accountability*:** Regulations compel businesses to inform users of their data practices in a clear and understandable manner. For instance, the GDPR encourages accountability in businesses by requiring users to be aware of their rights and have access to their data. Due to legal requirements, transparency reports and privacy dashboards are made available to the public, assisting customers in making knowledgeable decisions regarding their data.
- ***Safeguarding Against Data Misuse*:** In order to reduce the possibility of data breaches and misuse, regulatory norms require businesses to implement strict data protection procedures. Preventing illegal use or cyber threats to personal and behavioural data of consumers provides an ethical goal. Stricter enforcement has resulted from high-profile examples like the Cambridge Analytica affair, which have brought attention to the significance of these measures.
- ***Ensuring Consumer Autonomy*:** By giving users the freedom to manage their data through opt-out choices, deletion requests, or data portability rights, the CCPA and GDPR both strengthen consumer autonomy. These rules place a strong emphasis on user agency, enabling people to control their online personas and communicate with businesses anyway they see fit. The right to be forgotten under the GDPR, for example, enables users to delete data they believe is no longer pertinent or that may be misused.
- ***Supporting Fair Business Practices*:** Regulations stop companies from unfairly benefiting from the unauthorized use of customer data. For instance, businesses are prohibited from utilizing personal data for behavioural targeting without the user's knowledge under the GDPR's stringent consent requirements. This ensures that competitive advantage is founded on high-quality services rather

than data exploitation, levelling the playing field.

- ***Regulations such as the CCPA and GDPR are essential tools for establishing moral behaviour in behavioural analytics.*** These rules safeguard customers while encouraging confidence and responsibility in data-driven businesses by establishing explicit guidelines for data acquisition, consent, and transparency. These frameworks ultimately push businesses to embrace responsible data practices that put consumer autonomy, security, and ethical integrity first, even in the face of compliance issues. Transparent, ethical data use will remain crucial as companies navigate different regulatory environments in order to win over customers and comply with the law.

BALANCING BUSINESS INSIGHTS WITH ETHICAL PRACTICES

Businesses now understand and interact with their customers in a completely new way thanks to the incorporation of behavioural analytics into daily operations. To protect consumer rights, privacy, and trust, however, using data for insights must be balanced with moral behaviour. This section looks at how companies should prioritize ethical data use, maintain accountability, and foster trust by integrating ethics into their data strategies.

Integrating Ethics into Data Strategies

Incorporating ethics into data strategies involves embedding ethical considerations into every stage of data collection, processing, and analysis. Ethical data strategies aim to leverage insights without compromising consumer rights or privacy.

Ethical Data Collection and Processing: As shown in Fig. (**1**) , businesses should only gather information that is essential to achieving their goals. A retail business that wants to tailor recommendations, for instance, can prioritize past purchases over superfluous personal information, lowering privacy concerns. By following data reduction guidelines, businesses can obtain insightful information while protecting the privacy of their customers.

Fig. (1). Ethical data life cycle.
Source: Self-designed

***User-Centred Consent Practices*:** Obtaining explicit, informed consent is essential to ethical data strategies. By ensuring consent forms are easy to read and provide users with explicit explanations of the data being collected and its intended use, ethical businesses go beyond the law's obligations. As a sign of their dedication to flexible, informed consent, some businesses, like Microsoft, have created consent dashboards where consumers can modify their data-sharing options.

***Regular Ethical Audits*:** Regular audits of data procedures can guarantee compliance with changing standards and help identify potential ethical issues. To lower such risks, a business may, for example, examine its data retention procedures to make sure that outdated data is erased or anonymized. Data security, permission procedures, and third-party sharing agreements are a few topics that should be covered in audits.

***Ethics Training for Data Teams*:** It is crucial to make sure data teams are aware of the ethical ramifications of their work. They can identify instances in which data practices may violate privacy or result in bias thanks to their training. For instance, businesses might reduce unintended bias in behavioural analytics by teaching employees to recognize and address algorithmic bias.

The Importance of Accountability

In order to make sure that businesses handle customer data ethically, accountability in ethical data practices is essential. Establishing clear duty structures is essential to this, such as designating a Data Protection Officer (DPO) to supervise data processes and ensure compliance with ethical and legal requirements. Another factor is transparency, which is reinforced by the yearly transparency reports that businesses like Apple and Google publish to update stakeholders on data usage and security measures. As demonstrated by Facebook's oversight board, ethics committees or review boards also assist in evaluating data initiatives for ethical alignment. Last but not least, following laws like the CCPA and GDPR promotes accountability by enforcing fair data practices and consumer rights [3, 4, 6].

Building Consumer Trust through Ethical Data Use

Building consumer trust is essential for long-term success, as users are more likely to engage with companies that they believe are protecting their interests. Ethical data use is fundamental in creating a trusting relationship between businesses and their consumers.

- ***Transparency in Data Collection and Use***: Transparency is the first step toward trust. Customers' trust in the organization's intentions is increased when they are given clear explanations of the data being collected, its purpose, and its intended use. For instance, LinkedIn's user settings offer a clear description of its data practices, empowering users to comprehend and control their data.
- ***Empowering Consumers with Control***: Building trust with customers requires granting them control over their data. Users can manage their personal information through features including data access, correction, and deletion rights. Users can easily access, manage, and remove their data *via* Google's My Account dashboard, giving them a sense of empowerment and increased security when using the platform.
- ***Ethical Marketing and Personalization***: Customers value when their information is used to create relevant experiences without feeling unnecessarily tracked or abused, so using data responsibly for personalization builds confidence. For example, Netflix's recommendation engine makes content recommendations based on viewing history without revealing more personal information about users than is necessary for content. Netflix preserves user confidence by emphasizing relevancy over intrusive data tracking.
- ***Protecting User Privacy and Data Security***: Strong data security procedures are

also essential to establishing confidence. If customers are certain that their information will be safely stored, they are more inclined to provide it. To protect sensitive data from breaches, for instance, banks and healthcare institutions frequently use encryption, access controls, and multi-layered security procedures. Customers are more likely to believe that their information is in good hands when data security is given top priority.

- ***Responsive Customer Support and Data Rights Requests:*** Companies show respect for user concerns by swiftly answering consumer questions about data use, privacy settings, and data rights requests. Trust is also increased by a prompt customer service team that can respond to inquiries about privacy policies or assist with requests for data rights. Microsoft, for example, provides specialized assistance for privacy-related questions, letting users know that their concerns are taken seriously.

Businesses using behavioural analytics must strike a balance between moral behaviour and business insights. Businesses can gain important insights while protecting user rights and privacy by incorporating ethics into data strategy, maintaining accountability, and putting customer trust first. This ethical balance improves customer relationships and trust while also assisting firms in staying compliant and avoiding reputational issues. In the end, businesses that prioritize ethical data use can build a strong, trusting relationship with their users and gain a long-term competitive edge.

CASE STUDIES: SUCCESSFUL ETHICAL PRACTICES IN BEHAVIOURAL ANALYTICS

As businesses navigate the challenges of using behavioural analytics responsibly, some companies have become exemplars in integrating ethics into their data strategies. Examining case studies of leading organizations that prioritize ethical practices offers valuable lessons and best practices for maintaining transparency, protecting user privacy, and fostering trust. This section explores specific examples, lessons learned, and the positive impact of ethical data use on business success.

Examples from Leading Companies

- ***Apple's Privacy-Centric Data Strategy***: Apple has positioned itself as a privacy-first company, setting itself apart from rivals by reducing user data collection and improving data security. For example, App monitoring Transparency (ATT), which enables users to choose not to have their apps tracked by third parties, is one feature of Apple's IOS that restricts monitoring. Furthermore,

Apple ensures privacy by design by anonymizing data used for tailored recommendations in Apple Music and the App Store.

- ***Microsoft's Trustworthy AI Principles*****:** Microsoft has put in place a strong foundation for ethical AI and behavioural analytics that emphasizes accountability, transparency, and equity. Microsoft places a strong emphasis on transparent data policies, objective algorithms, and user involvement through its Responsible AI Principles. Additionally, the business regularly evaluates the ethics of its AI models to make sure that data-driven decisions respect user privacy and are in line with user preferences.
- ***Salesforce's Ethical Use of Customer Data:*** Salesforce, a pioneer in cloud and CRM technologies, has established strict regulations for the moral use of data, especially when it comes to customer data management. Guidelines for responsible AI and data utilization are part of its Ethical Use of Technology Initiative, which aims to prevent abuse and excessive dependence on personal information. Additionally, Salesforce gives its customers the ability to adjust data-collection parameters, promoting openness and control over their behavioural data practices.
- ***Patagonia's Limited Data Collection Approach***: The outdoor apparel brand Patagonia is well-known for its dedication to sustainability, which is evident in its data practices. Patagonia focuses on client relationships and ethical marketing, limiting data collection to the most important customer information and employing minimal personalization strategies. The business prioritizes privacy and trust by using behavioural analytics only to identify general consumer preferences rather than tracking specific customers.

The Impact of Ethical Data Use on Business Success

Ethical data practices boost customer trust and loyalty, as companies like Apple and Microsoft demonstrate by respecting user privacy and enabling user control, which fosters stronger brand loyalty and advocacy. Compliance with regulations such as GDPR and CCPA also reduces legal risks, with companies like Salesforce actively aligning with these standards to avoid costly repercussions. Ethical data practices further enhance brand reputation, offering a competitive edge, as seen in Apple's privacy-first approach, which attracts privacy-conscious consumers. Internally, these practices improve employee morale and attract talent aligned with ethical values, as seen with Patagonia. Finally, ethical data use contributes to long-term sustainability by building trust-based relationships, ensuring resilience in regulatory landscapes, and fostering lasting customer loyalty.

FUTURE DIRECTIONS FOR ETHICAL BEHAVIOURAL ANALYTICS

Ethical practices in behavioural analytics are continuously evolving, driven by new data privacy regulations, advances in technology, and changing consumer expectations. This section examines emerging trends in data ethics, the role of technology in enhancing transparency, and predictions for the future of behavioural analytics.

Emerging Trends in Data Ethics

The data ethics landscape is being shaped by growing awareness around privacy rights, data sovereignty, and the ethical use of AI. Companies are under increasing pressure to adopt practices that prioritize consumer interests and fair use of data. Key trends include:

- **Data Sovereignty:** With regulations such as GDPR and CCPA requiring stricter data localization, businesses are increasingly adopting data sovereignty measures. This trend ensures that personal data is processed and stored within the user's own country or region, supporting greater control and protection.
- **Algorithmic Fairness:** As AI algorithms play a larger role in decision-making, ensuring fairness is essential to avoid biased outcomes. Organizations are investing in ethical AI development, auditing their algorithms to prevent discrimination, and ensuring that data used for training is representative and unbiased.
- **Increased User Control and Consent Mechanisms:** Users are gaining more control over their data through user-friendly consent mechanisms and tools that allow them to opt out of data collection. This trend reflects a broader shift towards consumer empowerment and transparency.

Emerging trends in data ethics are expected to see varying levels of adoption across organizations, driven by growing awareness and regulatory pressures. For instance, data sovereignty is anticipated to reach an adoption rate of around 65% (Fig. **2**), as global regulations like GDPR emphasize data localization and encourage organizations to comply by managing data within specific jurisdictions. Algorithmic fairness is likely to see a 75% adoption rate as initiatives promoting unbiased and fair AI gain momentum, pushing companies to prioritize ethical algorithms. Additionally, increased user control features, such as consent management and data access options, are projected to become standard in approximately 85% of businesses, responding to heightened demands for transparency and empowering users to manage their personal information.

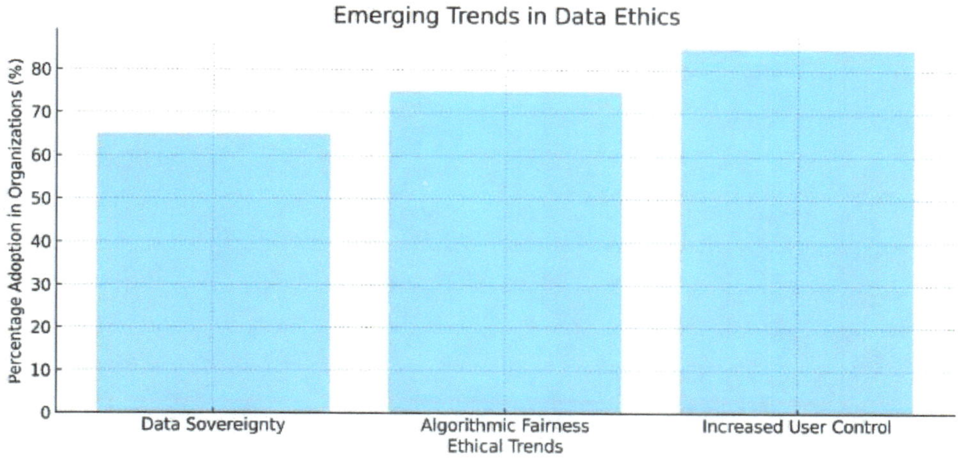

Fig. (2). Emerging trends in data ethics.
Source: Self-Designed

The Role of Technology in Enhancing Transparency

Technological advancements offer significant opportunities for enhancing transparency in behavioural analytics. Notable technologies include:

- **Privacy-Enhancing Technologies (PETs)**: PETs, such as differential privacy, homomorphic encryption, and federated learning, allow companies to analyse data while preserving individual privacy. These technologies ensure that even detailed analyses do not compromise user privacy.
- **Blockchain for Data Transparency:** Blockchain technology, with its decentralized and immutable architecture, is emerging as a potential tool for tracking data use and access. For instance, blockchain can be used to record user consent logs, providing transparency in how data is collected and shared.
- **Explainable AI (XAI):** Explainable AI frameworks are designed to make AI algorithms and models more interpretable, allowing users to understand how and why decisions are made. This technology is increasingly used to provide transparent insights, especially in fields like finance and healthcare.

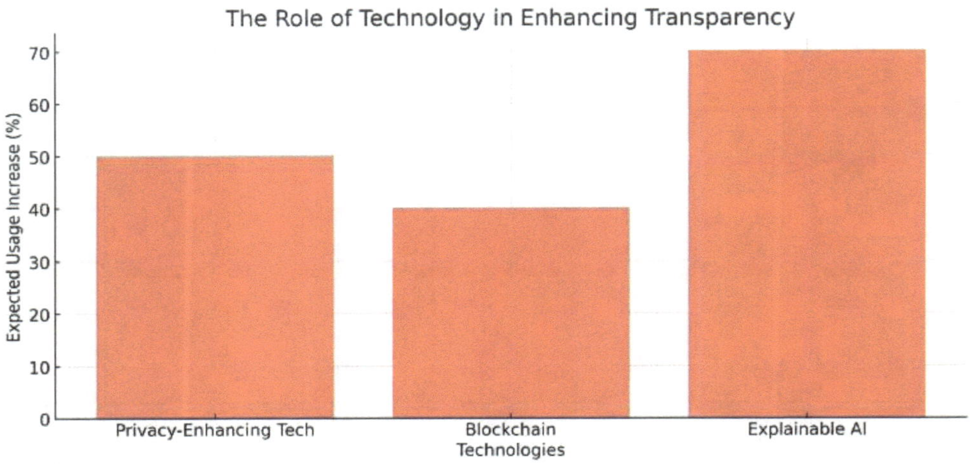

Graph 1: Graph showing the role of technology in enhancing transparency.
Source: Self-Computed

The role of technology in enhancing transparency is forecasted to grow, with various technologies seeing different adoption rates. Privacy-Enhancing Technologies (PETs) are expected to experience moderate adoption, with an anticipated 50% increase in usage as privacy concerns continue to escalate. Blockchain, while offering potential for transparency, remains in an early stage for these applications and is projected to see a more modest adoption rate of around 40% (Graph **1**). In contrast, explainable AI is anticipated to achieve significant uptake, with a 70% increase, as increased scrutiny of AI systems drives demand for transparent and interpretable AI frameworks.

Predictions for the Future of Behavioural Analytics

As businesses and consumers navigate the future of data use, several key predictions can be made about the direction of behavioural analytics:

- ***Regulations Will Strengthen and Expand Globally*:** With the success of GDPR and CCPA, more regions are expected to adopt strict data privacy laws, creating a global standard. This will compel businesses to prioritize privacy and ethical practices universally.
- ***Focus on Ethical AI and Reduced Bias:*** Businesses will increasingly prioritize ethical AI frameworks, reducing biases in their models and fostering greater inclusivity. This shift will likely encourage the development of certification programs for ethical AI, helping organizations validate their commitment to fair

data practices.

- ***User-Centric Data Models Will Emerge*:** Consumers will continue to demand more control over their data, leading to data models that prioritize user ownership. For instance, personal data vaults that store data under the user's control may become commonplace, changing the paradigm of data collection and use.

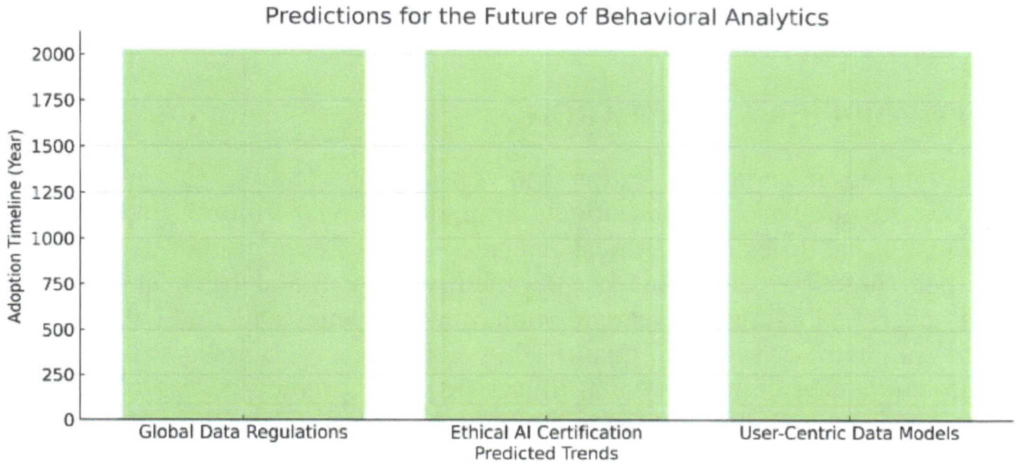

Graph 2: Graph showing future prediction of behavioral analytics.
Source: Self-Computed

Predictions for the future of behavioural analytics suggest adoption timelines influenced by regulatory trends, technological maturity, and market demand. By 2025, global data regulations may converge, following GDPR's lead toward a unified standard (Graph **2**). By 2026, we might see the emergence of standardized ethical AI certifications as the need for AI accountability grows. By 2027, user-centric data models focusing on consumer ownership and privacy are anticipated to gain traction, potentially becoming a new norm in data handling practices.

CONCLUSION

The conclusion highlights the key takeaways from this discussion on balancing ethical considerations with the benefits of behavioural analytics in modern business. By summarizing main insights, outlining the steps forward, and offering final reflections, this section reinforces the need for ethical approaches to data use and the potential for lasting value through consumer trust [6, 8, 15]. The delicate balance between harnessing behavioural analytics for business insights and upholding ethical standards reflects a growing need for businesses to view consumers as partners rather than mere data sources. An ethical approach fosters a trust-based relationship with customers, potentially enhancing brand reputation and long-term loyalty. As data use becomes more prevalent, the responsibility to protect consumer rights grows alongside it. By adopting a mindset focused on responsible data use, organizations can innovate and grow while respecting individual privacy and autonomy. As data ethics become embedded in corporate practice, companies not only align with the values of their customers but also contribute to the larger societal goal of a fair, transparent, and ethically responsible digital world.

SCOPE FOR FUTURE RESEARCH

In order to ensure both innovation and consumer protection, future behavioral analytics research should investigate frameworks that combine sophisticated analytical capabilities with ethical considerations. Research can evaluate how open data practices affect market competitiveness, brand trust, and customer loyalty over the long run. Research comparing companies with and without robust ethical policies can show quantifiable effects on company performance. Additionally, examining how consumers perceive privacy across cultures and demographics may help direct the alignment of global policies. It is important to consider emerging technologies such as AI-driven behavioral analytics for potential bias and unforeseen consequences. Best practices, legal frameworks, and long-term, trust-based business strategies can all benefit from such research .

REFERENCES

[1] A. Acquisti, L. Brandimarte, and G. Loewenstein, "Privacy and human behavior in the age of information", *Science,* vol. 347, no. 6221, pp. 509-514, 2015. [http://dx.doi.org/10.1126/science.aaa1465] [PMID: 25635091]

[2] C. O'Neil, *Weapons of Math Destruction: How Big Data Increases Inequality and Threatens Democracy.* Crown Publishing Group: New York, NY, USA, 2016.

[3] California State Legislature, California Consumer Privacy Act (CCPA), 2018. [Online]. Available: https://oag.ca.gov/privacy/ccpa

[4] European Parliament and Council, Regulation (EU) 2016/679: General Data Protection Regulation (GDPR), 2016. [Online]. Available: https://eur-lex.europa.eu/eli/reg/2016/679/oj

[5] European Union, "General Data Protection Regulation (GDPR) resources," 2016. [Online]. Available: https://gdpr.eu/

[6] L. Floridi, "The ethics of information transparency", *Philos. Technol.,* vol. 30, no. 1, pp. 1-6, 2017. [http://dx.doi.org/10.1007/s13347-017-0257-3] [PMID: 33717860]

[7] K. Martin, "Ethical implications and accountability of algorithms", *J. Bus. Ethics,* vol. 160, no. 4, pp. 835-850, 2019. [http://dx.doi.org/10.1007/s10551-018-3921-3]

[8] V. Mayer-Schönberger, and K. Cukier, *Big Data: A Revolution That Will Transform How We Live, Work, and Think.* Houghton Mifflin Harcourt: Boston, MA, USA, 2013.

[9] B.D. Mittelstadt, P. Allo, M. Taddeo, S. Wachter, and L. Floridi, "The ethics of algorithms: Mapping the debate", *Big Data Soc.,* vol. 3, no. 2, 2016.2053951716679679 [http://dx.doi.org/10.1177/2053951716679679]

[10] H. Nissenbaum, "A contextual approach to privacy online", *Daedalus,* vol. 140, no. 4, pp. 32-48, 2011. [http://dx.doi.org/10.1162/DAED_a_00113]

[11] F. Pasquale, *The Black Box Society: The Secret Algorithms That Control Money and Information.* Harvard Univ. Press: Cambridge, MA, USA, 2015. [http://dx.doi.org/10.4159/harvard.9780674736061]

[12] International Association of Privacy Professionals (IAPP) and Information Commissioner's Office (ICO), "Reports and whitepapers on data ethics and privacy." [Online]. Available: https://iapp.org/ and https://ico.org.uk/

[13] N.M. Richards, and J.H. King, "Big data ethics", *Wake Forest Law Rev.,* vol. 49, pp. 393-432, 2014.

[14] D.J. Solove, "Privacy self-management and the consent dilemma", *Harv. Law Rev.,* vol. 126, no. 7, pp. 1880-1903, 2013.

[15] S. Zuboff, *The Age of Surveillance Capitalism: The Fight for a Human Future at the New Frontier of Power.* PublicAffairs: New York, NY, USA, 2019.

CHAPTER 11

Integrating Digital Technology to Overcome Tourist Difficulties in Puri: A Solution-oriented Approach

Sobhana Tripathy[1] and **Ananya Mitra**[1,*]

[1] *School of Economics & Commerce, Kalinga Institute of Industrial Technology (KIIT) Deemed to be University, Bhubaneswar, Odisha, India*

Abstract: The Jagannath Temple in Puri, Odisha, is one of the holiest pilgrimage sites in India and a key destination in the sacred Char Dham circuit of Hindu culture, attracting millions of devotees annually. The Puri Jagannath Temple faces overcrowding, inadequate infrastructure, safety concerns, environmental issues, and post-pandemic travel hesitancy, affecting the spiritual experience. This study explores using digital technology to address these problems. A survey of 200 Generation Z respondents during the holy month of Kartik assessed the feasibility of a mobile app for managing temple visits. Strengths include personalized experiences, reduced physical contact, and streamlined access. Weaknesses include technological limitations, digital literacy challenges, and privacy concerns. Opportunities for crowd management and virtual booking are noted, while threats include technical glitches and resistance from traditional pilgrims. Results show that a Darshan Booking App can simplify booking, provide real-time information, and manage crowd density despite technical issues and privacy concerns. The findings highlight the need for targeted improvements for the app's success and broader adoption. The novelty of this paper lies in its pioneering approach to integrating digital technology for managing religious tourism activities at the Puri Jagannath Temple. Unlike previous studies that primarily focus on traditional management methods, this research investigates the feasibility and effectiveness of a Darshan Booking App, offering a comprehensive solution to mitigate challenges like overcrowding, safety concerns, and accessibility issues.

Keywords: Experience enhancement, Gen Z, Jagannath Temple JEL: Z32, Overcrowding, Religious tourism, Z12, O33.

* **Corresponding author Ananya Mitra:** School of Economics & Commerce, Kalinga Institute of Industrial Technology (KIIT) Deemed to be University, Bhubaneswar, Odisha, India; E-mail: ananya.mitrafhu@kiit.ac.in

Shradhanjali Panda, Leena Priyadarshini Singh, V. Ramasamy & S. Balamurugan (Eds.)

INTRODUCTION

Puri, renowned for the iconic Shri Jagannath Temple and its expansive golden beach, is one of the holiest destinations in India. It is part of the sacred Char Dham pilgrimage circuit, alongside Dwarika, Badrinath, and Rameswar. Known as Purushottama Kshetra, Puri is the abode of Lord Jagannath, his sister Devi Subhadra, and his elder brother Lord Balabhadra [1]. These revered deities are enshrined on the Ratna Simhasana, a bejeweled pedestal within the temple. The Shri Jagannath Temple, an architectural marvel built in the 12th century by King Ananta Varman Chodaganga Deva of the Ganga Dynasty, stands as one of Odisha's most significant monuments. Located by the sea, this magnificent temple is designed in the Kalinga architectural style and rises 65 meters above the ground on an elevated platform. Throughout the year, Puri hosts numerous vibrant festivals in honor of Lord Jagannath, attracting devotees and tourists from around the world [2]. Tourists visiting the Puri Jagannath Temple, one of the four significant religious sites in India, face several challenges that hinder their pilgrimage experience [3]. These difficulties stem from infrastructural limitations, environmental issues, and management of large crowds, all of which can diminish the sanctity and safety of the site. One of the major challenges identified is the overwhelming number of visitors, especially during peak religious events, which results in overcrowding. This not only causes discomfort for the tourists but also puts pressure on the existing infrastructure. The temple's limited space and the surrounding area's inadequate facilities exacerbate this problem, creating a chaotic environment that detracts from the spiritual experience [4, 5]. Efforts to improve infrastructure are ongoing, but remain insufficient to handle the volume of pilgrims [6]. Tourists also face safety concerns, particularly related to the temple's vulnerability to natural disasters. As Puri is located in a cyclone-prone region, safety measures for both devotees and visitors need to be robust. Inadequate preparedness for such events can cause panic, and recent cracks in the temple's boundary wall highlight the need for urgent restoration [7]. Furthermore, the risk of natural calamities like earthquakes or storms often leads to temporary closures or disruptions in temple activities, affecting the pilgrimage experience [8]. Environmental degradation in and around the temple site also poses significant challenges. Pollution, poor waste management, and the degradation of surrounding heritage sites reduce the aesthetic and spiritual appeal of the area. The poor condition of the local environment, especially air and water pollution, negatively affects both visitors' health and the temple's sanctity [9]. This ongoing degradation diminishes the overall tourist experience and raises concerns over sustainable tourism practices [10].

The COVID-19 pandemic led to a significant decline in the number of tourists visiting the temple, with many pilgrims hesitant to return due to health concerns.

This change in travel behavior, along with ongoing fears about overcrowding and inadequate health protocols, has continued to affect tourism recovery [11]. This travel avoidance has further strained the temple's economic model, which heavily relies on pilgrim tourism. A critical challenge discussed in the literature is finding a balance between facilitating tourism and maintaining the spiritual and religious sanctity of the temple. The influx of tourists, particularly non-devotees, has led to concerns that the temple may become too commercialized, thereby diminishing its sacred atmosphere. The pressure to develop more tourism facilities often conflicts with the temple's cultural and spiritual heritage [12 - 14].

RELIGIOUS TOURISM IN DIGITAL INDIA

Technology significantly shapes religious tourism in India, playing an essential role in crowd management, visitor experience, infrastructure, and safety. During large religious gatherings like the Kumbh Mela and Hajj, technologies such as Radio Frequency Identification (RFID), mobile applications, and wireless networks assist authorities in tracking crowd density and movement, helping prevent overcrowding and reduce the risk of stampedes. These tools enable real-time updates, allowing event managers to respond swiftly to ensure public safety and enhance the overall visitor experience [15]. Furthermore, digital tools like mobile apps and virtual reality have transformed how visitors engage with religious sites. These tools improve accessibility by offering navigation assistance, information on rituals, and virtual tours that deepen pilgrims' connections to sacred spaces before they arrive, contributing to a more informed and fulfilling pilgrimage experience [3].

Smart infrastructure is also a priority, as seen in policies like the Odisha Tourism Policy 2022, which promotes digital tourism to create seamless visitor experiences. Efforts include digital payment systems, automated check-ins, and interactive kiosks at major tourist locations, which together aim to create a responsive tourism ecosystem that aligns with sustainable tourism practices [8]. Health monitoring systems are also crucial, especially during events with high-density gatherings, where technology assists in emergency medical responses and the management of communicable diseases. Data analytics and digital health monitoring enhance safety by supporting timely interventions, especially in events with heightened health risks [15].

Additionally, government programs such as PRASAD (Pilgrimage Rejuvenation and Spiritual Augmentation Drive) and Swadesh Darshan are embedding technological advancements to develop and conserve pilgrimage sites. These initiatives enhance infrastructure, support public-private partnerships, and safeguard heritage through digital tools, making spiritual tourism in India both more accessible and sustainable [3]. Overall, technological advancements are not only improving safety and convenience but are also fostering a more integrated, responsive, and enriching experience for religious tourists in India.

OBJECTIVE

While the Puri Jagannath Temple remains a major pilgrimage destination, the difficulties faced by tourists—such as overcrowding, inadequate infrastructure, safety concerns, environmental issues, and post-pandemic travel hesitancy—pose significant barriers to a seamless spiritual experience. Keeping this in mind, the paper conducts a primary survey, collecting data on the feasibility of integrating digital technology to overcome difficulties faced by tourists at Puri Jagannath Temple as a solution-oriented approach.

METHODOLOGY

As the number of visitors continues to grow, these barriers create frustration, detracting from the overall spiritual journey, especially during auspicious seasons. Addressing these challenges is crucial to enhancing the pilgrimage experience, and digital technology may offer a promising solution to ease the difficulties faced by tourists. To explore how digital tools can mitigate these obstacles, a primary survey was conducted, focusing on the feasibility of implementing a mobile app for managing tourist activities at the Puri Jagannath Temple. The survey targeted a sample size of 200 respondents, all from Generation Z, who were surveyed during the month of 'Kartik', one of the holy and pious months as per the Hindu calendar. Gen Z is particularly tech-savvy, and their preferences and feedback are critical in assessing the potential for digital integration. The data collection period coincided with a peak in visitor numbers, providing valuable insights into how digital solutions could address immediate challenges like overcrowding and queue management, and providing real-time information about temple activities, crowd density, and safety protocols.

To assess the viability of using a mobile app, a Strengths, Weaknesses, Opportunities, and Threats analysis was conducted using a semi-structured questionnaire. The variables under the strengths of the app included its ability to provide personalized experiences, reduce physical contact, and streamline access to temple facilities, potentially enhancing safety and tourist satisfaction. The variables under weaknesses included technological limitations in remote areas, digital literacy challenges among older visitors, and concerns over data privacy that could hinder adoption. Opportunities included the potential for real-time crowd management, e-ticketing, virtual booking options, and better communication during peak events. On the flip side, threats included the risk of technological glitches during high-traffic periods, resistance to change from traditional pilgrims, and the need for continuous updates to keep the app relevant and user-friendly.

A range of statistical methods strengthens the robustness of the findings. Descriptive statistics summarize key sample characteristics, while skewness and kurtosis assess data distribution to ensure assumptions for further analysis. The Chi-Square test examines relationships between categorical variables, and correlation analysis explores connections between continuous variables. Principal Component Analysis (PCA) reduces dimensionality, uncovering underlying themes in attitudes. Together, these methods provide a comprehensive framework for drawing informed conclusions on the problem at hand.

RESULT ANALYSIS

The novelty of this paper lies in its pioneering approach to integrating digital technology for managing religious tourism activities at the Puri Jagannath Temple. Unlike previous studies that primarily focus on traditional management methods, this research investigates the feasibility and effectiveness of a Darshan Booking App, offering a comprehensive solution to mitigate challenges like overcrowding, safety concerns, and accessibility issues. By analyzing the responses collected from a primary survey of Generation Z respondents during a peak pilgrimage period, the study provides unique insights into the potential of mobile apps to enhance the spiritual experience, thereby addressing both the immediate and long-term needs of devotees.

Cronbach's Alpha, Kaiser-Meyer-Olkin, and Bartlett's Test of Sphericity Result

The Cronbach's Alpha of 0.978 indicates excellent internal consistency among the items in the scale. This high value suggests that the items are highly correlated and reliably measure the same underlying construct. The Cronbach's Alpha Based on Standardized Items is also 0.978, meaning the reliability remains strong even when the scores are standardized. Both values point to a very consistent and dependable scale. The Kaiser-Meyer-Olkin value of 0.920 indicates excellent sampling adequacy for factor analysis. Bartlett's Test of Sphericity is significant (p-value = 0.000), suggesting that the correlation matrix is not an identity matrix, meaning the variables are sufficiently correlated. Both results confirm that factor analysis is appropriate.

Descriptive Statistics Result

The app's ability to enhance the overall darshan experience through timely notifications and reminders received a mean score of 2.20, with a standard deviation of 1.099. The skewness value of 0.988 and kurtosis of 0.531 further highlight user ambivalence, indicating that the app's notification system needs enhancement to meet user expectations effectively. Furthermore, the reliability and security of booking through the app scored 2.34, with a standard deviation of 1.094, suggesting room for improvement in the app's security features. Results also pointed out several areas for improvement. For instance, many respondents found the user interface easy to navigate, as indicated by the mean score of 2.48 and a skewness of 0.649. However, the overall ease of use could still be enhanced, given the kurtosis value of -0.068, which implies slight negative kurtosis or flatness in the distribution. Additionally, concerns regarding digital literacy, privacy, and regional language support emerged as significant barriers, with respective mean scores of 2.35, 2.35, and 2.61. The data also reveals that while users recognize the potential benefits of the app, such as reducing overcrowding and enhancing the spiritual experience, the occurrence of technical issues and the lack of alternative support options pose challenges. The respective mean scores of 2.37 and 2.40, along with positive skewness values, highlight the importance of addressing these technical and support-related issues to ensure wider adoption and satisfaction among users. This comprehensive analysis emphasizes the need for targeted improvements in the app's functionality, user interface, and support systems to enhance its overall efficacy and user experience.

Chi-Square Test Result

The Chi-Square test results for the likelihood of using an app to schedule darshan based on gender show that there is no statistically significant association between the two variables. The Pearson Chi-Square value is 3.551 with 4 degrees of freedom and an asymptotic significance (2-sided) of 0.470, indicating that the relationship is not significant at the 0.05 level. Similarly, the likelihood ratio and linear-by-linear association tests also show non-significant results with p-values of 0.478 and 0.440, respectively. This suggests that gender does not have a significant impact on the likelihood of using the app, implying that both male and female respondents have similar attitudes towards the app's use for scheduling darshan.

Communalities Test Result

The major factors with the highest communalities highlight key features of the Darshan Booking App that enhance its overall success. Integration with local tourism services (0.839) and multilingual support (0.828) expand the app's value, making it accessible to a wider range of devotees, especially non-locals. The app's ability to provide valuable data for temple operations (0.821) and raise awareness about special events (0.801) improves both the user experience and temple efficiency. Features like timely notifications (0.820) and feedback mechanisms (0.820) ensure better communication and continuous improvement, while accurate darshan timings (0.709) build trust. Additionally, the app's convenience for remote devotees (0.752) and the need for regional language support (0.792) further enhance its accessibility. These factors collectively suggest that the app's potential for improving the temple visit experience lies in its ability to simplify the process, offer personalized features, and cater to the diverse needs of the devotee population.

Total Variance Explained Result

The Total Variance Explained result from the Principal Component Analysis (PCA) outlines how much variance each component explains in the dataset, both before and after rotation. The initial Eigenvalues show that the first component accounts for 52.07% of the total variance, a significant proportion, indicating that a single factor captures a large amount of the variation in the data. By the second component, the cumulative variance increases to 55.17%, and by the third component, it reaches 60.06%. These findings suggest that the first few components are highly influential in representing the underlying structure of the data.

After rotation, which maximizes the interpretability of the factors, the variance explained by the first few components remains high but is redistributed across additional factors. The first rotated component still explains 15.5% of the variance, and the second component explains 15.24%, contributing to a cumulative variance of 30.74%. This means that while the first component is dominant, multiple components are important for capturing the complex relationships in the data. The cumulative variance after rotation (around 70%) suggests that about 70% of the information is captured by the top 6-7 components, making them essential for understanding the structure of the dataset. This distribution of variance highlights the usefulness of dimensionality reduction techniques like PCA for simplifying complex data while retaining essential information.

Component Matrix Test Result

The factor loadings presented in the table provide valuable insights into the underlying components that explain the variance in respondents' perceptions of the Darshan Booking App. A key finding from the analysis is that Component 1 primarily captures the app's core functionalities and usability features. Variables such as security, user interface design, timely notifications, and simplification of the darshan booking process exhibit strong loadings on this component, reflecting their importance in ensuring a seamless user experience. These attributes are critical to user engagement, as they directly impact the app's reliability and ease of use. Moreover, features related to accurate darshan timings, convenience for distant devotees, and overcrowding management also load highly on this component. This suggests that the app's value proposition centers on enhancing the efficiency and convenience of the darshan experience. These findings underscore the significance of addressing functional performance, user navigation, and real-time communication to optimize the app's effectiveness.

In contrast, Component 2 appears to capture more socially and contextually sensitive issues associated with the app, such as digital literacy, exclusivity, and resistance from traditional devotees. Variables associated with these concerns—such as the lack of multilingual support, technical glitches during high-demand periods, and the complex payment process—indicate potential barriers to widespread adoption. These factors suggest that while the app offers significant utility, its successful implementation will depend on its ability to overcome social and cultural obstacles. Furthermore, Component 3 reflects concerns about the security of personal data, privacy issues, and potential regulatory challenges, which may affect users' trust in the platform. Together, these findings highlight the dual importance of optimizing the app's functional capabilities while addressing user concerns related to accessibility, privacy, and inclusivity. To ensure the app's widespread acceptance and sustained use, it is essential to balance technological innovation with a careful consideration of the diverse needs of its potential user base.

Rotated Component Matrix Result

Based on the Rotated Component Matrix, several key findings emerge regarding the use of a Darshan Booking App for scheduling visits to the Jagannath Temple. Firstly, the app is perceived to significantly simplify the booking process, with strong loadings on factors such as ease of navigation, timely notifications, and enhanced overall experience (Components 4 and 8). Users find the app useful in terms of convenience, particularly for those living far from the temple, and for improving the overall visitor experience. However, despite these benefits, several technical and accessibility issues persist. The app faces challenges like technical issues during high-demand periods and difficulties for users with low digital literacy (Component 1).

Moreover, the app's complexity and the lack of support options contribute to user dissatisfaction. Factors such as a cumbersome registration process, insufficient regional language support, and the need for better customer care options are significant barriers (Component 6). Additionally, there are concerns about the app creating exclusivity, disadvantaging those without smartphones or digital skills (Component 1). Privacy and security concerns also affect user trust and adoption rates (Components 1 and 4). Addressing these issues is crucial for enhancing user satisfaction and ensuring the app's success in managing temple visits efficiently.

Component Transformation Matrix Finding

The Component Transformation Matrix provides insight into how the original variables are transformed into the principal components. Here, the matrix shows the loadings of each original variable on the extracted components. Component 1 is strongly loaded by several factors, including ease of use, security, and overall convenience of the app. High loadings indicate that this component is crucial for understanding the primary benefits and functionality of the Darshan Booking App. It highlights how the app simplifies the booking process, provides timely notifications, and enhances the darshan experience, making it particularly valuable for those who live far from the temple or have tight schedules. Component 2, however, reveals some negative aspects, particularly related to the app's accessibility and usability issues. Negative loadings here suggest challenges such as technical issues, difficulties faced by users with low digital literacy, and the lack of alternative support options like customer care. This component emphasizes the need to address these challenges to improve user satisfaction and ensure wider adoption of the app among all devotees, regardless of their technical skills or access to smartphones.

FINDINGS

The objective of this study was to address the various difficulties faced by tourists at the Puri Jagannath Temple, such as overcrowding, inadequate infrastructure, safety concerns, and post-pandemic travel hesitancy, by exploring the feasibility of integrating digital technology as a solution. The methodology involved conducting a primary survey with Generation Z respondents to assess their preferences and the potential of implementing a mobile app for managing temple visits. The survey collected data during the holy month of Kartik, providing insights into how digital solutions could mitigate these challenges.

The findings indicate that digital technology, particularly a Darshan Booking App, can significantly enhance the pilgrimage experience by simplifying the booking process, providing real-time information, and managing crowd density. The app's strengths include its user-friendly interface, timely notifications, and the ability to offer personalized experiences, which contribute to overall tourist satisfaction and safety. However, the app also faces challenges such as technical issues, digital literacy barriers, and privacy concerns. Addressing these issues is crucial for the app's success and wider adoption. A SWOT analysis and various statistical methods, including PCA, highlighted the app's potential to improve visitor management while underscoring the importance of balancing technological innovation with accessibility and user concerns. Ultimately, the integration of digital tools can provide a more seamless and enriched experience for devotees visiting the Puri Jagannath Temple.

POLICY IMPLICATIONS

To optimize religious tourism through technology, policies should focus on enhancing safety, digital infrastructure, and environmental sustainability. Implementing real-time crowd management systems at major pilgrimage sites can significantly reduce overcrowding risks, ensuring public safety. Additionally, establishing robust digital infrastructure — including high-speed internet, digital ticketing, and smart kiosks — can streamline visitor services, making information more accessible and facilitating contactless transactions. Health and safety protocols are also essential; integrating wearable health-monitoring technology at high-density events would enable rapid responses to health emergencies, improving overall event safety. Policies should also encourage eco-friendly digital tourism, such as promoting virtual reality tours and off-peak virtual site visits, to manage the flow of tourists and protect sensitive sites. Strengthening public-private partnerships can further enhance digital innovation by providing ongoing maintenance and funding for sustainable technological improvements.

CONCLUSION

Lastly, providing digital training for local stakeholders, including religious authorities and tourism operators, ensures effective management and use of new technologies, creating a seamless and engaging experience for visitors. Together, these policies promote a safer, more efficient, and sustainable approach to religious tourism in India. By focusing on technology-driven solutions, the tourism sector can balance the demand for growth with the need for sustainability, improving both the visitor experience and the protection of sacred sites. The future roadmap for this paper envisions expanding the Darshan Booking App with advanced features like AI-based crowd prediction, multilingual support, and integration with navigation, accommodation, and emergency services. Collaboration with temple authorities, local vendors, and tourism boards will enhance adoption and inclusivity. Addressing privacy and cybersecurity concerns will be critical for user trust. Future research can explore pilot testing, user feedback analysis, and scalability for other pilgrimage sites across India. Incorporating AR/VR for virtual darshan experiences can engage remote devotees. The ultimate goal is to create a sustainable, technology-driven model of religious tourism that preserves tradition while enhancing safety, accessibility, and the spiritual experience.

REFERENCES

[1] R. Behera, and S. Nayak, "Safety measures during natural calamities at Shree Jagannath Temple", *J. Disaster Manag.,* vol. 12, no. 3, pp. 45-52, 2021.

[2] S. Das, *Lord Jagannath.* Sanbun Publishers: New Delhi, India, 2010.

[3] V. Gautam, V. Kumar, J. Gautam, and Ankush, "Role of technology on religious tourism: An indian perspective," 2024. [Online]. Available: https://www.researchgate.net/publication/378316021

[4] J. Kar, "Development of tourism in the religious town of puri: T he holy abode of lord jagannatha", *Int. J. Res. Anal. Rev.,* vol. 6, no. 1, pp. 581-582, 2019. [IJRAR].

[5] A. Mishra, "Balancing tourism and sanctity at shree jagannath temple", *Tour. Manag. Perspect.,* vol. 8, pp. 123-130, 2020.

[6] P. Mohapatra, and R. Senapati, "Restoration projects at shree jagannath temple", *Herit. Conserv. J.,* vol. 5, no. 2, pp. 78-85, 2019.

[7] L. Naveen, P.P. Pradhan, J. Biswas, and R.N. Subudhi, "Understanding travel avoidance of tourists to a heritage destination: case of puri pilgrimage after COVID-19 pandemic", *YMER Digital,* vol. 21, pp. 235-252, 2022.

[8] Odisha Tourism Department, *Odisha Tourism Policy* 2022, Cuttack, India: Government of Odisha, 2022. [Online]. Available: https://dot.odisha.gov.in/notifications/tourism-policy

[9] S. Panda, and A. Mitra, Pakhala in Jagannath Culture: An Amalgamation of Food, Heritage and Science
[http://dx.doi.org/10.1007/978-3-031-67360-3_4]

[10] R. Parida, "Sustainable tourism at religious heritage sites", *J. Sustain. Tour.,* vol. 24, no. 4, pp. 567-580, 2016.

[11] N. Sahu, and S. Patnaik, "Environmental degradation at Shree Jagannath Temple", *Environ. Sci. Technol.,* vol. 56, no. 7, pp. 234-242, 2022.

[12] G. Swain, and U.C. Mohanty, "Challenges faced by devotees at Shree Jagannath Temple", *J. Pilgrimage Stud.,* vol. 10, no. 1, pp. 15-29, 2023.

[13] G. Swain, U.C. Mohanty, and N. Sahu, "Infrastructure improvements for managing temple crowds", *Urban Plan. Dev.,* vol. 17, no. 2, pp. 89-102, 2023.

[14] G. Swain, A. Sahu, T. Bihari, and Swarnachud College, "Puri jagannath temple: Navigating the spiritual tourism landscape: Opportunities and challenges," *Int. J. Res. Humanit. Soc. Sci.*, vol. 11, no. 11, 2023.

[15] M. Yamin, "Managing crowds with technology: cases of Hajj and Kumbh Mela", *International Journal of Information Technology,* vol. 11, no. 2, pp. 229-237, 2019. [http://dx.doi.org/10.1007/s41870-018-0266-1] [PMID: 32289103]

SUBJECT INDEX

A

B

C

D

L

M

N

O

P

R

S

T

V

www.ingramcontent.com/pod-product-compliance
Lightning Source LLC
LaVergne TN
LVHW070951210926
848482LV00002B/179